The Heterodox
Yoder

The Heterodox
Yoder

Paul Martens

CASCADE *Books* • Eugene, Oregon

THE HETERODOX YODER

Copyright © 2012 Paul Martens. All rights reserved. Except for brief quotations in critical publications or reviews, no part of this book may be reproduced in any manner without prior written permission from the publisher. Write: Permissions, Wipf and Stock Publishers, 199 W. 8th Ave., Suite 3, Eugene, OR 97401.

Cascade Books
An Imprint of Wipf and Stock Publishers
199 W. 8th Ave., Suite 3
Eugene, OR 97401

www.wipfandstock.com

ISBN 13: 978-1-60899-551-6

Cataloging-in-Publication data:

Martens, Paul Henry.

The heterodox Yoder / Paul Martens

xii + 166 p. ; 23 cm. —Includes bibliographical references and indexes.

ISBN 13: 978-1-60899-551-6

1. Yoder, John Howard. I. Title.

BX8143.Y59 M37 2012

Manufactured in the U.S.A.

Permission has been granted by *Conrad Grebel Review* to reproduce a revised and expanded version—"Chapter 5: The New Shape of Ecumenism"—of Paul Martens, "The Problematic Development of the Sacraments in the Thought of John Howard Yoder," *Conrad Grebel Review* 24:3 (Fall 2006) 65–77.

Permission for publishing excerpts of John Howard Yoder's unpublished papers and letters that appear throughout this volume has also been granted by Martha Yoder Maust.

To B, C, Z, and T. You are totally awesome!

*It is normal for the newcomer to a debate
which is already in process
to accept the prevailing definitions of terms and
choose one of the existing sides,
whereas the wiser approach is to question the definitions.*

—John Howard Yoder, *The Christian Witness to the State*

Contents

Preface | ix

Acknowledgments | xi

ONE   Introduction: A Simpler Approach | 1

TWO   Foundational Theological Commitments | 19

THREE   The Prioritization of Politics | 54

FOUR   Reconstructing Jewish Christianity | 87

FIVE   The New Shape of Ecumenism | 116

SIX   Conclusion: The Heterodox Yoder | 141

Bibliography | 149

Name Index | 159

Subject Index | 163

Preface

READING JOHN HOWARD YODER has been a polemical affair. Standing in the midst of one of the most volatile conversations of the twentieth century—the role of the Christian in a world at war—Yoder forced his readers to pick a side: either nonviolence or violence; either faithfulness or unfaithfulness. One either had to resist his position or embrace it.

Of course, war and military conflicts of all kinds have not disappeared in the twenty-first century. Yet, shifting time, context, and voices have reshaped several of the foundational matters in the field of Christian ethics so that the choice of nonviolence or violence has been significantly modified and nuanced. For many, the debate between nonviolence and violence has been recast from a question that forces a single or isolated choice into a discussion about competing social or political practices that display a certain kind of character, habits, and virtue formed in particular and intentional communal contexts. Those who have embraced and appropriated Yoder have generally narrated the primary communal context for forming character and virtue as the church. And, in the course of rereading Yoder with these more robust concerns in mind, it has become clear that Yoder himself had begun presciently exploring this trajectory in his own way as early as the 1950s.

Yet, if Yoder's articulation of nonviolence in the 1970s had a tremendously galvanizing effect for a wide variety of pacifists (and by this I am broadly referring to the effects of the publication of *The Politics of Jesus* in 1972), the ongoing rereading of Yoder's foundational ecclesial and ecumenical convictions has provoked a much less unified reception. This book is one attempt to illuminate why this might be the case. Therefore, although I do not desire to denigrate individual texts that are deeply cherished, the argument contained in these pages is concerned with the overall shape and character of Yoder's corpus in a way that contextualizes his nonviolence within a larger theological matrix. Specifically, the argument traces the introduction and development of the foundational theological commitments that motivate and guide Yoder's relentless pursuit of a more faithful Christian existence, commitments that may have ended up being, by the mid-1990s, as provocative and contested as his nonviolent convictions were in the 1970s.

There are, of course, certain limits to this approach. First, following this sort of trajectory means that the book will not fall within a popular school of thought that operates on the belief that "works 'on' Yoder are best, not when he is described and discussed, but when he is used for ends beyond, but in sympathy with his own projects."[1] I am sympathetic with this position, and I am impressed by Richard Bourne's *Seek the Peace of the City*, Alex Sider's *To See History Doxologically*, and several other works that constructively appropriate Yoder in this manner. That said, I also believe that much of the current appropriation of Yoder selectively determines what "his own projects" are. This selectivity may be entirely defensible and appropriate, but it also rarely does justice to the complicated coherence of Yoder's own projects. For better or worse, it is this latter concern that occupies the following pages.

Second, from the opposite direction, this text is limited to the extent that not every one of Yoder's writings has been examined, thereby leaving the possibility that some of my readers will be dissatisfied, feeling that I have concluded this project too quickly. To be clear, I have no intention of being exhaustive; I simply intend to sketch what I take to be the key topographical features of the corpus. It is my hope that the rough map provided here will provoke and energize closer readings of Yoder's texts and deeper engagements with the questions he deemed most important. In this way, perhaps this book can contribute to the work of those who are interested in Yoder's projects and to the projects of those who are interested in going beyond Yoder.

---

1. Bourne, *Seek the Peace of the City*, ix.

Acknowledgments

As always, there are many people who have contributed to the final shape of this book. In a book pitched as a sympathetic critique of Yoder, I can imagine that some of my friendly interlocutors would just as soon not appear on this particular page. That is just too bad, as one cannot always choose which gifts he or she is given!

It would be fair to say that the first formal steps toward this book began during an independent reading course with Michael Baxter—a request he most graciously indulged—while I was a graduate student at the University of Notre Dame. Yet, it must also be acknowledged that even that beginning is rooted in an indirect debt to Yoder himself for creating a disposition in the Theology Department at Notre Dame that was open to welcoming a rather naïve Mennonite kid from Canada into the PhD program. Ever since these first formal engagements with Yoder at Notre Dame, Jerry McKenny has been and continues to be the voice of patient reason that encourages—and encourages responsibility. And, the final formal step in this process is indebted to Cyril O'Regan—thanks for the title . . . and so much more, of course.

Since I began working on the argument of this book in earnest, I have greatly appreciated the fruitful conversations with Jonathan Tran—a great friend and colleague—and the enjoyment of working together with excellent graduate students—Myles Werntz, Matthew Porter, and Jenny Howell—on various Yoder projects. I am also incredibly grateful for the time and care Dan Marrs invested in making this a much more readable and complete manuscript. Further, I want to thank Tim, Phil, Nick, Jordan, and Josh because, yes, this really is about a kingdom born upside-down.

I am also indebted to Mark Nation, Glen Stassen, Branson Parler, and Jamie Pitts for treating components of this argument that have been previously presented seriously enough to provide constructive criticisms. I doubt that this book will satisfy all of the concerns they have voiced, but it will provide a larger framework within which to continue discussion.

I would also like to take this opportunity to thank Anne Yoder and Martha Yoder Maust for energetically enabling and encouraging all of us to continue wrestling with these most important questions by making John's work readily available. In this same vein, I also want to acknowledge, with considerable gratitude, Charlie Collier's encouragement and willingness to ensure that the contested argument in this book will get a hearing.

Finally, I would also like to thank the Dean's Office of the College of Arts and Letters at Baylor University for providing a semester of research leave that enabled the completion of this book. It is always a pleasant challenge to work at a university whose motto stands at the same intersection as this book: *Pro Texana, Pro Ecclesia*.

ONE

Introduction: A Simpler Approach

Heterodox. It is rarely a good word, a positive word, or a complimentary word. It refers to the bringing together of two things that are of a different kind. And, usually on this basis, it also refers to something that is contrary to an accepted standard or tradition, unconventional, not orthodox. All of this is further complicated when cast in theological terms or within the history of the Christian church. In choosing *The Heterodox Yoder* as the title for this book, I am invoking this label in three interrelated respects.

The first evocation of heterodox concerns the selection of texts that I use to narrate Yoder's position. Several texts have achieved a definitive status in Yoder's corpus, beginning with *The Politics of Jesus* (1972) and followed by a group of secondary importance that includes *The Christian Witness to the State* (1964), *The Original Revolution* (1971), *The Priestly Kingdom* (1984), and *The Royal Priesthood* (1994). Occasionally, and depending on the context, *For the Nations* (1997), *Preface to Theology* (2002), and *Christian Attitudes to War, Peace, and Revolution* (2009) find a significant place in the conversation, but usually they are relegated to a level of tertiary importance. The rest of Yoder's corpus, for the most part, then serves an illustrative or supplementary role. How this hierarchy of texts came to be is not my concern in this context. That said, this book essentially ignores this hierarchy, first, by largely ignoring the relative weight placed on these particular texts within the current discourse and, second, by introducing a variety of other texts into this mix, texts that may be just as defining as those listed above.

A second evocation of heterodox emerges from the above, namely, a rather unorthodox narrative of Yoder's thought—both its foundation and its development—emerges when a wider variety of texts are mixed in and considered in a straightforward manner. Outlining this narrative in some detail is the central task of the chapters that follow.

Finally, and most importantly, this book is an attempt to raise the question of whether Yoder's thought, at the end of the day, is best described as heterodox Christianity. Of course, labeling something as "not" something else—as heterodox as opposed to orthodox—begs for a definition of that something else. Therefore, it would seem that I ought to define the criterion of orthodoxy before proceeding further. To dare to even get one's toes wet in this debate immediately exposes one to the multiple undertows or rip currents that can drag one unsuspectingly well beyond the safety of the shore, well beyond the safety of the solid familiarity of firm ground. Yet, this is precisely the turbulence in which one finds Yoder swimming. Because of this, a few summary comments are required to frame the following argument.

From certain perspectives, Yoder's free church convictions will be enough to provoke charges of heterodoxy. From other perspectives, his equivocal semi-embrace of the classic Christian creeds or his historicizing of Trinitarian affirmations slide rather far down the slippery slope towards a rejection of orthodoxy. Exploring these issues is helpful for clarifying what is at stake in Yoder's rendering of Christianity and, therefore, they cannot be ignored in this book. Yet, these are not the criteria I am referring to; my criterion is more basic and gives rise to these secondary issues. My criterion is the Christian affirmation of the particularity or uniqueness of Jesus Christ as a historical person and as a revelation of God. For those who have argued for years that it is precisely Yoder who has preserved the particularity or uniqueness of Jesus Christ against the acids of Constantinianism, modernity, or any number of other threats to Christianity, all I can do is beg for your patience and ask that you read my argument through to the end before rendering judgment.

Perhaps the best way to articulate the issue at stake is to appeal to Yoder's *Preface to Theology*. In the Introduction, he outlines several different modes of "doing theology." Among the modes he rejects is "dogmatic theology," which he defines as the interpretation of the statements made by or implied in the classic Christian creeds.[1] Alternately, he describes

---

1. Yoder, *Preface to Theology*, 33.

"historical theology," theology concerned with how Christian convictions came into being, how people first came to speak in a certain way, and why it happened. In *Preface to Theology*, this is the form of theological engagement Yoder adopts, with his face "turned toward the systematic agenda," and not merely for the purpose of providing a simple narration.[2] Beyond *Preface to Theology*, however, Yoder (1) remains loyal to the mode of doing theology he refers to as "historical theology" and (2) always rejects a simple narration in favor of an ethical or political agenda. His method is, throughout the corpus, inductive and historical. His method is to watch the theology of the early Christian church (often explicitly filtered through the sixteenth-century Anabaptists) and then draw conclusions about "how we ought to do theology from watching how it has been done in the past."[3]

In this way, Yoder attempts to affirm the particularity of following Jesus Christ in the manner of the early church, thereby providing a comprehensive and coherent reorientation of Christian theology. And, in this process, one might say that Yoder forces a reappraisal or reconfiguration of the very meaning of Christian orthodoxy.[4] My argument, however, is that it is precisely this reconfiguration that contains the seeds of Yoder's own devaluation of the particularity or uniqueness of Jesus Christ. As he continues outlining the methodology employed in *Preface to Theology*, he notes: "I said our method is 'inductive'; that means that instead of registering right answers already distilled, we go through the process of distillation observing variety as well as similarity."[5] In the pages that follow, I attempt to demonstrate that it is this attempt to "distill" the theology of the early church that leads to what I am calling Yoder's heterodoxy. To be as clear as possible at this point, I argue that Yoder's distillation amounts to a complex narration of the early Christian church in primarily ethical terms. Thus, his narration provides an account of the early church's particularity (a particularity that eventually earns the title of the politics of Jesus), but, as Yoder's corpus progresses, his narration of the early church's particularity eventually—and perhaps unwittingly—advocates an ethical or political particularity that becomes so "distilled" that the defining activities of the early church become abstracted into a general and universalizable,

2. Ibid., 34.

3. Ibid., 39.

4. I am gratefully indebted to Charlie Collier for this particular assessment of Yoder's approach to orthodoxy.

5. Yoder, *Preface to Theology*, 39.

not-particularly-Christian ethic: Jesus becomes merely an ethico-political example or paradigm within a form of ethical monotheism (at best) or a form of secular sociology (at worst).[6] This, in my judgment, is a heterodox account of the particularity and uniqueness of Jesus Christ. Moreover, the effects of Yoder's redescription of Jesus reverberates throughout the rest of his theology, providing occasions for what I take to be secondary disputes about Yoder's heterodoxy.

As one might suspect, my conclusions run contrary to many of the contemporary appraisals of Yoder's theological ethics. Branson Parler, speaking for a large contingent of Yoder readers, claims: "Part of Yoder's genius is his ability to see beyond the binary oppositions of many modern theological dilemmas."[7] As intimated above, I argue that it is precisely Yoder's attempt to overcome the prevailing dualisms in modern theology that leads him to unite theology and ethics, and this final move invites my third invocation of heterodoxy. To be clear, this does not mean that I am inferring that all resolutions of this alleged dichotomy are heterodox; it means that Yoder's idiosyncratic resolution of the tension between theology and ethics is heterodox. I will argue that his early statement of the relationship—"The Christian life is defined most basically in ethical terms"[8]—is, likewise, most basic to his lifelong redefinition of theology in

---

6. To reiterate, the issue is not that Yoder rejects particularity in terms of epistemological, ethical, or political claims. The issue is what sort of particularity he affirms (and this is one of my key disagreements with Mark Thiessen Nation. See Nation, "'Ecumenical' and 'Cosmopolitan' Yoder"). The ambiguity in Yoder's position appears starkly in "But We Do See Jesus," one of the texts frequently appealed to for his comprehensive vision of Christianity:

> For our world it will be in [Jesus'] ordinariness as villager, as rabbi, as king on a donkey, and as liberator on a cross that we shall be able to express the claims which the apostolic proclaimers to Hellenism expressed in the language of preexistence and condescension. This is not to lower our sights or to retract our proclamation. It is to renew the description of Christ crucified as the wisdom and the power of God. This is the low road to general validity. It frees us from needing to be apologetic in either the popular or the technical sense. It thereby frees us to use any language, to enter any world in which people eat bread and pursue debtors, hope for power and execute subversives. The ordinariness of the humanness of Jesus is the warrant for the generalizability of his reconciliation. The nonterritorial particularity of his Jewishness defends us against selling out to *any* wider world's claim to be really wider, or to be self-validating. (62)

7. Parler, "Spinning the Liturgical Turn," 179.
8. Yoder, "The Anabaptist Dissent," 32.

Introduction: A Simpler Approach 5

the direction of "'Christian-ness' as being an ethical matter."[9] In ways that will become clear as the argument unfolds, not only does Yoder overtly challenge what he takes to be the interests and conclusions of Christian orthodoxy, his thought is intentionally unconventional and contrary to tradition in its content from the earliest writings to the latest.

I do recognize, however, that making this argument convincing is going to be an uphill battle. Therefore, in order to articulate this case, certain assumptions that guide most readings of Yoder's corpus must be examined and challenged since these have been employed to ensure that Yoder falls within what his readers consider Christian orthodoxy. I refer to these preliminary assumptions as the "regulative framework" that has shaped the reception of Yoder's corpus. Challenging this familiar regulative framework makes room for the invocation of a heterodox Yoder: a heterodox approach that includes less familiar texts, elevates relegated themes, and yields a rich panoramic portrait of his thought.

Having stated my intentions up front in such a stark way, it may appear that this book intends to be a resounding rejection of Yoder. That is not the case; this book is not a simplistic rejection of Yoder as "representing a type of christomonistic sectarianism or politically naive pacifism or neo-liberal free church voluntarism" as has been done in the past.[10] Rather, this book intends to read Yoder sympathetically—yet critically—as a voice that never could reconcile itself with the dominant strain of thought that is usually referred to as "orthodoxy." That said, even Yoder recognized that "criticism is not rejection," that to criticize a thought is to take it seriously and to ask why its claims are to be believed.[11] Therefore, assuming a value judgment up front concerning either (1) the mode of reading Yoder utilized or (2) the construal of his thought as a whole contained in this book may be too hasty. Rather, it just may be that Yoder's heterodoxy is an equivocal blessing, a misguided attempt to rewrite Christian theology

---

9. Ibid., 29.

10. This is the phrase used by Kroeker in "Is a Messianic Political Ethic Possible?" 142. I also want to note, with great appreciation, the work of so many that have brought Yoder into mainstream theological conversations. It is this pioneering work that has led Christian thinkers like Richard Mouw to conclude that the views in Yoder's *The Royal Priesthood* "are not detestable," which is another way of saying that this work has enabled a serious reconsideration of Anabaptist thinkers like Yoder that is not governed by the lingering assumptions of the sixteenth century. See Mouw's "Foreword" in Yoder's *Royal Priesthood*, vii.

11. Yoder, *Preface to Theology*, 40.

and ethics that nonetheless helpfully provokes us all in certain ways. I have already stated the broad conclusion of this book, and I will leave the articulation of the supporting argument for the chapters that follow. For now, I will return to the preliminary deconstructive step that is necessary to clear the ground for a rereading of Yoder's corpus.

RETHINKING THE REGULATIVE FRAMEWORK FOR READING YODER

The introduction of any given author or subject is expected to begin by explaining or justifying why the particular book is needed. Introductions to books written about the thought of John Howard Yoder are no exception. Craig Carter's *The Politics of the Cross* begins with the claim that the "social-ethical thought of John Howard Yoder represents a major contribution to Christian theological ethics in the second half of the twentieth century, but it has not been taken with the seriousness it deserves at the level of disciplined scholarship."[12] Five years later, Mark Thiessen Nation began his introduction to *John Howard Yoder* with a reflexive appeal to another authority: "'Nineteen seventy-four, I believe, was the year I read John Yoder's *Politics of Jesus*.' James McClendon opens his three-volume systematic theology with this sentence, thereby signaling not only that John Yoder had made a substantial contribution to his thinking, but more importantly, that reading Yoder had transformed his whole approach to the enterprise of theology."[13]

It is natural to expect introductions of this nature in the decade following Yoder's passing, as they represent the attempt by sympathetic colleagues and students to consolidate, synthesize, defend, or extend Yoder's life and work. This introduction simply acknowledges the fact that a book on Yoder's thought no longer needs to be justified since that argument has already been made through the pioneering work of Carter, Nation, and many others.[14] Of course, acknowledging this fact simply pushes the justification to a second level: why is this particular book on Yoder necessary? In short, the purpose of this book is to examine carefully and critically

---

12. Carter, *Politics of the Cross*, 15.

13. Nation, *John Howard Yoder*, xvi.

14. See also Zimmerman, *Practicing the Politics of Jesus*, and the various collections of essays devoted to Yoder, including *The Wisdom of the Cross*; *A Mind Patient and Untamed*; *Power and Practices*; and *The New Yoder*.

whether Yoder's celebrated "rearranging [of] the theological landscape" in the twentieth century is an unmitigated good.[15]

In a sense, this book is part of the next logical step in the reception of Yoder's life and work, a step that has already begun piecemeal in several conferences and collections of essays.[16] Now that there have been several book-length attempts to introduce Yoder's thought comprehensively, it is possible to take a step back and evaluate the synthesis that has emerged. As I see it, during the first decade of consolidating the life and work of John Howard Yoder, there has been substantial agreement among many of his readers. This agreement is frequently rooted in a common approach to Yoder's corpus, a common approach that is often implicit, unstated, or only stated informally in more personal contexts. The power of this common approach cannot be underestimated, and one cannot attend a conference on Yoder or read very far in the secondary literature without discovering a few familiar refrains that frame this popular perception. The interpretive keys to this regulative framework could be listed as follows:

1. *The Politics of Jesus* is Yoder's defining text.[17] In a sense, yes, of course, this is Yoder's defining text in terms of readership, influence, and identity. This text, for many interpreters of Yoder, was the text that introduced them to Yoder and, therefore, has become the canon within the canon, so to speak, of Yoder's corpus. For example, in her thoughtful and articulate attempt to describe Yoder's theological research program, Nancy Murphy determines the "hard core" of his program (and the relation of this "hard core" to ethics) in reference only to *The Politics of Jesus*. Even though she may do

---

15. This is the phrase used by Zimmerman to denote the importance of Yoder's work in opening the first chapter of *Practicing the Politics of Jesus*, 23.

16. The conferences that have been most important in this respect are "Assessing the Theological Legacy of John Howard Yoder," University of Notre Dame, March 2002, and "Inheriting John Howard Yoder: A New Generation Examines His Thought," Toronto Mennonite Theological Centre, May 2007.

I would also consider *The New Yoder* as another example of a volume that assumes Yoder's importance and then takes an intentional step in demonstrating why he is still relevant with reference to select interlocutors. What is unique about *The New Yoder* is its relegation of the task of "making sense" of Yoder's work. Of course, the editors presume that making sense of Yoder is important, but not of primary interest. See *The New Yoder*, xv.

17. This statement is not the same as claiming that *The Politics of Jesus* is a "classic," a suggestion that Stanley Hauerwas has rightly argued against. See "When the Politics of Jesus Makes a Difference," 982–87.

so for good reasons, one ought to note that Murphy then introduces Walter Wink, Gustav Aulén, Stanley Hauerwas, and René Girard as interpretive lenses before a second text in Yoder's corpus is referenced.[18] Murphy may be entirely right in her reading of *The Politics of Jesus*, but to assume that this stands as the foundation of a comprehensive account of Yoder's defense of Christian pacifism demands further examination.

It is unlikely that Yoder thought of this text as the key to his corpus, or if there was a single defining text in his corpus.[19] Near the end of his life, he unflatteringly described *The Politics of Jesus* as a text assigned by the Institute of Mennonite Studies (Elkhart, Indiana) that was intended to present a "peace witness" Mennonites would recognize as their own, but one that was directed at non-Mennonite readers through a nondenominational publisher.[20] Of course, *Politics* is not "just any text," but in any appeal to *Politics* as definitive, one ought to qualify the appeal with the recognition that Yoder had been writing for two decades prior to its publication, and that he continued writing for a quarter of a century subsequently. As I hope to demonstrate in chapter 3, this matters.

2. **Yoder never changed his mind or, expressed with more nuance, Yoder is a very logical and systematic thinker.**[21] Another way to express this refrain is to claim a "substantial unity" in Yoder's work.[22] This claim is linked to the first in that the unity of the corpus is usually tied to the defining features of *The Politics of Jesus*, though one

18. See Murphy, "John Howard Yoder's Systematic Defense of Christian Pacifism," 45–68.

19. See, for example, Yoder's comments in the preface to the second edition of *Politics of Jesus*, published in 1994: "There are of course numerous points where my original statement in the 1972 text would need to be corrected or retracted. There are others where it would be fitting to defend it against misinterpretations or to argue against interlocutors who understand it correctly but disagree" (viii). See also Hauerwas, "When the Politics of Jesus Makes a Difference," 982, though Hauerwas also seems to slide into equating *Politics* with the significance of Yoder.

20. Yoder, "The Politics of Jesus Revisited."

21. For an expression of the former, see Reimer, *Mennonites and Classical Theology*, 291; for an expression of the latter, see Carter, *Politics of the Cross*, 18.

22. See Michael Cartwright's introductory essay in *The Royal Priesthood*, 3. Even the editors of *The New Yoder*, Peter Dula and Chris K. Huebner, assume that Yoder's work was "remarkably consistent over the course of a long career" (ix).

rarely finds it stated as baldly as Carter dares when he suggests that the rest of the corpus is devoted to (1) working out the implications of *Politics* and (2) demonstrating that the thesis of *Politics* has been taken seriously in history by the Anabaptist tradition.[23]

The implication of this refrain is that the possibility of disagreement or tension in Yoder's corpus is usually foreclosed from the start.[24] Yet, evolution, tension, and disagreement in Yoder's development are claimed by Yoder himself, illustrated both in his later reflections on the first edition of *Politics*[25] and in conceptual shifts that appear within the corpus (e.g., his use of middle axioms in *The Christian Witness to the State* and their later rejection in *For the Nations*).[26]

The examples cited above are not superficial and should not be easily written off. Yet, the issue under consideration in this challenge is really not the question of whether Yoder changes his mind. Of course he does. Ultimately, the question is, *about what* does Yoder change his mind? To be clear, I am convinced that there are several convictions that remain constant in his thought, and it is precisely his repeated return to these constants that allows an evolving appreciation, interpretation, and application of these very constants. Please allow a brief digression outlining the constants that this book will illuminate though the course of the argument.

a. *The Central Theological Conviction.* If there is one conviction that undergirds Yoder's thought in its entirety it is this: "God is

---

23. Carter, *Politics of the Cross*, 243.

24. Further, to preserve the unity of Yoder's thought, certain portions of the corpus are often simply ignored, especially some of Yoder's later writings such as *Body Politics: Five Practices of the Christian Community Before the Watching World*. Carter is to be commended here, however, for not shying away from this late text in his "Beginner's Guide to Reading John Howard Yoder." See *The Politics of the Cross*, 246.

25. See note 7 above. Noting this, however, does not mean that I am suggesting that there are radical seismic events that change the face of his thought overnight. Rather, I will attempt to demonstrate how Yoder's thought slowly and incrementally shifts—often with considerable overlap—through time.

26. In *Christian Witness to the State*, Yoder calls for the use of middle axioms to "help translate into meaningful and concrete terms the general relevance of the lordship of Christ for a given social ethical issue" (32). Thirty years later, in "The New Humanity as Pulpit and Paradigm," Yoder seems to retract this claim in his appeal to the notion of a paradigm that "points to the awareness that the way most communication works is not by projecting and then reassembling a maximum number of atoms of information, nor of axioms and maxims, but by pattern recognition." See Yoder, *For the Nations*, 43.

sovereign over history."[27] Or, to restate, "The Rule of God is the basic category."[28] For much of his corpus, this is also expressed in christological terms: "Jesus is Lord," or "Jesus is Messiah and Lord."[29]

This claim, however, is not an abstract dogmatic claim. It is a political claim; it is a claim about history; it is a claim about power; it is a claim about the body of Christ. For example, in *The Christian Witness to the State*, Yoder describes it as follows: "The triumph of Christ has already guaranteed that the ultimate meaning of history will not be found in the course of earthly empires or the development of proud cultures, but in the calling together of the 'chosen race, royal priesthood, holy nation,' which is the church of Christ . . . The meaning of history . . . lies in the creation and the work of the church."[30]

Clearly, for Yoder, the claim that Jesus is Lord entails a claim not only about the cosmos in abstract, but about the world in which we live as part of that cosmos. To claim that Jesus is Lord is to live in the world in a particular way, to join a particular community, to exist with a certain style, to participate in the work of the church. After all, Yoder was not afraid to claim that "God too is ecclesiocentric."[31] In this sense, Nancy Murphy is right to claim that, for Yoder, "the point of the New Testament witness, *tout court*, is first of all moral and political (as opposed to metaphysical, doctrinal, mystical)."[32] And this moral and political New Testament witness is the communal witness of the church. In sum, the core conviction driving Yoder's corpus is the conviction that God's kingdom is political, historical, and social. How this conviction plays out in the corpus, however, is continually revisited and reformulated. For Yoder, one defining expression of Christ's lordship in history is contained within the Anabaptist tradition, and, therefore, his distillation of "true Anabaptism" is also the distillation of true

27. Yoder, *For the Nations*, 67.
28. Yoder, *Priestly Kingdom*, 54.
29. See, for example, Yoder, *Royal Priesthood*, 131; *Politics of Jesus*, 235–36; *Original Revolution*, 58; and *Christian Witness to the State*, 8–9.
30. Yoder, *Christian Witness to the State*, 13.
31. Yoder, *For the Nations*, 240.
32. Murphy, "John Howard Yoder's Systematic Defense of Christian Pacifism," 48.

Christianity, a definition he will use normatively and critically as he continually seeks the restitution of Christianity.

b. *The Driving Issue.* If the claim that "God is sovereign over history" is the central theological conviction in Yoder's thought, this conviction extends beyond the church. Yes, to claim Jesus as Lord is to assume a particular ethical and political posture. But this is only part of the story. Yoder identifies the rest of the story in *The Priestly Kingdom*: "The message cannot remain in the ghetto [among believers] because the good news by its very nature is for and about the world. The good news is not information which will remain true even if people in a ghetto celebrate it only for themselves; it is about a community-building story for which the world beyond the ghetto is half of the reconciling event."[33]

Here we can see that the driving issue in Yoder's corpus is simply this: how ought one to think about the relationship between the church and the world if God is sovereign over history?[34]

The sectarian description of Anabaptism by Ernst Troeltsch in the early twentieth century, and later by both Reinhold and H. Richard Niebuhr, provided the intellectual crucible for one of Yoder's college mentors, Harold S. Bender.[35] The opening paragraphs of Bender's defining *The Anabaptist Vision* are haunted by this charge, for how else can one explain a complete and utter lack of humility concerning one's own self-consciously humble tradition when he boldly claims, "There can be no question but that the great principles of freedom of conscience, separation of church and state, and voluntarism in religion, so basic in American

---

33. Yoder, *Priestly Kingdom*, 55. In "The Otherness of the Church," Yoder frames the relationship in a way that has made the ontology of peace posited by "Radical Orthodoxy" rather appealing to his readers: "But behind or above this visible dichotomy [of the church and the world] there is a believed unity. All evidence to the contrary notwithstanding, the church believed that its Lord was also Lord over the world... This belief in Christ's lordship over the *exousiai* enabled the church, in and in spite of its distinctness from the world, to speak to the world in God's name, not only in evangelism but in ethical judgment as well." See Yoder, *Royal Priesthood*, 56.

34. It is precisely this conviction that James Davison Hunter does not adequately account for in his tendentious summary of Yoder and "neo-Anabaptists" in *To Change the World*.

35. The charge of sectarianism remains alive and well late into the twentieth century. See, for example, James Gustafson, "The Sectarian Temptation."

Protestantism and so essential to democracy, ultimately are derived from the Anabaptists of the Reformation period, who for the first time clearly enunciated them and challenged the Christian world to follow them in practice."[36] This, too, is part of the Bender legacy that left a deep imprint on the young Yoder, who in his dissertation dared to suggest that it was not the Anabaptists but the Protestant state churches in the second half of the sixteenth century that were, in fact, sectarian.[37]

For Yoder, it is not pacifism that is the driving issue in his thinking, but rather the church's relationship to the rest of the world.[38] One of the obvious signs that this issue permeates Yoder's thought lies in his book titles, which betray his basic conviction as clearly as Reinhold Niebuhr's binary labels betray him. How else can one explain *The Christian Witness to the State*, *Discipleship as Political Responsibility*, *The Priestly Kingdom: Social Ethics as Gospel*, *Body Politics: Five Practices of the Christian Community for the Watching World*, and *For the Nations: Essays Public and Evangelical*, to name just a few? Certainly, each of these texts provides a slightly different account of the interaction between the church and the world, yet the issue is the same: the church is related to the world and must tell the world that God is sovereign over history.

c. *The Perennial Question*. Given the above, how is the church to share this conviction? One difficulty with Yoder's corpus is that there is not one single answer as to how the church ought to speak or witness (or whether the church ought to speak or witness) to the world around it. Sometimes Yoder argues that the church ought

---

36. Bender, *The Anabaptist Vision*, 3–4.

37. Yoder, *Anabaptism and Reformation*, 136.

38. This is evident in both his constructive and critical arguments. For a fine example of the latter, see the open and harsh challenge to some of his postliberal and Mennonite friends (much like the title of the collection of essays in which it appears—*For the Nations*). In this context, Yoder rejects the possibility that the church cannot or should not speak to the world in stating: "The 'communitarians' of our time, for whom all meaning is internally self-authenticating, may be taken to stand for the people whom Paul in this passage calls 'Jews.' They will not risk the challenge of telling the world that servanthood, enemy love, and forgiveness would be a better way to run a university, a town, or a factory. They pull back on the grounds that only they have already experienced the power and novelty of that threefold evangelical cord in the worship and ministry of the church. They affirm integrity but at the cost of witness." See *For the Nations*, 49.

to use middle axioms; sometimes he argues that the church ought to use paradigmatic practices; sometimes he argues something else in between. Yet, in all cases, Yoder rejects the sectarian label and demands that the church share the truth, the good news, with the world. But it is precisely here that Yoder's Anabaptist posture of loving humility also affects his communication, an evolving dialogical communication that is ruled by the claim that God is sovereign over history.

In laying out what I take to be the three interrelated and constant elements of Yoder's logic, I am attempting to specify the things about which Yoder did not change his mind. Most readers of Yoder's work will agree that these are absolutely central elements of his thought. Granting this formally, however, still requires further specification of how these get fleshed out. On this issue, the question of how the church communicates with the world introduces some equivocation. As Yoder dialogues with those within and outside of his own tradition, and with those within and outside of Christianity, his articulation of how the church relates to the world slowly evolves. Recognizing the possibility for development and innovation, therefore, opens the possibility of discerning the potentially problematic elements of Yoder's legacy, and therefore the probability of disagreement between my reading and that of several of his sympathetic readers.

3. **Yoder only wrote on topics that he was assigned.** Certainly, as exemplified above concerning *The Politics of Jesus*, there is ample evidence that Yoder wrote many of his lectures, articles, and books at the request of certain organizations, institutions, or groups. This observation, however, takes on a certain interpretive power when it is coupled with the assumption that Yoder adapted his tone or language to address the particular audience he was assigned to address.[39]

On one hand, this claim relates to the previous—the unity in Yoder's thought—in that this is one means of overriding possible dissonance in Yoder's corpus (e.g., "Yoder is just using different language to explain the same thing," or "If he were addressing Mennonites he

---

39. The argument usually made here is that Yoder is a conversational writer who begins where the reader is in order to begin the conversation. After all, as Yoder himself says, there is no "from scratch" to begin a conversation. See Yoder, *For the Nations*, 10.

would have said such and such,"⁴⁰ or "That [book/article/lecture] was never intended to be read in this way or by this group"—all of which I have heard in one form or another on multiple occasions). On the other hand, this is also the dialectical counter to the previous interpretive key—the unity of Yoder's thought—in that this third claim preserves Yoder from becoming a systematizer or methodologist, which are both derogatory words for most readers of Yoder.⁴¹ Taken together, these conclusions provide a way of allowing a high level of confidence in constructing "Yoder's position," even if there may appear to be equivocations in language, emphases, or themes.

There are, however, several difficulties with this position. First, the usually unstated implication here is that Yoder was not entirely in control of the production of his corpus and, therefore, certain claims, statements, phrases, and ideas can be ignored—or at least marginalized—while others can be supplied in the face of a perceived lack. Logically and textually, however, this conclusion and its implications are problematic. On a very simple level, even if a topic was assigned to him, Yoder was still responsible for preparing the content of his books, articles, and lectures. Further, archived correspondence indicates that there was usually some flexibility in selecting topics for lectures. And Yoder certainly also had preferences and interests that he sought to attend to in his research, most clearly evident in his application for various fellowships to study the history of Jewish-Christian relations.⁴²

---

40. Again, Yoder himself provides warrant for this approach in, for example, *The Priestly Kingdom*. At the conclusion of "The Kingdom as Social Ethic," he states: "The imperatives of dialogue with majority mentalities have skewed this description toward the problematics of weakness and effectiveness. An authentic portrayal of 'the peace church vision' from the inside would have spoken more of worship and servanthood, reconciliation and creativity, *Gelassenheit* and the Power of the Light, 'heartfelt religion' and transforming hope, and the person of Jesus Christ. But if this paper had been thus affirmative then the reader would have wondered why any of that should be 'sectarian.'" Yoder, *Priestly Kingdom*, 101.

41. See, for example, Huebner, "The Christian Life as Gift and Patience."

42. For example, in 1983, Yoder applied for both Guggenheim and Rockefeller Fellowships for the purpose of bringing together and synthesizing contemporary developments in understanding the history of the church in "the epoch of 50–150" and its relevance to the situation at the end of "the age of Christendom" (see the "Minimal Prospectus for a Research Project").

Second, in terms of language, Yoder was very explicit in his later works that he was seeking a new kind of language—analogous to Yiddish—that provides a third way between his "native" language and the language of the world around him.[43] Third, and relatedly, the idea of "getting behind" Yoder's language to grasp the kernel of what he really means assumes that the reader possesses the true definition of the terms, that the reader grasps what Yoder really intended. Yet, as the epigraph for this volume suggests, Yoder called definitions of many things into question, not merely the definitions of terms used by those on one side of an argument. In the face of this position, the working principle of this book is that Yoder had considerable control and intention in the language he used and the writing of his corpus, certainly more than this third regulative principle implies.

4. **To understand Yoder you must place his thought in its "proper historical context," which is Anabaptism**. This principle is closely related to the previous. It is not by accident that Nation, Carter, and Zimmerman all begin their exposition of Yoder's thought with chapters devoted to the mid-twentieth-century Anabaptist context in which Yoder emerges. Especially relevant in all their narratives is Yoder's embrace of Bender's *The Anabaptist Vision*. At one level, this is the right way to begin since Yoder did emerge in this context, and he was deeply and permanently formed by it (and this book, too, must deal with Yoder's relation to his formative Anabaptist context). Aside from the familiar difficulties with Bender,[44] it is generally assumed that Yoder appropriates and expands a form of the three essential characteristics of *The Anabaptist Vision*: the believers church, discipleship, and pacifism. Therefore, it is understandable that a version of the Anabaptist world is the context that one may comfortably assume fills in the perceived gaps that Yoder was not able to address anywhere in his corpus (especially if one assumes he was too busy attending to issues that he had been assigned).[45]

---

43. See Yoder, *For the Nations*, 4.
44. See Nation, *John Howard Yoder*, 20–21.
45. For example, Carter sympathetically explains Yoder's account of baptism as dependent on his believers church context in this way: "If Yoder were giving a systematic account of theology, instead of writing on the specific topic of the retrieval of the ethical meaning of Christian doctrines and practices, it would be a serious omission to leave out the meaning of baptism to the person baptized . . . While I would not want to accuse

Yet, Yoder's constructive understanding of Anabaptism is singular, narrow, and not necessarily to be equated with his own Mennonite tradition. Therefore, invoking an unspecified notion of Mennonitism or Anabaptism to replace what has been rejected or challenged by Yoder (a category that includes significant elements of Yoder's own Anabaptist and Mennonite heritage) becomes a tenuous and tricky enterprise.

Perhaps more could be added to this list, but these four claims suffice to characterize the broad assumptions held by a majority of Yoder's sympathetic interpreters today. The difficulty with this list of interpretive keys is that they are true, but not entirely true. With the little bit of explanation noted above, I have sought to demonstrate that (*a*) a form of each claim can be located within Yoder's corpus, (*b*) all of these claims work together to support a certain interpretation of Yoder, and (*c*) all of these claims can also be overstated. The purpose of this book is to destabilize or relativize this regulative framework in order to avoid what I take to be the simplistic synthesis that they allow within Yoder's corpus, thereby opening the possibility of new readings of Yoder. Ignoring these principles and turning to the texts themselves, the following is a brief sketch of the shape of this book that attempts to follow diachronically the introduction and development of foundational themes in Yoder's corpus. In taking Yoder's evolving voice seriously, I am attempting to respect a rich corpus, one that betrays a thoughtful and questioning mind and that cannot and should not be forced into a prescribed consolidation or synthesis. In doing so, I intend to dispense with the defensive gnosis that has governed much of the interpretation to date and to question Yoder patiently and persistently as Yoder questioned those who had gone before him.

A BRIEF COMMENT ABOUT THE SHAPE OF THIS BOOK

This book roughly follows the development of the central theological themes in Yoder's corpus. To begin, the first chapter examines the foundational theological commitments that emerge in Yoder's early years—the years before the appearance of his more recognizable texts, the years when he was working in France and studying in Basel. It traces the prevalence

---

Yoder of reductionism, it must, nevertheless, be noted that his account of baptism is incomplete and needs to be incorporated into a systematic believer's church theology so that its implications can be worked out and clarified." See Carter, *Politics of the Cross*, 199.

of discipleship as an ethical category in its relation to the work of Christ, moral freedom, biblical interpretation, and the work of the church, and concludes that all of the elements in Yoder's theology are best understood within a certain free church understanding of ecclesiology.

Working from the conclusion of the first chapter, the second proceeds to reexamine the contributions of the texts that immediately precede *The Politics of Jesus*. It begins by demonstrating how Yoder's description of the church as "the original revolution" enables both a particular ecclesiology and a specific kind of witness to the state. The chapter then returns to *Politics* by contextualizing its pacifism within these broader concerns. Reconsidering *Politics* in this context, however, illuminates how the conviction that discipleship is primarily ethics is beginning to play itself out in ways that constrict not only the biblical texts but also the definition and practices of the church.

The third and fourth chapters then trace out the increasingly problematic accounts of ecclesiology, ecumenism, ethics, and Christology that emerge in the years following the appearance of *Politics*. The third chapter traces the evolution of his reconstruction of Jewish Christianity to the point where the politics of *diaspora* becomes the normative style of a minority existence in the world for original messianic Judaism; the fourth traces the intra-Christian discussion of ecumenism that becomes focused upon sacraments as the most effective social processes that unite Christians and build the kingdom of God.

As I have already indicated, I will argue that this trajectory eventually yields a certain heterodoxy; the conclusion explains why this is so by returning to the original foundational themes found in Yoder's early writings. In this process, I hope to show that the difficulty with Yoder's corpus is not that there are a few trees that are out of place. Rather, the difficulty is that Yoder's corpus may actually be a different forest than many think they are seeing.

Two final notes: First, as this book is devoted to explicating the logic of Yoder's corpus, engagements with secondary material will generally be limited to the footnotes. Further, it is already clear that there will be occasional disagreements (of varying degrees) between my interpretation of Yoder's corpus and those interpretations offered by Nation, Carter, and others. Rather than repeatedly highlighting these, I will generally assume that the interested reader can search these out on his or her own. In the final chapter, I will make some general comments concerning this text in relation to (1) other renderings of Yoder's theological ethics and (2) the context of ongoing conversations within the larger field of Christian ethics.

Second, as this book is an attempt to trace a broad chronological trajectory in Yoder's thought, the manner in which his texts are footnoted will resist the current practice. For reasons outlined above and because each of the following collections spans many years, I will refer to individual articles contained within *The Original Revolution*, *The Priestly Kingdom*, *The Royal Priesthood*, *For the Nations*, and *The Jewish-Christian Schism Revisited*.

TWO

Foundational Theological Commitments

While he was a student at Goshen College, Yoder apparently enjoyed breaking dress conventions—it is said he would wear a necktie with a T-shirt or use his necktie as a belt. And, to the chagrin of professors everywhere and always, he would sit through lectures and participate in class discussions while also reading a book.[1] Of course, these observations have little material relevance to the foundational commitments I am addressing in this chapter. They may, however, have some formal resonance with the content of this chapter, as these overtly tactless actions illuminate the independent and perhaps irreverent streak that freed Yoder to pursue his vocation boldly, to chart a path that no one had walked before. Whatever the case may be, it is most helpful to remember that there was already a considerable amount of youthfully energetic groundwork completed in Yoder's thought before the monumental *The Politics of Jesus* became the book that it is. This chapter is an attempt to introduce some of the central features of the foundation that were taking shape in Yoder's dynamic early years.

Earl Zimmerman, referring to the publication of Yoder's dissertation on Swiss Anabaptists, suggests that Yoder had developed his basic theological commitments by 1962. He then goes on to claim that the maturing of this vision is "best seen in three books that he wrote in the next ten years," namely, *Christian Witness to the State* (1964), *The Original Revolution* (1971), and *The Politics of Jesus* (1972).[2] Selecting 1962 as the

---

1. Zimmerman, *Practicing the Politics of Jesus*, 42.
2. Ibid., 174. Reimer articulated a similar position: "His *The Politics of Jesus* (1972)

year in which Yoder's convictions coalesced is somewhat arbitrary because that particular date is simply attached to the publication of Yoder's dissertation. But Zimmerman's point is that these issues were basically settled in Yoder's mind before the publication of his more familiar writings. On this point, Zimmerman stands with the majority of Yoder scholarship. Yet, if this claim is correct, then it is very important to have a clear understanding of what Yoder was up to in the years leading up to 1962. If this claim is not correct, then it is important to have a clear understanding of where Yoder changes his mind or develops beyond his early writings. Either way, the theological commitments that undergird the initial years of Yoder's scholarship provide the foundation for his subsequent reflections.

In another expression of his idiosyncrasy, Yoder had written and published a substantial amount by the time he published his dissertation. His first scholarly article—"Caesar and the Meidung"—was published already in 1949, and it was quickly followed by several other lasting scholarly contributions, including but not limited to "Reinhold Niebuhr and Christian Pacifism" (1955), *The Ecumenical Movement and the Faithful Church* (1958), "The Otherness of the Church" (1960), and *Peace Without Eschatology?* (1961). Alongside these he also published dozens of popular essays and wrote a number of unpublished papers. Therefore, Zimmerman has a considerable amount of material to work with when he claims that Yoder had developed his basic theological commitments by this time.

Speaking of the results of Yoder's dissertation, which was, in turn, the culmination of his formative years, Zimmerman notes: "The two key concepts of Anabaptism, according to Yoder, were *community* and *discipleship*."[3] Yoder, at this stage, rooted his own position within the Anabaptist trajectory, and it is also true that these two concepts stand at the center of his own emerging theology; the texts examined below bear this out extensively. Therefore, in this chapter, I will use these related concepts as the means to unpack the theological convictions grounding the corpus. In short, I will begin to unfold how these two concepts are defined and appropriated by Yoder in a way that illuminates these early years and also paves the way for developments in the later years of Yoder's authorship—the years following the publication of *The Politics of Jesus*—that I would consider to be the complete maturation of these

---

was simply a working out of his Concern Group theology of the 1950s and 1960s." See "Mennonites, Christ, and Culture," 6.

3. Ibid., 164.

early convictions. As a preliminary description of discipleship is helpful for understanding Yoder's church community, I will proceed to address the themes in this order.

DISCIPLESHIP: A PREAMBLE

The notion that discipleship is central to Yoder's thought is impossible to challenge. An examination of the concept can be attempted from several directions. On one side, the concept of discipleship ties Yoder to his former teacher and mentor at Goshen College, Harold S. Bender. In Bender's classic, *The Anabaptist Vision*, he emphatically states: "First and fundamental in the Anabaptist vision was the conception of the essence of Christianity as discipleship."[4] Certainly, the young and occasionally petulant Yoder was critical of elements of Bender's practical application of Anabaptism as it pertained to the building of denominational institutions and identities, but on the centrality of discipleship there is deep sympathy.[5] One example of the elder mentor's influence is found in Yoder's contribution to a collection of essays that served as a "Sixtieth Anniversary Tribute" to Bender. In his contribution, Yoder argued that what the Anabaptists called discipleship was simply the claim that Christ is authoritative in ethics in the same way that the Reformers understood Christ as authoritative in soteriology.[6] In his early years, Yoder believed that "the structural connection between Christ and ethics" was the theological key that nearly all Christians had missed. Therefore, for Yoder as with Bender, to the extent that the Anabaptists held a high view of Christ in both ethics and soteriology, they also stood in prophetic dissent against both Catholics and Reformers in the sixteenth century.[7]

---

4. Bender, *The Anabaptist Vision*, 20. The second point of emphasis in Bender's retrieval of Anabaptism is the concept of the voluntary church, and the third is nonviolence. I do not want to overstate the debt Yoder has to Bender here, but a form of the logic of this order also seems to be present in Yoder's thought, as I will illustrate below. In a footnote in his "The Prophetic Dissent," Yoder pointed to Bender's *The Anabaptist Vision*, Ethelbert Stauffer's "The Anabaptist Theology of Martyrdom," and Bender's "The Anabaptist Theology of Discipleship" as expositions of "discipleship as the formal principle of Christian ethics." See Yoder, "Prophetic Dissent," 100.

5. See Zimmerman, *Practicing the Politics of Jesus*, 42–50, and Nation, *John Howard Yoder*, 10–29.

6. Yoder, "Prophetic Dissent," 100.

7. In these early texts one cannot ignore Yoder's rather facile descriptions of other— i.e., non-Anabaptist—Christians. For example, in this particular discussion, he states:

On another side, the concept of discipleship can be approached from the direction of Yoder's critique of Reinhold Niebuhr.[8] Yoder's relationship with Niebuhr is complex, as Niebuhr is also responsible for articulating and validating a certain form of pacifism rooted in the life and teachings of Jesus within the contested conversations of twentieth-century Christian ethics. In "Reinhold Niebuhr and Christian Pacifism," Yoder clearly notes that one of the reasons Niebuhr matters is "because he talks to us," because he addresses the question of pacifism and nonresistance, "using it in fact as the clearest case of the essential problem of all Christian ethics."[9] Working in the wake of Niebuhr's Christian Realism, Yoder is pressed into the precarious position of affirming that Niebuhr was right to construe Jesus' life and thought as pacifist and yet wrong in his "realistic" limiting of the imitation of Jesus to one's personal life and excluding it from social life and, therefore, from history.[10] Or, to restate, Yoder argued that Niebuhr was right about Jesus but he was wrong in his contextualization of the imitation of Jesus within the rest of his theology

---

"The Reformers were so fully conditioned by their anti-Catholic polemic that they fell prey to the temptation to affirm simply the opposite of what the Roman Church had taught. Against Catholic immanence they leaned toward an almost Docetic transcendentalism; against Catholic legalism they tended toward antinomianism" ("Prophetic Dissent," 100). Or, one page later: "With Augustine, the Reformers identified the millennium with the Christianization of the Roman Empire" (101).

These sorts of sweeping oversimplifications cannot be ignored, and others have taken note of the problem as well. See, for example, Leithart, *Defending Constantine*, 284–85. That said, recognizing these deficiencies in his understanding does not automatically discredit the constructive argument that he is attempting to articulate. Looking at this particular case, whether he is right or wrong about "the Reformers," "Catholics," or a selection of "the Reformers" or "Catholics," his articulation of discipleship is not automatically disqualified from being cogent and compelling, even if less polemical. And it is also helpful to recognize that as Yoder matures, these sorts of generalizations become less frequent and more qualified.

8. See, for example, Wright, *Disavowing Constantine*, 57, who includes Yoder's encounter with H. Richard Niebuhr's thought as definitional.

9. Yoder, "Reinhold Niebuhr and Christian Pacifism," 101.

10. See, for example, Niebuhr's claim that "the ethical demands made by Jesus are incapable of fulfillment in the present existence of man." Importantly, Niebuhr's rationale is rooted in a view of the eschatological context of Christian action, as he continues: "They proceed from a transcendent and divine unity of essential reality, and their final fulfillment is possible only when God transmutes the present chaos of this world into its final unity." Niebuhr, *Interpretation of Christian Ethics*, 35.

(or, some would suggest, his lack of theology).[11] In response, Yoder's criticism is sharp. Yoder demands discipleship:

> The acceptance of the *cross*, i.e., the full cost of utter obedience to the loving nature of God, is the path to the accomplishment in history, not of perfection, but of action which can please God and be useful to men. The triumph of love over sin is not reserved for some Platonic realm (such as Niebuhr's "superhistory") where the eschatological judgment takes place. Sin is vanquished every time a Christian in the power of God chooses the better instead of the good, obedience instead of necessity, love instead of compromise, brotherhood instead of veiled self-interest.[12]

On another side, one could approach Yoder's discipleship from the context of his studies at the University of Basel, especially his relationship to Oscar Cullman and Karl Barth. As Zimmerman rightly notes, Yoder seems to affirm Barth's reading of the Bible as a narrative centered in Jesus Christ, thereby making the particular story of Jesus decisive for discipleship and ethics.[13] Further, the biblical exegesis of Cullman also appears to have had a profound influence on Yoder's description of discipleship through (*a*) an articulation of the notion of the "reign of Christ" as a viable replacement for two-kingdom theology, (*b*) his research on Jesus' relationship to the Roman and Jewish parties in first-century Palestine, and (*c*) his research on the politics of Paul.[14]

Wherever one wishes to begin the discussion, it is clear that discipleship permeates Yoder's early thought, and its persistent presence cannot

---

11. See Hauerwas (with Michael Broadway), "The Irony of Reinhold Niebuhr."

12. Yoder, "Reinhold Niebuhr and Christian Pacifism," 116.

13. Zimmerman, *Practicing the Politics of Jesus*, 104. Zimmerman also highlights that Barth also affirmed the rejection of natural theology as a source independent of the story of Jesus and the distinction between the church and world for all social and ethical reflection. Craig Carter develops a more expansive list of eight "areas of agreement and similarity" with a further attempt to describe Yoder's "postliberal" approach to social ethics as a creative synthesis between the Anabaptist theological heritage and Barth's theological method (Carter, *The Politics of the Cross*, 89). In this context, I only intend to provide a brief gesture toward genealogical debts. That said, I think Zimmerman's caution that one ought not to overemphasize Yoder's indebtedness to Barth is appropriate given all of the other converging influences bearing upon the young Yoder. See also Yoder, *Karl Barth and the Problem of War*.

14. Ibid., 104. I am borrowing the articulation of these three particular contributions from Zimmerman, as I believe he has done an excellent job of illuminating the relevance of Cullman for grasping the evolving formulation of Yoder's theological categories.

be attributed to only one cause. Complicating the discussion further is the pervasive assumption that we all understand what Yoder meant when he used the term "discipleship." Of course, shorthand overlapping analogues like "obedience," "the imitation of Christ," and *Nachfolge* are frequently used, and certain understandings of these terms partially capture the depth of what Yoder meant. But his use of the term was intentional and specific, implying a theological background that belies the term's familiarity. It is precisely the concept of discipleship that occupied Yoder's contribution to the first volume of *Concern* in 1954, namely, "The Anabaptist Dissent: The Logic of the Place of the Disciple in Society." He began as follows:

> This essay attempts, in the context of current ecumenical discussions of the church's responsibility in society, and with special reference to the problems involving the use of violence, to elaborate a doctrine of social responsibility logically consistent with the concept of discipleship as understood and interpreted within the Anabaptist-Mennonite tradition . . .
>
> Discipleship is here understood as denoting a particular attitude toward the Christian life, whose major emphases are:
>
> a. That the Christian life is defined most basically in ethical terms. While forgiveness, membership in a social order, participation in worship, or receiving a revelation may all be very relevant factors, they do not rob *obedience in ethics* (*Nachfolge*) of primary rank.[15]
>
> b. That valid ethical instructions are given in the New Testament, on the basis of which we may reliably know the precise content of the obedience which is expected of us. This attitude will be seen to contrast with other uses of the terms "obedience" and "discipleship" which are unrelated to precise ethical formulations, and which leave the content to be determined by a sort of enlightened opportunism.[16]

This statement is not only clear, it is bracing in its boldness. To those who have come back to the early Yoder after passing through Hauerwas and the liturgical turn in contemporary Christian ethics,[17] this statement will be jarring in its assertion that the Christian life is, most basically, defined as ethics. And the relegation of worship, forgiveness, and receiv-

---

15. See also the subsequent comment: "The disciple [is] the Christian who sees his 'Christian-ness' as being an ethical matter." Yoder, "The Anabaptist Dissent," 32.

16. Yoder, "The Anabaptist Dissent," 29.

17. See, for example, *The Blackwell Companion to Christian Ethics*.

ing a revelation (and any number of other unnamed elements of the Christian life) to subordinate roles under ethics further complexifies several sympathetic readings of Yoder.

In the remaining pages of this book, I intend to demonstrate that this definition of discipleship—even though increasingly nuanced and refined—remains normative for Yoder throughout his life, and that this conviction initially gives birth to a fresh and polemical understanding of Christian existence but, as the years progress, also matures into a problematic account of Christian particularity as it continues to pursue the primacy of ethical existence that is shaped by "precise ethical formulations." As we will see, the development of this story is complex. Yet the thread of the primacy of the ethical remains strong and central throughout, especially as we turn to Yoder's articulation of community. Before moving in that direction, however, please allow a brief examination of three theological convictions that mutually support his account of discipleship: (*a*) the redefinition of soteriology in light of the elevation of discipleship, (*b*) moral freedom, and (*c*) the unity and clarity of the New Testament ethical demands understood in light of discipleship.

Discipleship and the Work of Christ

It is generally assumed that Yoder does not engage in systematic theology, and in terms of method, this is generally true. In 1954, however, he presented a short unpublished paper titled "A Study of the Doctrine of the Work of Christ" that comes as close to a systematic exposition of a doctrine as can be found in the corpus. The starting point for this study, according to Yoder, is the revolutionary effect accomplished by the introduction of discipleship as a guide to understanding the Christian life, and the purpose of his seminar paper is to examine what sort of soteriology is required to affirm and enable the centrality of discipleship. He explains:

> This undertaking is rendered all the more necessary by the fact that often the Work of Christ is so understood as to undermine the concern for discipleship. Ever since Luther stated man's problem as "how to get a gracious God" and found the answer "by Grace," it has been felt that any effort to take ethics seriously was self-justification and a misjudgment of the atonement. It must therefore be ascertained whether discipleship and atonement are

thus opposed; and if they are not, it must be seen wherein the Lutheran view made a wrong move.[18]

Here we find Yoder directly addressing the issue that appears in print a few years later in "The Prophetic Dissent of the Anabaptists." Even at first glance, Yoder's commitment to the primacy of discipleship in the definition of the "Work of Christ" is evident, as, clearly, any opposition between the two—discipleship and Christ's work—must be attributed to Luther's wrong move. To proceed to resolve this opposition, Yoder outlines two methodological criteria: the first is negative, the second positive.

First and negatively, Yoder rejects the necessary normativity of what he took to be medieval formulations of the doctrine of Christ. Provoking a discussion among Anabaptists that is still hotly contested because it strikes at the core question of theological identity, Yoder emphatically states: "In the Anabaptist–free church context, where the marriage of church and world consummated under Constantine, Constantius, and Theodosius has come to be known as the 'Fall of Christianity,' we are not bound to any special reverence for the doctrinal formulations worked out by the medieval Catholic church. This is as true for certain aspects of the Nicene Creed (where Constantine himself suggested as a compromise the wording finally accepted) as for the Augustinian eschatology, the Anselmian soteriology, or the Thomistic ontology."[19]

I sometimes wonder whether Yoder would be more amused or confused by the debate that has emerged concerning his adherence to the creeds, but, be that as it may, one can see in this brief introductory statement that Alain Epp Weaver's position on this matter—"Yoder explicitly did not contend . . . that the creeds are theologically suspect simply because they took shape under Constantine"—is too strong.[20] On the other hand, the above statement seems to support J. Denny Weaver's claim that Yoder's "analysis of Nicene-Chalcedonian Christology opened the door

---

18. Yoder, "A Study in the Doctrine of the Work of Christ," 1. (Hereafter, "A Study.")
19. Ibid.
20. Weaver, "Missionary Christology," 434. Weaver, in making this claim, is protesting against Reimer, who argued that "Yoder understands the fourth-century theological debates primarily within a socio-political framework (both ecclesiastical and imperial), and this makes him suspicious of them." See Reimer, "Trinitarian Orthodoxy," 254.

Yoder's statement, cited above, does seem to challenge the absolute claim, offered by Craig Carter, that "Yoder's approach to social ethics is rooted in the classical, orthodox Christology that the ecumenical creeds affirm as the meaning of the Scriptures." See Carter, *Politics of the Cross*, 93, 113–26.

to seeing the particular context of these formulas and their specific link to Constantinian ecclesiology."[21] In this comment, one ought to note that J. Denny Weaver claims that Yoder merely "opens the door" (and does not necessarily walk through it in the same way as Weaver) and that Yoder himself stipulates that only "certain aspects" can be excluded from special reverence. Therefore, A. E. Weaver is also not wrong to argue that Yoder does use traditional Christian creedal statements in ecumenical and missional contexts. And this is also to say that there are elements of the Nicene Creed that Yoder will hold as definitive for Christianity, even if these elements of the creed are further specified or redefined beyond traditional understandings, such as his subsequent claim that his position is "more radically Nicene and Chalcedonian than other views."[22] But getting back to the point of Yoder's comment, it is important to note that Yoder does not hold certain elements of the Nicene or Chalcedonian Creed as authoritative because they are in the creed. Rather, to the extent that certain elements of the creeds capture what he takes to be the teachings of the Bible, particularly the teachings of Jesus, just to that extent do the creeds—and the rest of what was consummated under the "Fall of Christianity"—become authoritative.[23] With this recognition we arrive at the positive criterion for the doctrine of Christ.

21. Weaver, *Anabaptist Theology in Face of Postmodernity*, 44. In this statement, Weaver seems to be merely echoing Yoder's later claim that issues of theology in the Constantinian church were, in the end, "dealt with on the political level. That is what made an issue serious in that age of the church." See Yoder, *Preface to Theology*, 215.

22. See Yoder, *Priestly Kingdom*, 8–9.

23. In his posthumously published lecture notes that were used between the early 1960s and 1981 (and that reflect "the state of scholarly opinion in 1960"), Yoder outlines the relationship between Bible and Creed as follows:

> If we look back at the politics between 325 and 431, at some of the theologians' methods and motives, at the personal quality of Constantine, or if we ask in what sense he was a Christian when he dictated this dogma, then we have to be dubious about giving the movement any authority. If we call into question the acceptance of Hellenistic thought forms foreign to the way the Bible thinks, which fit with neither the Hebrew mind nor, for that matter, with the modern mind, then again we have to challenge whether the creed does us much good . . .
>
> For the Believers Church tradition, and for modern readings of the story, it seems that the only claim of the Nicene Creed is to have provided the best answer to an intellectual problem. The doctrine is not authoritative, but the claims of Jesus who creates the problem are.

See *Preface to Theology*, 204–5.

The second and positive criterion is defined as "the Bible," or perhaps more accurately, as "the NT teachings." I will return to a fuller account of this criterion below, but in this context, a few words are necessary. Yoder's basic contention is that exegesis, "for centuries," has been hindered by the presuppositions of the exegetes in such a way that prevented them from allowing the texts to "speak for themselves." The presuppositions that have crippled exegesis are, as one might expect, theological presuppositions that have been constructed in the context of Constantinian Christianity and, therefore, have led exegetes to ask the wrong questions. Here again the concept of discipleship comes to the rescue: "Abandoned by Christendom since patristic times, [the perspective of discipleship] can provide the key to the puzzle, and thus a coherent and meaningful understanding of the Work of Christ may be found which will deal more satisfactorily with the facts than the theories heretofore submitted have done."[24] Fortunately, Yoder does recognize how pretentious this claim is, as it is a claim to have "rediscovered the truth," lost since the early church, about the work of Christ.

Having established the appropriate criteria for explicating the work of Christ, Yoder then moves on to deconstruct Anselm's satisfaction theory of the atonement. As I want to spend time with Yoder's positive redefinition, I will abstain from tracing the details of his critique in this context.[25] To begin his own account, rather than focusing on sin as the central problem of the atonement, Yoder poses two foci: (*a*) separation from God and (*b*) the incapacity to do good. Salvation, therefore, is not primarily concerned with the remission of guilt or the cancellation of punishment for sin that one has committed. Rather, salvation is concerned with "reconciliation (reestablishment of communion) and obedience,

---

This position also looks much like Yoder's description of Anabaptist hermeneutics, which elevated the role of the congregation (which we will return to shortly): "The other necessary implication of thus placing theological authority in the hands of the congregation was that the congregation must not be bound by tradition or former creedal statements, nor by the supervision of government authority. The congregation will recognize the assistance of the teaching tradition, and learn from it as long as it is in accordance with Scripture . . . There was no denial of history; but there was a refusal to be bound by tradition." Yoder, "The Hermeneutics of the Anabaptists," 301.

24. Yoder, "A Study," 3.

25. To follow this conversation further, one should begin with Rachel Reesor Taylor, "Yoder's Mischievous Contribution to Mennonite Views on Anselmian Atonement."

i.e., discipleship."[26] "Every strand of NT literature makes clear that God's purpose with man is to establish obedience in his communion, not to deal with guilt."[27] To this end, redemption is understood as a "change of masters."[28] The work of Christ, then, is best understood as the fullest expression of what God meant humans to be: "The work of Christ is, at its center, obedience (Philippians 2 *et al.*). Christ was exactly what God meant man to be; man in free communion with God, obeying God and loving mankind with God's love. This is the truth which the Nicene Creed seeks to safeguard; this man Christ Jesus was really God working, was man in perfect communion with God. Nicaea affirms the reality of God's working in Christ's obedience."[29]

Rather than addressing the unity between God and humans in ontological and metaphysical terms (the allegedly false move toward the world of Greek thought exemplified in creedal orthodoxy), Yoder argues that the unity between God and humans, for lack of better terms, is a unity in will and action.[30] Therefore, "unity in Christ" and "abiding in Christ" are

26. Yoder, "A Study," 4.

27. Ibid.

28. Yoder, as he frequently did, cited textual evidence here, drawing on 1 Cor 6:20; 7:23; Rom 6:17-22.

29. Yoder, "A Study," 8.

30. In "Let the Church Be the Church," Yoder explicitly uses the language of unity between Jesus and the Father in "will and deed" (129). This formulation helps us understand Yoder's later comments concerning the problem with Christmas. In an effort to separate himself from the metaphysical claims of creeds, he makes the following rather bold claim in "On the Meaning of Christmas": "If in the effort to save Christmas, we bring to it the full weight of the miracle of God-made-infant, we fall into the docetic heresy, affirming the full divine presence apart from the *story* of the man. Divine sonship is clearly proclaimed first at Jesus' baptism; before that the Gospels only point to its promise. For the sake of the real meaning of incarnation we must, like the Gospels, see the cross behind the cradle" (19).

His point is simple: "Not the innocence of the infant but the obedience of the Man, Jesus, saves us" (18). That said, Yoder is also keen on not being identified as representing adoptionism (see *Preface to Theology*, 124).

It seems that Yoder is still finding his theological home while working within the exegetical framework offered by Cullman (see *The Christology of the New Testament*), which limits his claims on these matters to what he defines as the "real meaning" (as above) or, later, as the core of the New Testament content: "It is that Jesus, the Word in Jesus, is genuinely of the character of the deity and genuinely human, and that his work is the work of God and yet the work of man" (*Preface to Theology*, 201). In this statement, it is also clear that, in a manner not too distant from many nineteenth-century theologians, Yoder's *Preface to Theology* also utilizes the notions of a discernable and definable

not mystical assertions but ethical statements about how human actions align with the actions of God revealed in Jesus, actions that include laying down one's life in suffering and death.[31] This is the theological root of Yoder's nonviolence, namely, that God is nonviolent.[32]

To complete the transformation of soteriology so that it aligns with discipleship, Yoder returns to the language of repentance and faith:

> Man's appropriation of the Work of Christ is by repentance and faith, but neither of these terms is to be understood as orthodoxy understood them. Repentance means ethics, not sorrow for sin; it is the turning-around of the will which is the condition of obedience . . .
>
> Faith, likewise, must be understood biblically and de-Anselmized. It is not the acceptance of the proclamation that Jesus dies because of our guilt; it is rather the committal to the faith-union of obedience made available to us through the perfect and triumphant obedience of Christ. In Pauline usage faith is identification with Christ's offering of himself in obedience to God; in Hebrews faith means believing enough to obey when it looks hopeless . . . in both uses faith means discipleship.[33]

With this conclusion, Yoder then claims that his view of salvation as restored communion and restored capacity for obedience fits—better than Anselm's view—all the New Testament expressions of atonement.[34] And, in the same way, "there is thus no gap between justification and

---

"biblical center" (202), of "essence" (128), and even of "kernel" (170). Certainly, the "real meaning" is ethical and not an eternal idea. Yet, it is this "real meaning" that then must be returned to in order to legitimate or challenge subsequent theology as it stumbles through history, and this includes his challenge to the creation of the creeds as well.

31. A few years later, the language of "solidarity" becomes important in Yoder's description of this theme. See *Preface to Theology*, 123.

32. This statement will begin to make more sense once Yoder's understanding of moral freedom is clear. In the meantime, it is necessary to remember that he understands Jesus' obedience unto death as "conformity to the nature of God. The reason Jesus had to die to save man, is that God *is* that way." See the unpublished "The Wrath of God and the Love of God," 8. Unfortunately, these early writings by Yoder have remained unpublished, leading to conclusions that may not yet be complete. See, for example, Stoltzfus, "Nonviolent Jesus, Violent God?"

33. Yoder, "A Study," 9.

34. In this way, the position of one in sin (to use the familiar nomenclature) is defined as being in unfaith-alienation-disobedience. For Yoder, this is the position that "the world" is in. For this reason, sin for a Christian is a "contradiction in terms." See Yoder, "A Study," 9.

sanctification,"[35] between soteriology and discipleship. To be entirely clear, Yoder's version of discipleship is not added on to a Lutheran or Anselmian version of justification or atonement; Yoder's version of discipleship rejects and redefines Lutheran or Anselmian (not to mention any other) accounts of justification or atonement.

Before leaving Yoder's unpublished "A Study of the Doctrine of the Work of Christ," it is imperative to address one of the essential components of discipleship that has been indirectly introduced already, namely, human moral freedom.

Moral Freedom

There are cases in which Yoder looks much like a child of the Enlightenment; his approach to moral freedom is one of those cases. Yoder would, of course, reject the aspersion and, like Bender, point behind the Enlightenment to the radical biblicism of the sixteenth-century Anabaptists as justification for his position. Taking up this mantle, he logically begins with "The Bible sees man as always in a context of choice."[36] Already in 1989, Charles Pinches asked the following questions of Yoder: "Why is human freedom so important? And, is its existence morally significant enough such that the existence of evil which (indirectly) follows from it can be thought to be morally justified?"[37] Pinches' reading of Yoder is sympathetic, and he asks the questions in the most respectful way in order to rescue the notion of theodicy from analytic philosophy and recast it in more robust theological terms. Yet it is clear that Yoder's answer to the questions does not entirely satisfy Pinches.

For Yoder, the answer is simple: one must either obey or disobey God. He elaborates: "Unless these commands of God are nonsense . . . they mean that man is really placed before a decision." Or, "Man's freedom . . . means that, in the context of choice before God, which is the condition of man, both obedience and disobedience are real possibilities."[38] Certainly, Yoder is aware that freedom is a contested term, but as one can

---

35. Ibid.
36. Yoder, "A Study," 6.
37. Pinches, "Christian Pacifism and Theodicy," 251.
38. Yoder, "A Study," 6. As Pinches points out, there are other places in Yoder's corpus where this position can be found (and most of the material he points to was published over a decade later, especially *The Original Revolution*).

easily see, he will "continue to use it, conscious of its shortcomings."[39] For Yoder, freedom is the root of morality and also the key to understanding how God relates to humanity. In fact, Yoder's understanding of freedom is fundamentally theological. Allow me to explain further.

First, if one were attempting to sketch Yoder's version of a theodicy, the basic problem would be articulated as follows: "The problem of evil can be traced no further back than this; the possibility of disobedience is the sole condition for the reality of human freedom and personality. Why then did God take the risk when it would have been so easy, so much simpler, not to have created the problem?"[40] This is the basic shape of the question that undergirds all further reflection on nonviolence, and I take this to be essentially in line with Pinches' articulation of Yoder's position. Yoder, however, rejects his own form of the question as "out of order, if not sacrilegious." He turns to affirm, immediately, that "the only answer is that God is *agape* and *agape respects the freedom of the beloved.*"[41] He follows this claim by launching into a fascinating and adamant account of God's respect for human freedom:

> This last statement is the one solid point where no exceptions may be made; it is the starting point of theology, of history, of ethics, of church order, of every realm where agape matters. Agape respects the freedom of the beloved even to lose himself. The first revelation of agape was thus the creation of human freedom; and no theology or ethics which denies this freedom can be true (universalism denying man's freedom to turn away from God, Constantinianism denying the freedom not to be a Christian, monism denying man's real existence, totalitarianism and utopianism denying the freedom of choice (and sin) in society), for each such system denies the problem it set out to solve.[42]

In short, God respects human freedom to the extent that God will never violate it. If this lets evil in by the back door, this is "too bad," because there is no other way. God, because of his agape, took that risk, and continues to take that risk. With this foundation, it is not a long stretch to

---

39. See also Yoder, "The Wrath of God and the Love of God," 2–3.
40. Yoder, "A Study," 7.
41. Ibid.
42. Ibid.

arrive at Yoder's conclusion that agape must require nonresistance, bearing—literally—one another's sins, even unto the cross.[43]

If we can return, for a moment, to the work of Christ, Yoder is also willing to claim that the resurrection is both an ontological and psychological affirmation that vindicates the way of discipleship since "Death couldn't hold him down (Acts 2:24)." The point is that no matter what humans attempt, God will respect their freedom, since their freedom, even at its worst, cannot destroy God's love.[44] This is, of course, to state the use of freedom in terms of evil, the framing assumed in questions of theodicy. But there are also positive or "right" ways to express one's freedom. Here lies the bedrock of Yoder's account of the free church, the obedient community that has chosen obedience, the community that has chosen to express its freedom lovingly to "influence reality, to express [itself] in history" through discipleship.[45] Before moving directly to Yoder's early articulations of Christian community that make up the second section of

---

43. In "The Wrath of God and the Love of Man," Yoder also sketches various ways in which God's respect for human freedom can be short-circuited. These include (*a*) universalism (because it means history is a farce), (*b*) predestination (because it precludes the capability of "talking back" to God), (*c*) Constantinianism (because it forecloses the possibility of choosing to be a Christian), (*d*) certain kinds of pacifism (because they do not require repentance, forgiveness, and a new birth to "live in the path of peace"), and (*e*) concern for human justice. Although the first four ways seem relatively intuitive, this final one deserves further explanation at this point. To explicate how a concern for human justice impinges on God's respect for human freedom, Yoder states:

> "We may well agree (with the New Testament) that this function of government somehow stands in God's hands; and yet at the same time, once we have understood something about the wrath of God, and once we have seen that its nature is precisely that which permits man to create chaos and destroy himself and the world around him, we see that there is a sense in which human justice, by preventing that chaos from going its normal course, and preventing the worst kinds of sins, and the worst kinds of crimes from being carried out unhindered, interferes with the freedom which God has given man." (5)

It is helpful to remember that, in 1956, Yoder had neither utilized Hendrik Berkhof's *Christ and the Powers* nor written *The Christian Witness to the State* (both of which allow him to nuance the brashness of this early position). That being said, one also ought to note that this is the position Yoder holds in order to claim that "God's love and his wrath are the same thing," that God's love does not miraculously intervene in existence but allows humans to lose themselves.

44. Yoder, "A Study," 8.

45. Ibid., 7.

34 THE HETERODOX YODER

this chapter, please allow one more circling back to the role of the Bible in constituting the content of discipleship.

Discipleship and the Bible

Earlier, when beginning to sketch Yoder's understanding of discipleship, I quickly passed over the claims that (*a*) the valid ethical instructions of discipleship are given in the New Testament and, on this basis, (*b*) we may reliably know the precise content of the obedience that is required. As with everything else dealt with thus far, these are claims that will continue to be revisited and refined throughout Yoder's corpus and, therefore, this book. Additionally, I have already noted a considerable amount in the footnotes about Yoder's use of the Bible. Therefore, it is high time to present at least a preliminary sustained reflection on Yoder's perception of the Bible's role and relevance in his own terms.

Perhaps most basic and assumed is the claim that the Bible is authoritative for Christians.[46] But as Yoder himself recognized, most Christians could assent to this claim in some form. So, what further qualifies Yoder's reading of the Bible? Stated most bluntly, his position, drawing on the history of Anabaptism, could be summed up in a statement such as the following: "The Anabaptists . . . maintained the absolute supremacy of Christ and the apostles as authority, not only against the later church, but also over against the earlier revelation in Judaism."[47] As usual, this particular claim is couched in polemics against both the Catholic and the Reformed traditions, but I would prefer to prescind from evaluating whether Yoder was correct in his historical assessment here in order to attend to the constructive account of biblicism that he (along with David Shank) sought to provide already in 1955.

Behind Yoder's initial forays into this debate stands a threefold need that, again, is directly tied to discipleship. The need, betraying the confusion current in the mid-century Mennonite context, is described as

1. the need for a clearer idea of biblicism in order to present to the world and to other Christians a clear witness for discipleship;
2. the inadequacy of simply saying that we obey all New Testament commands, since they are not all applied in the same way, and some that are obeyed are not as clear in the New Testament as others;

---

46. Yoder, "What Are Our Concerns?" 168.
47. Shank and Yoder, "Biblicism and the Church," 77.

3. the inadequacy of an attitude to New Testament practice that draws a sharp line between that which is commanded expressly and that which is not.[48]

In order to address this profound need, Yoder and Shank provide six principles of a "Consistent Biblicism," an approach that provides a foundational framework to which subsequent claims can be related.[49]

The first principle is a negative principle, namely, the principle that the Reformers' biblicism was problematic—and could therefore be challenged—because it grew out of unquestioned assumptions that were rooted in the identification of church and society. Or, stated in more general terms, Yoder and Shank suggest that this "preliminary analysis of partly unconscious presuppositions is the first step toward a consistent Biblicism."[50] Logically, therefore, the negative principle is merely the first chronological step in Yoder's analysis and not the true first principle, as there is a positive position that one must hold (or at least be aware of) from which one can challenge the presuppositions of a church-society identification.

This positive position is found in the second principle: "the insistence on the unique authority of the Incarnation as attested by the apostolic writings, i.e., the New Testament."[51] This position entails that (*a*) the person of Christ is authoritative and (*b*) the apostolic writings give reliable testimony to this person. It is also helpful to remember that the early Yoder does not have a flat New Testament in that he is willing to write, as he did in 1954, "Granted, we would have the Gospel if we had only the Synoptics, Acts, Peter, and James, but how much poorer we would be!" He then goes on to suggest that what Paul, John, and Hebrews do in the New Testament is what theology aims to do: organize the raw materials of the

---

48. Ibid., 74.

49. Attention to Yoder's early writings, such as this one, would enrich current conversations that struggle to make sense of Yoder's use of Scripture. See, for example, Hauerwas and Huebner, "History, Theory, and Anabaptism," 396–97.

50. Shank and Yoder, "Biblicism and the Church," 78.

51. Ibid. Yoder did not shy away from this claim in early ecumenical discussions, fully aware that his rejection of "the attribution of authoritative character to any particular historical development" and his demand for a "mutual abandon of any attempt to have recourse to any particular evolution as a canon of interpretation" would offend certain interlocutors. Whether one agrees with Yoder or not, there seems to be a bit of irony in Yoder's making this claim within an essay self-consciously written from a "historic free church perspective." See Yoder, "Nature of the Unity We Seek," 225.

gospel events into an "intellectually graspable whole" to meet contemporary problems.[52]

What exactly it means that "the person of Christ is authoritative" dominates much of Yoder's thought in the ensuing years. Because of this it is important to recognize something of an implicit and assumed meaning in these early statements—and, therefore, the relative imprecision of the claim at this point, an imprecision that finds resolution later in *The Politics of Jesus* and other writings. All that said, it is important to note that the fundamental issue here is the question of what, precisely, is authoritative and what is not.[53]

The third principle, again evident in later writings, is that one must not hesitate to utilize the fruits of historical, archeological, and linguistic study of the New Testament texts. With rather bold confidence, Yoder was willing to agree that "on almost everything that really matters, New Testament exegetes have come to a great degree of agreement as to what the New Testament means by what it says, and what the life of the New Testament church was like."[54] But, again, it is important to note that this evaluative claim is conditioned by the priority of discipleship; assuming that an "objective" reading of the New Testament will support his own position, he continues: "The fact remains that one of the strongest witnesses for discipleship in modern Christendom . . . comes . . . from the exegetical theologians who have the scholarly equipment to read the Bible with both microscope and telescope."[55]

52. Prefatory letter attached to the previously noted Yoder, "A Study."

53. Interestingly, Yoder later credits Marcion for raising this question in a helpful manner. In *Preface to Theology*, he writes of the context of the early church: "What is the criterion which can show us the truth in this pluralistic mess of many kinds of literature, saying many kinds of things, even contradictory things? How is the church to find its way? Well, Marcion says, let us do it by distinguishing between the authoritative literature . . . and the rest" (115).

Of course, that is not to say that Yoder agreed with Marcion on which books or which concepts should be authoritative. But, it is to say that he identifies with Marcion's search for a norm that one can continually loop back to (to use the language of *Preface*), for a root against which its branches can be judged (to use the language of "The Authority of the Canon"), or both (to use the language of *The Priestly Kingdom*). See also Miller, "In the Footsteps of Marcion."

54. Shank and Yoder, "Biblicism and the Church," 79. It is this principle that would later move towards a position closer to "Biblical Realism." See Yoder, "Authority of the Canon," 271, and Carter, *Politics of the Cross*, 63–65.

55. Ibid. Challenging "traditional advocates of an orthodox doctrine of Inspiration," Yoder and Shank then go on to name the select scholars they have in mind: Cullman,

The fourth principle is simple and, to some extent, dependent on the previous: "we must question seriously the validity of a distinction of level between New Testament command and example."[56] The point of Yoder and Shank here is not, as one might expect, to elevate the example of Jesus' life to that of his commands. Rather, the purpose of this principle is to relativize the authority of direct commands found in the New Testament (for example, the command that women should not braid their hair in 1 Peter 3:3, which was regularly ignored in Mennonite circles). They continue by explaining that both command and example were "time-bound in that they represented responses to problems in a first-century surrounding; both command and example were based on principle."[57] This recognition invites debate and, therefore, opens the door for the fifth principle, namely, that one must be clear about what sort of modifications of the New Testament commands and examples might be legitimate to adjust to a changing world. For a modification to "be clear" requires meeting three criteria, which together constitute the fifth principle:

1. The change must be made by a studied and prayerful decision of the church community (and not solely the leader).[58]

2. There must be clarity about (*a*) the principle involved in the New Testament command or example, (*b*) why that principle is no longer served by the expression which was adequate in New Testament times, and (*c*) why the new proposal is a faithful expression of the principle in the contemporary context.

3. The question facing the new proposal must always be "Does it edify?" and not whether it is forbidden.[59]

Finally, after prying discipleship from obedience to New Testament commands and examples in their most literal form and then tying them to a principle behind the text, Yoder and Shank offer the sixth principle:

Eichrodt, Taylor, Rowley, Hunter, Stewart, Minear, Miller, and Bright. Again, it is difficult to downplay the superficial assumption that these names constitute the fullness of "New Testament exegetes" but, regardless, it is clear what they are driving at with this principle.

56. Ibid.

57. Ibid.

58. In this criterion we also find one of the very familiar themes in Yoder's corpus—communal hermeneutics—and this will be addressed further in the second part of this chapter.

59. Shank and Yoder, "Biblicism and the Church," 79–80.

the presence of a pattern of faith and life that is perfectly conformed to the New Testament is *not* necessarily a sign of the true church.[60] This final principle (*a*) provides a platform for criticizing certain literal imitations of the Bible and (*b*) encourages humility in the face of traditions that have developed differently than Anabaptists.

The Consistent Biblicism outlined by Yoder and Shank, therefore, is much less straightforward than one might assume. It presumes that we can distill the "principles" behind the text. It presumes much of the previous discussion on moral freedom, as full knowledge, agreement, and understanding are necessary for following through with interpreting the Bible according to these principles.[61] And it presumes these for the purpose of bringing forth a clear and refocused expression of the work of Christ that, in turn, calls forth repentance and faithfulness, that is, discipleship. Yet, as obliquely indicated in the discussion thus far, discipleship is not a concept that can be isolated from community. In the following pages, I hope to illuminate why discipleship and community, together, dominate Yoder' early writings.

THE CHURCH: THE HEART OF THE MATTER

In *Christian Ethics: A Historical Introduction*, Philip Wogaman introduces Yoder as follows: "The Christian pacifist tradition gained unusually articulate interpretation in the twentieth century through the work of John Howard Yoder."[62] This is true, but to focus on this as if it was Yoder's focus—especially the early Yoder—is to predispose the reader to a deficient reading of Yoder. And if this is how one begins to introduce Yoder, one usually concludes, as Wogaman does, by leaving Yoder behind:

> But Yoder believes that sin cannot be destroyed by sin. Only God, using the faithfulness of loving people, can ultimately destroy sin.
> Yoder thus places a high premium on the company of faithful Christians. Influenced by this, a number of other Christian ethicists and theologians—such as Stanley Hauerwas and James William McClendon—have structured Christian ethics around the reality of a more faithful church.[63]

---

60. Ibid., 81.
61. Ibid.
62. Wogaman, *Christian Ethics*, 233.
63. Ibid., 234.

Foundational Theological Commitments

My point in citing Wogaman here is not to suggest that he is wrong on any of these individual facts; my point is that Wogaman is one of many readers who understand Yoder as, essentially, a pacifist paving the way for other theologians and ethicists to push further and contextualize his pacifism into a fully developed ecclesiology.[64] This view of Yoder's contribution to theology and ethics is somewhat inadequate and does not do justice to his understanding of the church community as the locus of discipleship, of nonviolent love, of the politics of Jesus.[65] Yoder himself, already in the 1950s, seemed to sense something of a bifurcated interest in the *Concern* pamphlets and their authors (his own work included). Rather presciently, he noted that the published pamphlets and the annual study conferences made themselves heard "outside the Mennonite Church mainly in matters having to do with nonresistance, and inside Mennonitism thus far mainly in matters having to do with church order."[66] In the next few pages, I hope to demonstrate that Yoder's ecclesiology cannot be ignored by those outside "Mennonitism" and, in fact, that much of what Yoder had to say about theology and ethics are, understood appropriately, aspects of his ecclesiology.

Interestingly, Yoder's first writing on the church indirectly revealed the position he would later develop directly. In 1949, the year after he graduated from college, Yoder published an article in *The Mennonite Quarterly Review* about a legal case between a former member of an Old Order Amish Mennonite congregation and the elders of the same congregation. With the title "Caesar and the Meidung" (*Meidung* means "shunning"), the obvious antithetical construction of the interlocutors—the contest between church polity and civil law—is revealing. In short,

---

64. In noting this pattern, I do not want to assume an antagonistic reason for excluding attention to Yoder's free church ecclesiology (though that may be a contributing factor). It seems more likely, however, that the popularity of *The Politics of Jesus* and its emphasis on Christian pacifism has been definitive here, leaving Yoder's other contributions in the relative background.

65. On this point, it also appears that Nathan Kerr's critique of Hauerwas' rushing too quickly to identify the "politics of Jesus" with the "politics of the church" seems to misunderstand Yoder's insistence that these are not separable. Certainly, Kerr may be correct in attempting to separate Yoder's "politics of Jesus" from Hauerwas' "politics of the church," but to claim that there is, in Yoder's thought, an identifiable distinction between these two is to misunderstand either his church or his politics. This is evident here but will also become clearer in subsequent chapters. See Kerr, *Christ, History and Apocalyptic*, 130.

66. Yoder, "What Are Our Concerns?" 164.

the case concerned the shunning of the former Amish congregant and, in the midst of Yoder's analysis, a glimpse of his future position emerges: "I am led to agree with the Amish that [the former member] was free to be a member of the church, and he was free not to be a member of the church, but he cannot claim the freedom to be at the same time both a member (economically) and not a member (religiously); for participation in the Christian social fellowship is not thus divisible."[67]

The unity of "economics" and "religion" suggested here gestures bluntly in the direction of his later writings, including those written in the 1950s. In this final section, I explore the depth of Yoder's ecclesiology by letting his own articulation of the attributes of the church structure serve as my summary. In this way, I hope to demonstrate that it is rather difficult to distill any of his theological and ethical contributions or articulations apart from their ecclesiological context.

In 1957, Yoder publically gave voice to what the participants in the Concern movement held in common. Rather unoriginally yet appropriately, the title of the article ended up being "What Are Our Concerns?" Recognizing that others might frame these concerns differently (using biblicism or pneumatology as key concepts, for example), Yoder chose to articulate the concerns as attributes of the church.[68] As usual, he cast his discussion of the attributes of the church against the misunderstandings of other Christians. Therefore, when asserting what he understood to be the attributes of the church, he was conscientious in noting that they are not sacraments and hierarchy (Roman Catholicism), right preaching and sacraments—and perhaps discipline ("the churches of the Reformation"), good intentions (liberalism), true doctrine on select questions (fundamentalism), or indefinable interiority (spiritualism).

What is left? With confidence, Yoder then moves to indicate the position that not only unified the Concern participants, but the position that constitutes the church's message *within and without* Mennonitism.[69] The annotated list provided by Yoder includes six attributes. Building from the backdrop of discipleship and concluding with momentum in

---

67. Yoder, "Caesar and the Meidung," 90.

68. By choosing to use the term "attributes" rather than the more familiar language of "marks" (*notae*), Yoder already indicates something about his ecclesiology. In 1966, he would explain why the traditional language of "marks" is insufficient. See Yoder, "Let the Church be the Church," 116–17.

69. Yoder, "What Are Our Concerns?" 165.

the direction of his ecumenical reflections, I would like to address each of these in their original order.

a. *The church is the fellowship of those who have responded to the call of discipleship.* Framing the attribute this way, we can now understand that discipleship is not separate from the church (which he would describe as legalism or liberalism) but discipleship calls people into the church. The church finds its unity in its discipleship and not correct doctrine (orthodoxy) or fellowship with God (Lutheranism). The stark contrasts evident here reveal both the polemical and the missional stance of Yoder's church: it does not claim perfection, but it demands it, and if it is demanded, obedience is possible. He explains: "*Simul justus et peccator* is allowable as an historical observation; but it is illegitimate in the realm of faith and ethics."[70]

As we have seen above, concrete ethical teaching is possible within the discriminating community and, therefore, discipline is possible within the community. After all, contra the recent emphasis on the Eucharist in Christian ethics, the fellowship is based on "the common conviction that the unity of the church is unity in discipleship."[71] For this reason, moral freedom must be assumed: as one must choose to follow Christ, one must choose a new beginning. And, for this reason, infant baptism is contested. Several years later while speaking in South America, Yoder emphatically articulated this conviction: "It is sure that if we insist that membership in the people of God is a matter of new birth and that mere conformity to the standards and behavior patterns and ideas of the people of God without personal conviction is no help, this is the needed safeguard. The refusal to baptize infants or the immature remains a most appropriate symbol of the refusal to forsake that missionary character that the church is called to retain."[72]

---

70. Ibid., 167. Yoder also frames this same sentiment in terms of the church as a whole: "The Gospel does not say anything about sin as an unavoidable phenomenon in all human existence; it says 'Repent!' which, being interpreted, does not mean 'continue in sin, but sorrowfully,' but rather 'STOP IT!' The Church's not being the Church can not be discussed in the indicative; 'Repent and be the Church' is the only thing to say." Yoder, "Light to the Nations," 18.

71. Ibid.

72. Yoder, *Revolutionary Christianity*, 9. Commenting further on the place of children

Whatever one thinks about Yoder's understanding of a voluntary church, it cannot be ignored. For Yoder, it is the first and founding conviction that the subsequent attributes assume and, in many cases, are contingent upon.

b. *The "unit of action and authority" within the church is the local congregation.* Intentionally, this attribute rejects confessionalism (too doctrinal); Episcopal or Presbyterian-synodical views (too mechanical); geographic, national, or other provincialism (Constantinian); and pietism and cell movements (separate congregation from church). Yoder, however, does not deny the notion of a "Church Universal" that has no fixed sociological form and is made up of all believers. Rather, he suggests that the Church Universal becomes "really visible" in terms of action and authority when there is (*a*) sufficient temporal continuity, (*b*) geographical continuity, and (*c*) an exchange of convictions and concerns for a unity to form whose core is a common commitment to discipleship.[73] With an implicit nod to Bender, this attribute recognizes the utility of denominations to the extent that they serve as an instrument of fellowship, study, service, or witness . . . and do not take themselves as the church. That being said, this attribute is functionally predicated on the following, so further comment will be reserved until the third attribute is stated.

c. *The Bible is the authority in the church.* As we have seen above, this is not a very descriptive claim in and of itself, though one ought to note the singular source of authority.[74] What Yoder has in mind here is the continued relevance of the Bible not only to provide answers but also to ask questions of its readers. In an attempt to articulate this, Yoder produces a preliminary sketch of a communal hermeneutic. Speaking of the Anabaptists as the

---

in the church, Yoder has the boldness to continue this train of thought: "If the children of believers are thought of as already within the community of faith, the unavoidable result is that within two or three generations the focus of attention changes from winning of those outside the people of God to educating and holding those who were born into Christian families. With the passage of time, this has in the past always resulted in the geographic identification of one area as 'Christian' and of other areas as 'pagan.'"

73. Yoder, "What Are Our Concerns?" 167–68.

74. This is a very early statement of the claim that he would develop in a more nuanced form later in "The Authority of Tradition."

resource for imitation against the model of the Reformers, he states: "The Anabaptists came quickly to definite positions, but by a more circular and less final study process; Scripture's answer to the first question is carried to the church, and thus serves to formulate a new question for which an answer must be sought, thus progressively purging out of the system one's unconscious presuppositions and getting more objectively at what the Bible itself is interested in."[75]

The implication is that the Anabaptists were best able to get at what the Bible was really about because they lived in a certain way, because they had the right sort of community. A few years later, Yoder would restate this principle, or something quite similar: "Only he who is committed to the direction of obedience can read the truth so as to interpret it in line with the direction of God's purposes."[76] Again, Yoder is persistent in his critique of orthodoxies that want to settle on final doctrinal answers in place of biblical objectivity too quickly. To this end, he makes some claims that will rankle many of his contemporary readers. For example, he claims that rationalism "forced what orthodoxy refused; its positivistic objective analysis asked the Bible what it really had to say." And continuing, "The tradition of honest and technically capable scholarship is coming to maturity at a position nearer to Anabaptism than to either orthodoxy or liberalism."[77]

Whatever rhetorical and theological gymnastics Yoder performs in order to attach his own hermeneutic theory to the movements of the day, one cannot lose sight of the thrust of this attribute—namely, that biblical authority is not a doctrine but a way of living according to what the Bible says. With that, one can loop back to the second attribute—the unit of the local congregation—for the means of executing that authority. Moving forward in the list, however, also entails a looping back to the first attribute concerning the voluntary church.

75. Yoder, "What Are Our Concerns?" 169.

76. Yoder, "Hermeneutics of the Anabaptists," 307.

77. Yoder, "What Are Our Concerns?" 170. Rather than exhort Anabaptists to Biblical Realism alone, however, Yoder suggests that the answer to this question lies somewhere between Fundamentalism and Biblical Realism (and that "between" may or may not be a large area, depending on one's point of view).

d. *The Church is a Separation.* What is implicit in the first attribute receives its own treatment here. Evoking the specter of *The Schleitheim Confession*,[78] Yoder makes the now familiar claim that it was the Anabaptists who gave theological meaning to the concept "world."[79] The point here is that, in Yoder's view, Christendom did not see the church and the rest of the world as separate. Once one had to choose the church voluntarily (i.e., after the Radical Reformation), one decided between an existence apart from the church and an existence in the church. The "apart from the church" is the "world." There are three interrelated claims wrapped up in the claim that the church is separate from the world: (*a*) the church and the world deal with evil differently; (*b*) the church and the world have different understandings of eschatology; and (*c*) the church knows the world better than the world knows itself. Each of these claims demands further elaboration here.

First, to reiterate the obvious, once one chooses the life of discipleship in the church, one also adopts a new way of existing. For Yoder, this entails "nonresistance, nonswearing, nontribunals, non-participation in government; all of this is a refusal to deal with evil the way the world does."[80] This is what Yoder means when he states that "Christian ethics is for Christians."[81] Working within a largely descriptive Troelstchian framework, Yoder is not afraid of the language of sectarianism on this matter, calmly admitting that "this view may be summed up by saying that the 'sectarian,' knowing that discipleship is a matter of individual calling and response, does not expect Christian ethics of the non-Christian."[82]

Of course, there are certain things that any given society—"in its unbelief"—will consider necessary (the use of violence for self-preservation is presumed by Yoder as one example). In this way, the world is not simply chaotic but becomes what Yoder calls "structured unbelief," a position that can be instantiated in many

---

78. See the edition of *The Schleitheim Confession* translated and edited by Yoder.

79. Yoder, "What Are Our Concerns?" 171.

80. Ibid., 172. Yoder's list also entails other forms of nonconformism, including rejection of luxury, alcoholism, ambition, and artificial politeness (although one may wonder about the adjective "artificial" here).

81. Yoder, "Otherness of the Church," 62.

82. Yoder, "Anabaptist Dissent," 30.

forms (and Yoder is most concerned about those forms of the world—like Christianized Germanic Europe—that appear to be Christian in name or symbol).[83] In none of the world's structured social manifestations, however, is the church to be confused with the world. Against the pleading of those sympathetically concerned with the world, Yoder responds: Christians must be wary of participation in it because "the church's responsibility to and for the world is first and always to be the church."[84]

Second, and fleshing out the previous claim further, the differences between the present actions of the church and the world are also rooted in their competing views of eschatology and history.[85] In these early writings, the two central and competing options in Yoder's thought are Constantinianism and the true church.[86] Thus far in my summary, I have assumed a basic understanding of Constantinianism as the synthesis of church and nation. At this point, this definition is no longer adequate, as Constantinianism is a fairly specific concept. In its early formulation, the concept is predicated on a theological reading of history that is divided

---

83. This is the same reason that Yoder rejects H. Richard Niebuhr's use of the term *culture* in his monumental *Christ and Culture*. "Culture," for Yoder, has no intrinsic ontological dignity and cannot be spoken of apart from Christ. See "Otherness of the Church," 62.

84. Yoder, "Otherness of the Church," 61. One ought to remember, at this point, Yoder's conviction that God allows people to "talk back," and it is precisely this patience that allows evil in the form of denials of Christ to become incarnate structurally in the world (62).

85. Yoder, "What Are Our Concerns?" 172.

86. This prevalent duel profoundly reflects Yoder's western European and North American context, as he does not consider secularism, paganism, or any other religion (Islam, for example) as among the most pressing temptations for Christianity. At times, it is almost uncomfortable how much the drive to overcome Constantinianism distracts him from worrying enough about other dangers threatening the church. For example, in 1966, he penned the following:

> From the perspective of the church of believers, there is a certain sense in which we can with gratitude accept the "secularization" that characterizes the modern age. To the extent that this means Christian faith is being disentangled from a particular civilization, a particular part of the world, a particular social structure, and especially to the extent to which it is being disentangled from identification with the total membership of any one social group or nation, this development "clears the decks" for a restatement of what it means for the church to be in but not of the world.

See Yoder, *Revolutionary Christianity*, 11.

into two "aeons": "These aeons are not distinct periods of time, for they exist simultaneously. They differ in nature or in direction; one points backward to human history outside of (before) Christ; the other points forward to the fullness of the kingdom of God, of which it is a foretaste. Each aeon has a social manifestation: the former in the 'world,' the latter in the church or the body of Christ."[87]

Despite the claim that they exist simultaneously, there is a "radical break" between them. Because a particular social manifestation is attached to each aeon, one cannot participate in both at the same time. The old aeon entails the politics of nationalism and pragmatism, of "being responsible"; the new aeon entails the politics of discipleship, of loving "in the way of the cross and in the power of the resurrection."[88] This is, however, not yet the contest between Constantinianism and the true church but something like the clash between pagan Rome and the early church. For Yoder, the true church exists according to the politics of the new aeon, which is a straightforward assertion (and the language of "politics" in this sense becomes more explicit and entrenched later in *Christian Witness to the State*). Constantinianism, however, is fallacious precisely because it attempts to hold the ethics of both the old and new aeons at the same time:[89] it attempts to hold violence and Christian love (or violence as Christian love) together in the same ethic.[90] For Yoder, this is but one more specific expression of "the world."

---

87. Yoder, "Peace Without Eschatology?" 146–47. For Yoder, there is no straightforward reading of history because of this contest of aeons. Rather, history reveals "as much of the Antichrist as of Christ." See "The Otherness of the Church," 55.

88. Ibid., 151. At this point, Yoder claims that nonresistance is right because it anticipates the triumph of the Lamb that was slain and "not because it works." Later, he will reconsider this claim in terms of a new kind of efficacy.

89. Ibid., 153. The key problem with this synthesis is that God has not yet removed sin and evil from the world. Therefore, sin has been taken up into the church in a way that assumes its presence. For Yoder, this is the reason why the sacraments were instituted in the early medieval church: to attempt to overcome the sin that was intentionally incorporated into the church. One can probably guess that Yoder did not think this either a biblically sufficient answer.

90. Despite his problematic description of the historical emergence of what he takes to be Constantinianism, this is the core concept he is working with. And, whether one agrees with Yoder or not, Leithart's suggestion in the direction of a "purified" Constantinianism does not get to the heart of the matter. See Leithart, *Defending Constantine*, 342. For

In terms of eschatology, then, Constantinianism is heretical because it believes that God's kingdom is realized in the union of church and world and through the means of the conquest of the world by the state or other political body.[91] In one of his less-than-sympathetic readings of history, this is the position that Yoder attributes to the medieval church (and to most of church history to the present).[92] Clearly and emphatically, Yoder rejected the idea that the meaning of history could be carried by any group of people (whether nation, race, or family) other than the church. Why? Because the church, in imitating the suffering love of God, anticipates the triumph of the Lamb proclaimed by the resurrection.[93] Through the proliferation of *The Politics of Jesus*, this theme has become increasingly familiar. Yet, in regard to this earlier context, I would like to pause and note two things before moving on: (1) again, the nonviolence of God (and not merely the commands of Jesus) emerges as central because "only by respecting this freedom [of the sinner] to the bitter end can love give meaning to history"[94]; and (2) the old aeon will not be defeated until the *parousia*, and for this reason history will remain the field of battle between the old and the new aeon until God intervenes to vindicate human obedience.[95]

The third claim entailed in the attribute of the church as separate from the world is that the church knows the world better than the world knows itself. Building on what has been said already, Yoder moves toward articulating how the church—even if separate

---

further reflection on Yoder's use of Constantinianism, see also Heilke, "Yoder's Idea of Constantinianism," and Sider, "Constantinianism Before and After Nicea."

91. Yoder, "Peace Without Eschatology?" 154.

92. See his later nuancing of this claim in "Constantinian Sources of Western Social Ethics," 135-47.

93. Yoder's use of "eschatology" refers to "a hope that, defying present frustration, defines a present position in terms of the yet unseen goal that gives it meaning." See "Peace Without Eschatology?" 145.

94. Yoder, "Peace Without Eschatology?" 151.

95. Ibid., 152. Yoder says very little about this idea, and it is not clear how he imagines this working. In "Peace Without Eschatology?" he appeals to Revelation 19 (a rather non-nonviolent chapter) to gesture in the direction of God's intervention, yet, given his strong stance on God's nonviolence and the freedom allowed for sinners, this construal of a final consummation of "the war of the lamb" fits, at best, rather uncomfortably.

from and in contest with the world—can speak to the world. In "What Are Our Concerns?" Yoder explains the logic of his position as follows: "If [the sixteenth-century Anabaptists] had had time they would have worked out, in line with their church-world understanding, the lines of prophetic witness to the state; telling the statesman that if he refuses to accept the Gospel, he should at least be an honest statesman."[96]

Given what we have seen of Yoder's description of the separation of church and world, it seems that he could make the case that, yes, the church knows the world better than the world knows itself, and, yes, the church stands as a prophetic witness against the state, and even, yes, the church calls political leaders to follow the gospel. But the piece that seems to be arbitrarily inserted into this explanation is the claim that the church can call a political leader to be "at least an honest statesman."[97] After all, the logic of this statement seems to run directly in the face of the logic of Yoder's formulations of Christian ethics thus far, namely, that sin cannot be considered when making indicative statements. How is one to make sense of this novel and anti-sectarian feature of Yoder's claim?

The answer to this question begins with Yoder's view of Christ as not only the head of the church but also the Lord of history. For Yoder, the old aeon, despite its status as rebellion against Christ, continues to be ruled by Christ. What Yoder means by this is that Christ continues to "channel" evil to serve God's purposes. He provides this example: "Vengeance itself, the most characteristic manifestation of evil, instead of creating chaos as is its nature, is harnessed through the state in such a way as to preserve order and give room for the growth and work of the church. Vengeance is not thereby redeemed or made good; it is nonetheless rendered subservient to God's purposes, as an anticipation of the promised ultimate defeat of sin."[98]

This example, however, does not yet explain why the political leader needs to be admonished to be honest (and, for that matter,

---

96. Yoder, "What Are Our Concerns?" 172.

97. I take Yoder to mean honesty in the straightforward sense here and not in reference to the political leader's "refusal to be honest with the absolute priority of church over state in the plan of God," which is described later in *Christian Witness to the State* (17).

98. Yoder, "Peace Without Eschatology?" 149.

just). As it stands, one could also assume, according to this example, that God will use and redeem the evil of political leaders regardless of whether they are honest or not. Yoder then continues to explain that the state itself is the incarnation of semi-subdued evil (recall his earlier claim that the world is "structured unbelief").[99] What he means is that if force is used to protect the innocent and punish evildoers, then a positive evaluation of the state—as the state—can be assessed because it is playing its appropriate role under the reign of Christ by limiting evil rather than adding evil to evil.[100] But it does seem odd that a positive evaluation can be offered for what is openly acknowledged as demonic rebellion without "intrinsic ontological dignity," to use the language of "The Otherness of the Church."[101] And what criteria would one use to determine such a positive?

It must be admitted that this early account of the church's mandate to speak to statesmen is undeveloped and, at times, seems to be at odds with itself theologically. In the ensuing years, however, Yoder seems to have sensed the inner tension here. He sought to address precisely this issue in more detail in *The Christian Witness to the State* in 1964, and frequently returned to this theme throughout his corpus, eventually reframing the relationship between church and world in a significantly different way. For this reason, I will leave further comment to the next chapters. After this lengthy excursus, it is time to return to the fifth attribute of the church.

---

99. In "Otherness of the Church," Yoder describes the world as "the fallen form" of creation. The state, therefore, is "a demonic blend of order and revolt" that has no ontological dignity. For this reason, one cannot ask what the world or the state "really are." See "Otherness of the Church," 56–57.

100. Yoder, "Peace Without Eschatology?" 150. There is a sense in which Reinhold Niebuhr's understanding of the "balance of egoism" still plays a substantial role in Yoder's positive description of the state. See "Peace Without Eschatology?" 153.

101. Granting that the early church understood that the world was under Christ's rule does not, however, logically seem to entail that the church demand "not Christian righteousness but human *justitia*" from the state (which Yoder describes as the church taking "prophetic responsibility for civil ethics without baptizing the state"), especially if Yoder denies an appeal to "a universal innate moral sense." What Yoder seems to need to make this work is some positive account of human justice, but all that can be said positively in the state's (or the world's) favor is to note its "preservative function," which is also gestured to rather vaguely. See Yoder, "Otherness of the Church," 56.

e. *The church is missionary and led by the Spirit.*[102] In an uncharacteristic turn, Yoder goes on to note that these are "well enough admitted to need little further development." In fact, his reason for including this attribute (which is probably a combination of two attributes) is to "demonstrate that they cannot be taken seriously without drawing certain other conclusions, such as separation from the world and congregationalism."[103] Certainly, enough has been said above concerning the missionary nature of the church in its separation from the world. One can also grasp how the Spirit is necessary for communal interpretation and discernment in the congregation, as has been indicated above.[104] Beyond this, however, the last comment concerning congregationalism and the gifts of the Spirit is further fleshed out years later in his writings challenging the professionalization of the clergy.[105]

Recognizing that I have already said more than Yoder did in explaining this attribute, I believe one final proviso is in order: although Yoder readily acknowledges at this stage that the Holy Spirit is the "down payment" on the coming glory, he is, as one might expect of a theologian articulating a form of a *theologia crucis*, also very nervous about attributing too much attention to the Spirit beyond the life of suffering. One can immediately feel this in "Peace Without Eschatology?": "The Holy Spirit is the 'down payment' on the coming glory, and the new life of the resurrection is the path of the Christian now.[106] But before the resurrection there

---

102. Yoder, "What Are Our Concerns?" 172.

103. Ibid.

104. In his critique of Reinhold Niebuhr, the Holy Spirit is a key issue as well. Yoder argues that resurrection, the church, and regeneration are works of the Spirit. And, in this, he affirms that the Spirit imparts power as a "working reality within history and especially within the church." In this way, new possibilities are open that Niebuhr cannot see. See "Reinhold Niebuhr and Christian Pacifism," 116. This principle is also at work in Yoder's *What Would You Do?*, although, in this later context, Yoder usually uses the language of Providence rather than referring directly to the Holy Spirit. See, for example, *What Would You Do?*, 34–36.

105. See, for example, "The Fullness of Christ."

106. This is also entirely in line with Yoder's emphasis on the kenotic theme of humiliation preceding resurrection that permeates the biblical language about Christ, best displayed in Philippians 2. See *Preface to Theology*, 73, 104, 124, 215.

was the cross, and Christians must follow their Master in suffering for the sake of love."[107]

f. *The Church is bigger than our own backyard.*[108] In this final attribute, what was already implicit in Yoder's identification of the visible church with the local congregation is developed further. He begins with the indicative: Christians and churches should have fraternal relations in common work in service and witness, in common worship, in acquaintance with one another's needs and concerns, in reciprocal admonition, and in occasional organizational union.[109] The rest of his account, however, attempts to argue that the free church is the only church that has been, can be, and is now consistently ecumenical. Perhaps the boldest part of this claim is stated as follows:

a. Territorial or confessional churches cannot by definition be ecumenical; the most they can do is to recognize one another as being *also* valid churches.

b. Episcopal and Orthodox churches are even less capable of being fraternally open; since the historical continuity that they alone possess is their definition of the church, the only way to have unity is to join them. This is real sectarianism.[110]

Of course, this evaluation is predicated on a certain understanding of "ecumenical," and Yoder, again, is not shy about proposing a sharpened reinscription of a familiar term. For Yoder, unity is rooted in following Christ, which means that "we lay upon those who confess him the claims which Christ lays upon those who confess His name."[111] In short, this is what he meant when he wrote that "*Christian unity is not to be created, but to be obeyed.*"[112] Or, to rephrase: those who claim to follow Christ should obey him—that is the source of true ecumenical unity. The more contentious point, however, is his specification of what Christ lays upon those who confess his name, namely, "Christian obedience,

---

107. Yoder, "Peace Without Eschatology?" 148.
108. Yoder, "What Are Our Concerns?" 172.
109. Ibid., 173.
110. Yoder, "What Are Our Concerns?" 173.
111. Yoder, *The Ecumenical Movement*, 36.
112. Ibid., 21.

biblical baptism, separation from the world, and the rest of what the Gospel implies."[113] In a word, discipleship.[114] And if discipleship—which is defined most basically in ethical terms—is where unity is instantiated, then Yoder's claim concerning the superiority of the free church in its consistent ecumenicity begins to make sense.[115] With this background, we can then understand his positive evaluation of the sixteenth-century Anabaptists as models of ecumenism and not, as frequently understood, examples of the "break-in-order-to-be-faithful" principle.[116] Perhaps Yoder states it most transparently in the final pages of *The Ecumenical Movement and the Faithful Church*: "The Anabaptists accepted in their midst men who sometimes were too original and too daring in the attempt to rethink traditional doctrine in light of discipleship. They accepted them, without accepting their doctrinal deviations, because of their conviction that discipleship mattered first. Likewise, the Anabaptists accepted separation from the state churches, with whom they agreed about everything on the fundamentalist checklist; once again, because discipleship comes first."[117]

In 1957, when Yoder published these six attributes of the church, he had hope for the ecumenical church. "What Are Our Concerns?" concludes with a positive assessment of the current "interchurch" situation: other churches are willing to have a conversation. And, until the free church witness is refused, Mennonites ought not to withdraw from the conversation.[118] It is important to note, of course, that it takes two

113. Ibid., 36.

114. Mark Thiessen Nation is entirely on target here when he subtitled his chapter on ecumenism "A Call to Unity in Disciplined Discipleship." See Nation, *John Howard Yoder*, 77–108.

115. In this context, the shaping role of Yoder's dissertation—*Anabaptism and Reformation in Switzerland*—comes to the fore. Yoder, throughout his analysis of the dialogues between Anabaptists and Reformers, demonstrates that it was not the Anabaptists who precipitated the break with the church; rather, they continually sought to continue the conversation until Zwingli forced them to choose between either the unity of Zurich or the faithfulness of the church (which, in effect, means that Zwingli left the church and not the Anabaptists). See "The Turning Point in the Zwinglian Reformation," 140, and *Anabaptism and Reformation in Switzerland*, 121–30.

116. See Yoder, *Ecumenical Movement*, 29.

117. Ibid., 40.

118. Yoder, "What Are Our Concerns?" 176. See also Yoder, "Nature of the Unity We Seek."

participating parties to have a real conversation. And on this basis Yoder humbly acknowledges that his own position must be open to revision (he notes that there are sixteenth-century Anabaptist examples of this as well).[119] In the ensuing chapters, I intend to indicate certain points where Yoder alters his position following sincere conversations with willing interlocutors. That said, Yoder also energetically spoke and wrote in order to articulate his own positions with the hope that others would embrace them. None of these articulations gained more of an audience than *The Politics of Jesus*, and it is this particular articulation that culminates the development of the next chapter.

CONCLUSION

If it is true that Yoder developed all of his basic theological commitments by 1962, it is somewhat ambitious to assume that one chapter can distill and summarize everything. Yet, for better or worse, this chapter has attempted to approximate that task. Of course, there are many related elements and extensions of his thought that have been either ignored or merely intimated, especially some of his polemical descriptions of the failures within the history of Christianity. Throughout the chapter, my intention has been to focus on the themes of discipleship and the church community in order to illuminate the extent to which these themes form an interdependent foundation for all of his other theological commitments. Following a preamble on Yoder's definition of discipleship devoted to revealing its reliance on a particular understanding of the work of Christ, human moral freedom, and the authority of the Bible, this chapter situates Yoder's theology and ethics, following his own lead, as an outgrowth of a particular ecclesiology, a free church ecclesiology that contextualizes theology and ethics within a discussion of the attributes of the church.

Against this background, the next chapter will turn to the first examples of really "famous" Yoder texts such as *Christian Witness to the State*, *The Original Revolution*, and, of course, *The Politics of Jesus*. Rather than treat these individually and in isolation—although some of this will be necessary—I will attempt to frame these texts within further developments of Yoder's ecclesiology. In this process, I hope to provide a fuller reading of Yoder's theological and ethical development and, thereby, to relativize and contextualize pacifism appropriately within this larger context.

---

119. See Yoder, *Anabaptism and Reformation in Switzerland*, 121.

THREE

The Prioritization of Politics

WITH LITTLE FANFARE, *The Politics of Jesus* was published in 1972. World events that stand behind its contextual purview include the Cold War hostilities in Vietnam, the beatings and bombings in Northern Ireland and England, and the American-sanctioned destabilization of select Central and South American governments and economies. For many people living in the early 1970s, the challenges and effects of these violent events were immediate, and Yoder's text, written at the right time and published by the right press (and perhaps promoted by the right friends[1]), provided a coherent and accessible Christian pacifist position that was much needed. It is, therefore, not surprising that *The Politics of Jesus* has become a profoundly important text, both in terms of the fields of theology and ethics and in terms of the intellectual and moral development of its individual readers. Because of this, it was the de facto entry point into Yoder's corpus for many, and the center around which many of Yoder's other writings were subsequently read.

At one level, the text is a self-confessed attempt to respond to "the ways in which mainstream Christian theology has set aside the pacifist implications of the New Testament message."[2] Building on the pacifist trajectory of the previous years—*Karl Barth and the Problem of War* (1970), *Nevertheless: Varieties of Religious Pacifism* (1971), and *The Original Revolution: Essays in Christian Pacifism* (1971), for example—*Politics* has

---

1. This is, of course, a gesture to the persistent praise offered by Stanley Hauerwas. See, for example, his autobiographical comments in this vein in *A Better Hope*, 133–35.

2. Yoder, *Politics of Jesus*, x.

occasionally been understood as summarily articulating the central issue in Yoder's thought, namely, Christian pacifism. To elevate pacifism as a discrete concern in this way, however, does not seem to mesh with Yoder's own delineation of the pacifist trajectory of these years. One year before the publication of *The Politics of Jesus*, Yoder provided the following explanation for the compilation of *The Original Revolution*, and it seems to me that a similar explanation would suit *The Politics of Jesus* as well. In the Preface to *The Original Revolution*, he describes the situation: "There is a growing awareness in churches and seminaries that the problem of war is at the heart of much of the sickness of modern society, and a growing recognition that the traditional Christian approaches to this problem, namely, the just war and the crusade, are becoming increasingly inadequate as sources of moral guidance and are beginning to look as if they never were adequate." He then continues recounting the paucity of recent attention to the matter by historians, theologians, and denominations, concluding: "It is thus more under the vacuum of a particular need than under the pressure of any conviction of personal apostolate that I have accepted the invitation to gather a body of essays which seek to restate in various moods and modes the conviction that the renunciation of the sword to which Jesus called his disciples is one of the keys to the rest of the problem of Christian faithfulness and to the recovery of the evangelical and ecumenical integrity of the church in the age of the atom."[3]

In this chapter, I intend to describe Yoder's pacifism in the context of his broader concern for Christian faithfulness, for "the recovery of the evangelical and ecumenical integrity of the church" as it is expressed in his prolific post-dissertation years as an administrator for the Mennonite Board of Missions in Elkhart and, by 1965, as a full-time professor at Goshen Biblical Seminary.[4] To do so, I will begin by attending to what he calls "the original revolution; the creation of a distinct community with its own deviant set of values and its coherent way of incarnating them."[5]

---

3. Yoder, "Original Revolution," 8–9.

4. A brief biographical note is probably helpful to place Yoder during these years. Yoder finished his graduate studies in 1957, taught at Goshen Biblical Seminary for the 1958–59 academic year, and then worked for the Mennonite Board of Missions from 1959–65. From 1960–65 he also taught part-time at the Mennonite Biblical Seminary in Elkhart, and, from 1960–69, he worked in several official roles with the National Council of Churches. Also, as early as 1967, Yoder taught occasional courses at the University of Notre Dame, where he later became a full-time professor in 1977.

5. Yoder, "Original Revolution," 28.

Following this, a brief interlude addressing Yoder's continued reflections on the church's relationship to the state will be introduced, especially as it appears in *The Christian Witness to the State*. To conclude the chapter, I turn to Yoder's attempt to appropriate more fully the language of politics as normative for the Christian community.[6] As indicated earlier, these texts represent, according to Zimmerman, the "mature version" of Yoder's theology, the "flowering of his early work."[7] To begin to work toward evaluating this conclusion and what it entails concerning Yoder's specification of the politics of Jesus, I need to introduce a narrative thread that becomes foundational in its own way: the story of Abraham and his children.

THE ORIGINAL REVOLUTION AND ITS DEVIANT VALUES

Throughout his early work, Yoder spends a considerable amount of energy clearing the way for his constructive program. On occasion, it almost seems that narratives concerning the devolution of Christianity dominate his thinking.[8] Given the context and his intended audience, this is understandable. Yet, Yoder is more interesting and usually more careful when articulating a positive counter-narrative, a constructive alternative to what he takes to be the Constantinian deformation of the church. By the late 1960s, this Christian counter-narrative had become attached to the Old Testament, or at least to the story of Abraham. Later, it is also intimately attached to Jeremiah, but that is a development that will be addressed in a subsequent chapter.

One of the critical issues facing Yoder's construal of Jesus is the question of the relationship between the Old and New Testaments. Anxious to avoid the charge of supersessionism on one hand (i.e., attending only to the New Testament as authoritative) and the affirmation of divinely sanctioned violence on the other (i.e., uncritically accepting the entirety of the Old Testament as authoritative), Yoder turned to Abraham to find a narrative thread in which Jesus would make sense, both as rooted in the

---

6. Although this order does not follow a formal chronology (at least according to the order of the central texts I will discuss here), the logic of this chapter uses texts that span approximately eight years—beginning in 1964 with the publication of *The Christian Witness to the State* and ending in 1972 with the publication of *The Politics of Jesus*—and follows a thematic emphasis that is predicated on the conclusions of the previous chapter.

7. Zimmerman, *Practicing the Politics of Jesus*, 174.

8. See, for example, Leithart's comments concerning Yoder's Constantinian narrations as playing a too significant role in *Defending Constantine*, 320–21.

Old Testament and as definitive for the New. The first step in his argument begins within Jesus' immediate context. It asks what Jewish means were available for his establishment of the kingdom of God. In a foreshadowing of *The Politics of Jesus*, Yoder's "Original Revolution" outlines a typology of the four possible social strategies for retaining Jewish identity in the first century: (1) realism—acceptance of the current situation as definitive for what is possible (Herodians and Sadducees); (2) righteous revolutionary violence—direct opposition of the current establishment on its own violent terms (Zealots);[9] (3) withdrawal—self-conscious relocation of the kingdom (Essenes); and (4) proper religion—select rules of segregation to retain purity amidst participation in the current political context (Pharisees).[10]

Yoder's Jesus rejects all of the above yet retains his Jewish religious roots. How does he do so? By adopting a fifth social strategy that looks "back to what God had been doing or trying to do for a long, long time." This fifth strategy is historically rooted in the following biblical story or, more accurately, in what Yoder takes to be *the* biblical story:

> The Bible story really begins with Abraham, the father of those who believe. Abraham was called to get up and leave Chaldea, the cultural and religious capital of the known world in his age, to go he knew not where, to find he knew not what. He could not know when or whether or how he could again have a home, a land of his own. And yet as he rose to follow this inscrutable promise, he was told that it was through him that the nations of the world would be blessed. In response Abraham promised God that he would lead a different kind of life: a life different from the cultured and the religious peoples, whether urban or nomadic, among whom he was to make his pilgrim way.[11]

This is the initial eruption of the original revolution, the inauguration of an intentional community with an alternate set of values. These

---

9. For a solid examination of Yoder's treatment of the Zealot position as a real temptation for Jesus, see Klassen, "Jesus and the Zealot Option," 131–49.

10. Yoder, "Original Revolution," 18–27.

11. Ibid., 27. In "Let the Church Be the Church," Yoder also offers the following pregnant quip: "*God's pattern of Incarnation is that of Abraham, and not of Constantine.*" See "Let the Church be the Church," 112. In *Revolutionary Christianity*, Yoder sketches a genealogy of God's wandering people that begins with Abraham, includes Joseph and "his immigrant brothers" and Moses' "refugee caravan," and then introduces Jesus—the homeless rabbi who was also exiled to Egypt—before moving to Pentecost and the dispersion of the young church. See Yoder, *Revolutionary Christianity*, 161.

people became known as "Hebrews" because they were "the people who crossed over."[12]

The remainder of the Old Testament, according to Yoder's narrative, is then understood as God's creative faithfulness to the promises made to Abraham and his children, even though the likelihood that his descendents would become the instrument of their fulfillment became less and less evident. When Jesus finally emerges on the scene, he again takes up the task that God had attempted through Moses, Gideon, and Samuel; namely, the task of gathering his people around God's word and will.[13] Avoiding the four temptations of his day, this is precisely what Jesus accomplishes: he gathers a "society like no other society mankind had ever seen."[14]

With this claim, however, an equivocation seems to sneak into Yoder's argument. The question that must be asked is this: How can Yoder make this last statement about the uniqueness of the society that was gathered around Jesus and yet hold to the previous claim that the family of Abraham was, in fact, "the original revolution"? Further complicating this relation is Yoder's statement that "Jesus did again what God had done in calling Abraham or Moses or Gideon or Samuel: he gathered his people around his word and his will."[15] In locating Jesus within a reading of the Old Testament in this way, Yoder clearly avoids the blunt charge of supersessionism. Yet, the task that remains is differentiating Jesus'

12. Yoder, "Original Revolution," 28.

13. See also Yoder, "If Abraham Is Our Father," 103.

14. Yoder, "Original Revolution," 28. Earlier, in his essay "Peace Without Eschatology?" Yoder similarly suggested that what was "centrally new about Christ was that these ideas [i.e., the resurrection, God's victory over evil, and the selection of a faithful remnant] became incarnate" (148–49).

Yoder also addresses this issue in *The Politics of Jesus* by asking what the violent "legends" of the Old Testament might have meant for Jesus and his contemporaries. In that context, he draws the conclusion that the central theme of the legends is that "God himself will take care of his people." On this basis, Jesus' relation to violence in the Old Testament is construed as follows: "When, therefore, Jesus used the language of liberation and revolution, announcing a restoration of 'kingdom' community and a new pattern of life, without predicting or authorizing particular violent techniques for achieving his ends, he need not have seemed to his listeners to be a dreamer; he could very easily have been understood as updating the faith of Jehoshaphat and Hezekiah, a faith whereby a believing people would be saved despite their weakness, on condition they 'be still and wait to see the salvation of the LORD.'" Yoder, *The Politics of Jesus*, 84.

15. Yoder, "Original Revolution," 28. At this point, it becomes clear that the simple identification of the instauration of the new aeon with Jesus is complicated. Although Yoder never addresses the terminological question directly, perhaps this is why the language of old and new aeons disappears from Yoder's corpus rather early.

community from anything else in the history of God's relationship to his chosen people in such a way that the church is, in fact, understood as the truly new society that Yoder claims it is.[16] Echoing several of the ecclesiological themes present in the previous chapter, Yoder names three broad qualities of this community: the community is (*a*) voluntary, (*b*) mixed in composition, and (*c*) requires a new way of living. I will briefly comment on each of these in order to move toward a refined description of Yoder's ecclesiology.

1. *A Voluntary Society.* Again, echoing the free church stance of his earlier years, Yoder clearly states that one can only become part of the society by repenting and freely pledging allegiance to the king. Framed in this way (and against the backdrop of an ethnic understanding of Jews as God's people), the revised political and social nature of Yoder's revolutionary community becomes readily apparent. In the previous chapter, we saw how Yoder sought to discipline the language of repentance. In this context, not only repentance but the definition of the gospel is disciplined, and, in the process, entrance into the church is also clarified. As one might expect, Yoder recognizes and appeals to the enduring relevance of the biblical refrain drawn from Mark 1:15: "Repent and believe the good news!"[17] To understand this refrain properly requires a close examination of the terms involved, and for the sake of clarity I will begin with a brief summation of Yoder's notion of repentance as the prerequisite for entering the church.

In short, to repent is "not to feel bad but to think differently."[18] While we might acknowledge the straw man character of equating repentance with feeling bad as the lone alternative, Yoder's point is that repentance is "a transformation of the understanding (*metanoia*), a

---

16. Perhaps the best way to understand the relationship between the Old and New Testaments in Yoder's thought in these years is spelled out in an essay—"The Hermeneutics of the Anabaptists"—written in 1967. In that context, Yoder states that behind the relationship between the Old and the New Testament is a "still deeper" question: the question of the relationship of God's purposes in history. Although Yoder states his position in terms of a question (and perhaps a rhetorical question), the answer is clear: we understand "God's purposes to be working themselves out through history so that a meaningful movement from the Old Testament to the New can be a fundamental part of God's plan." See Yoder, "The Hermeneutics of the Anabaptists," 306–7.

17. Yoder, "Original Revolution," 31–32.

18. Ibid., 31.

redirected will ready to live in a new kind of world."[19] But what is this new kind of world? For Yoder, this is the good news, the gospel, the *euangelion*, the "revolution." In short, it is "*the judgment of God upon the present order and the imminent promise of another one.*"[20] This is what Jesus proclaimed: "He accepted the phrasings John [the Baptist] made current; he proclaimed the coming kingdom and let himself be called (though reticently, and subject to misunderstandings and redefinitions) the Anointed One (*Messiah*), or the Awaited One."[21] The good news is that the kingdom is coming, yet it is an "intentional community."[22] The question that must be faced is, what ought one do about it? Yoder's prescriptive answer: this choice for change "will involve attitudes, so it can be called 'repentance,' *metanoia*, 'turning-the-mind-around.' But it also involves social practices, 'fruits worthy of repentance,' new ways of using possessions and power. The promised coming change involves social and personal dimensions *inseparably*, with none of our modern speculative tendency to dodge the direct claim on us by debating whether the chicken or the egg comes first."[23]

19. See Yoder, "Political Axioms of the Sermon on the Mount," 38. In this context, Yoder also appeals to Matthew 4:17: "Repent; for the kingdom of Heaven is upon you." Recall the claim made in the previous chapter: "Repentance means ethics." See Yoder, "A Study," 9.

20. Yoder, "Original Revolution," 18. It is important to note, too, that Yoder develops his definition of "gospel" out of Mary's Magnificat (Luke 1:49–53), claiming that "the change Mary was rejoicing in is 'gospel.'" See "Original Revolution," 15. This, of course, is good news for the poor and bad news for the proud and the rich (16).

21. Ibid.

22. Ibid., 28. He also suggests that today (that is, in 1971), it might be called "an underground movement, or a cell movement," both of which require voluntary involvement.

23. Ibid., 17. One ought to notice that although Yoder does not treat it specifically in this context, "belief" would probably fall under the same sort of volitional redescription that is applied to repentance. It is also important to note that Yoder, taking aim at "evangelical Protestantism," goes out of his way to distinguish the kingdom from the perceived benefits of the kingdom. Yes, repenting may do something for one's aimlessness in life; it may (*a*) clear one's conscience of guilt and anxiety, (*b*) alleviate intellectual confusion, (*c*) provide "doctrinal meat" to digest, (*d*) illuminate a heritage to appreciate, (*e*) strengthen moral resolve, and (*f*) give one a sense that God cares "about helping me squeeze though the tight spots of life." Yoder then continues: these are not wrong: "They have their place. BUT ALL OF THIS IS NOT THE GOSPEL. This is just the bonus, the wrapping paper thrown in when you buy the meat, the 'everything' which will be added, without our taking thought of it, if we seek first the kingdom of God and His righteousness." See "Original Revolution," 31–32.

And, in this way, Yoder passionately articulates the single, indivisible means of entry into Christian life, that is, into the faithful church.[24] In this way, Yoder also implicitly turns away from centuries of theological attempts to classify Christianity as a species of religion by reclassifying it as a species of morality—Jesus' revolution is a "moral revolution."[25]

2. *Mixed in Composition.* In the summary of the previous quality of the church, the emphasis lay on the mode of entry into the coming "kingdom of God" while leaving the content of the kingdom relatively unexamined. With this second quality, Yoder starts to flesh out the particular quality of this new kind of community. To begin, further differentiating the Christian community from earlier Old Testament examples, this new community was mixed: "It was a society which, counter to all precedent, was mixed in its composition. It was mixed racially, with both Jews and Gentiles; mixed religiously, with fanatical keepers of the law and advocates of liberty from all forms; with both radical monotheists and others just in the process of disentangling their minds from idolatry; mixed economically, with members both rich and poor."[26]

As one examines this mélange, it becomes clear that several criteria are identified as absolutely not central in the establishment

---

More recently, Stephen Dintaman has reacted strongly to precisely this characterization of the gospel, arguing the general point that Yoder's definition illustrates that there are "reductionist tendencies at work in Mennonite academic settings." Dintaman readily acknowledges that the behaviors required for and within the life of discipleship (including the practice of nonresistant love) have become considered as the core of Anabaptist identity. Yet, he argues in Yoder's own language and rhetorical use of capitalization: "This is not a call for us to forsake social awareness and active work for social change, but just a reminder that ALL THIS IS NOT THE GOSPEL!" See Dintaman, "The Spiritual Poverty of the Anabaptist Vision," 207. One could consider this but one example of disagreement within the Anabaptist community on this matter.

24. In a related manner, Yoder suggests thinking about salvation, too, as "a unity of a status and a life" in *Preface to Theology*, 123.

25. Yoder, "Political Axioms of the Sermon on the Mount," 39.

26. Yoder, "Original Revolution," 28. In "If Abraham Is Our Father," Yoder also notes that this trajectory is latent in the Old Testament with profound results: "Through the incorporation of persons of non-Israelite blood into the tribe, through the expansion of the world vision to include other nations, through the prophets' criticism of and history's destruction of kingship and territorial sovereignty as definitions of peoplehood, the movement continued through the centuries which was ultimately to culminate at the point where John the Baptist opened the door for Jesus." See "If Abraham Is Our Father," 103.

of this community. The proscribed list includes race, ethnicity, religious orientation (in terms of ritual and worship),[27] and economic status. So, if these criteria are of no significance in determining this new community, what binds it together? The answer is the heart of Yoder's vision: the new way of life Jesus gave to its members that would, among other things, enable it to remain mixed in composition.

3. *A New Way of Living.* Finally, we arrive at the prescriptive summary of the "deviant values" that constitute this revolutionary community. Specifically, Jesus modeled and gave the community forgiveness (a new way to deal with offenders), suffering (a new way to deal with violence), sharing (a new way to deal with money), gifts for every member (a new way to deal with problems of leadership),[28] a new order (a new way to deal with corrupt society), and a radical new vision of what it means to be a human person (a new pattern of relationships, including those with the state and the "enemy nation").[29] This is a new style of life in which the very existence of such a group is itself a "deep social change."[30]

The language of "dealing with" appears very frequently in Yoder's description here, and some might want to read this as a sign of resentment or resignation. I would suggest that we read this language sympathetically as an inflection that presupposes that these new ways of living, by definition, entail a relationship with the world. Or, to restate, these are all gifts that demand social relationships and require "dealing with" the neighbor in love. And thinking about them in this way helps explain how this community that claims such revolutionary values cannot be a withdrawn community. Therefore

---

27. In a preemptive gesture against later developments in Christian theology, Yoder intentionally notes: "Jesus did not bring to faithful Israel any corrected ritual or any new theories about the being of God. He brought them a new peoplehood and a new way of living together" ("Original Revolution," 31). One can already sense the impending directions of his later writings on the Jewish-Christian schism, directions I will discuss in the fourth chapter.

28. This particular concern is addressed in some length in "The Fullness of Christ."

29. Yoder, "Original Revolution," 29.

30. Ibid., 31.

Yoder's exclamation: "In that apartness, how present!"[31] Or, alternately, "Our deeds must be measured . . . by what they 'say.'"[32]

Looking back at the list, again, one also notices the comprehensive scope of the new values, a scope that includes but is not limited to pacifism. In *The Original Revolution*, this is the vision cast in the opening chapter, which both rhetorically and theologically sets the stage for the subsequent essays on Christian pacifism. And, with a return to pacifism, it seems that the difference between the community gathered by Jesus and the community of Abraham's children is finally differentiated.[33]

At this point in his thinking, Yoder seems to hold to a sort of historical development in which the perceived unity of the Old Testament was evolving in the direction of relativizing a given ethnic-political peoplehood. We saw this above in Yoder's account of the mixed nature of the church foreshadowed in Judaism, and we can see it coming to its logical conclusion in the new pattern of relationship demonstrated by Jesus, one that trusts God for the security and identity of his people to the extent that even the notion of holy warfare is translated into the willingness "to renounce those definitions of one's own people and of the enemy" that gave holy warfare its original meaning.[34] That is to say that God's gathering of his people to himself through Abraham, Moses, Gideon, and Samuel is quantitatively different in a manner that also entails a qualitative difference from his gathering through Jesus.[35] This gathering has been on its way, to use Yoder's phrase, in a "positive movement along coherent lines," but it has now arrived.[36] With Jesus, history is finally at

---

31. Ibid., 28.

32. Yoder, "Political Axioms of the Sermon on the Mount," 41.

33. By this I mean that the slow development from what is "novel" in Old Testament holy war finally ends in what is "novel about the man Jesus." See "If Abraham Is Our Father," 103.

34. Yoder, "If Abraham Is Our Father," 104.

35. Yoder's recognition of the importance of Jeremiah for understanding Jewish pacifism is still several years away.

36. Yoder, "If Abraham Is Our Father," 103. It is precisely on this point that Kerr appears to have overstated the "independence," "uniqueness," and "singularity" of Jesus. Certainly, he is right to oppose Yoder's apocalyptic Christology to certain mid-twentieth-century theologies, and I am generally sympathetic to his argument against "the presumed universalizing and ideological mechanisms of control" evident in the powers. See Kerr, *Christ, History and Apocalyptic*, 145. But Kerr's rhetorical polemics also tend to elide the increasingly extensive effort Yoder makes to tie Jesus firmly within the history of Judaism and within the grain of the universe that contextualize and illuminate Jesus' uniqueness.

the point where even the unqualified love of the neighbor, including the enemy—to the point of readiness to suffer unjustly at his hands—appears not only understandable but possible as the most appropriate testimony to the nature of God's love and his kingdom. After all, to recall one of Yoder's foundational commitments from the previous chapter that also appears in *The Original Revolution*: "We do not, ultimately, love our neighbor because Jesus told us to. We love our neighbor because God is like that. It is not because Jesus told us to that we love even beyond the limits of reason and justice, even to the point of refusing to kill and being willing to suffer—but because God is like that too."[37]

And, with that, we can now turn to a few summary comments concerning Yoder's ecclesiology in order to ensure that unwarranted assumptions have not sneaked into the discussion of the three qualities.

The Definition of Church

Having provided an account of the components that constitute the "the original revolution," it is time to identify its ramifications for understanding Yoder's ecclesiology. In this context, Yoder's concern is identifying the faithful church as the culmination of God's calling of a people, and the attributes developed in the previous chapter ought to be assumed as the foundation for this discussion. But, rejecting preconceived ritual, metaphysical, or ontological predicates, Yoder pushes his previous descriptions further in the direction of the priority of social ethics, stating that "the word which Jesus used [for church] does not mean a gathering for worship nor an administration; it means a public gathering to deal with community business. Our modern terms *assembly, parliament, town meeting*, are the best equivalents."[38] The church is God's people gathered to do business in God's name, to "find what it means here and now to put

---

37. Yoder, "Political Axioms of the Sermon on the Mount," 51. In *Discipleship as Political Responsibility*, a generally underappreciated text, Yoder provides an overlapping account that thickens his ecclesiology: "The essence of following Jesus is not grasped if we view it primarily as a commandment to become the same as Jesus, or to act the way Jesus did; rather, following Jesus really means basing our actions on our participation in Christ's very being" (61).

38. In "Original Revolution," Yoder does not actually provide the Aramaic or Greek word he claims to be referring to when he uses the term "church" (30). He has in mind, however, the Greek term *ekklesia*, which also receives a nearly identical definition in "Binding and Loosing," 9. See also his definition of *qahal* and *ekklesia* in *Christian Witness to the State*, 18.

into practice this different quality of life which is God's promise to them and to the world and their promise to God and service to the world." Understood this way, if this new community lives faithfully, it then becomes "the most powerful tool of social change."[39]

With this definition, one can see both Yoder's negative rejection of what he understood as cultural accretions to the church and his positive concern for wider social renewal. And, as we have seen, Yoder's church does not have a social agenda; the church is a social agenda; the church is what the church does. Against this broad backdrop, Yoder also has a considerable amount to say about the church and its relations to the state in the late-1960s. So, it is natural to turn in that direction in order to demonstrate how Yoder specifies one example of the church's witness.

THE CHURCH AND THE STATE

In the previous chapter, I briefly introduced Yoder's "Peace Without Eschatology?" in order to illuminate the importance of the separation of the church and state, especially as it pertains to eschatology and Yoder's utilization of the concept of distinct "aeons." After summarily sketching Yoder's attempt to explain how Christ is the Lord of history and not merely the church, I suggested that he was still a little unclear as to why a statesman ought to be honest. Whether it is my misunderstanding or Yoder's opaque argument, it seems that I am not alone in my puzzlement since Yoder begins *The Christian Witness to the State* with a lengthy excerpt from "Peace Without Eschatology?"—followed immediately by the claim that *The Christian Witness to the State* is an exposition of precisely this excerpt. Someone else must have needed further clarification, too! Nonetheless, please allow me to reproduce the claim that Yoder himself deems worthy of further exposition: "It is possible for the Christian or the Christian church to address to the social order at large or to the state criticisms and suggestions concerning the way in which the state fulfills its responsibility for the maintenance of order."[40]

Of course, there are many in the Christian tradition for whom this claim is a given that needs no further explanation. Recognizing this illuminates a certain context and audience and, as it turns out, *The Christian Witness to the State* was the product of an assignment given to Yoder by

---

39. Yoder, "Original Revolution," 31.

40. Yoder, *Christian Witness to the State*, 5. The cited passage preceding the claim is drawn from "Peace Without Eschatology?" 158–60.

the Institute for Mennonite Studies in 1958–59. The task and uniqueness of the book lies in its exposition of this claim while maintaining a pacifist stance. Therefore, the purpose of the text, stated most sharply, is: "To analyze whether it is truly the case that a Christian pacifist position rooted . . . in Christological considerations is thereby irrelevant to the social order."[41] If the title of the text does not give away the answer already, the answer is no, the pacifist position is not irrelevant. To make this argument, however, the grounds for the witness must be justified and the form of the witness must be explained.

1. *The Ground for Witness to the State.* In *The Christian Witness to the State*, Yoder does not start with an abstract analysis of the state in itself. Why? The easy answer is that he simply cannot define the state without prior theological considerations. In short, he must begin with the New Testament claim that Jesus Christ "is now exercising dominion over the world."[42] The world, as we have seen earlier, is divided into two aeons: the present (characterized by sin) and the coming (the redemptive reality that entered history in an ultimate way in Christ). But, to state the obvious question, if Christ is Lord, how is it possible for the present aeon to be characterized by sin? To answer this question, Yoder turns to Paul's language of "powers,"[43] to which he will return frequently in the ensuing years.

In short, the powers govern the realm that the Bible refers to as world (*kosmos* or *aion houtos*). They are referred to in the Bible in many ways: thrones, principalities, powers, archangels, and dominions; they invisibly determine human events; in modern terms, they

---

41. Yoder, *Christian Witness to the State*, 7.

42. Ibid., 8. Yoder is adamant that the witness to the state "has never been *based on* a theory about what the state is and should be in itself, nor has it been rendered *for the sake of* the state 'in itself'" (77). In *Discipleship as Political Responsibility* (initially published in German in 1964, the same year as *The Christian Witness to the State*), it appears as though Yoder does begin his analysis with "The Mandate of the State." Upon closer examination, however, it is clear that this investigation is modified by "according to the New Testament," thereby affirming his refusal to treat the state as an "objective" or "autonomous" institution that can be separated from theological delimitations. See *Discipleship as Political Responsibility*, 17–20.

43. Although Yoder has used the language of powers and principalities since at least "Peace Without Eschatology?" he draws particularly on Hendrik Berkhof's *Christ and the Powers* for his understanding of the powers in the mid-1960s. Not only did he translate *Christ and the Powers* in 1962, he also quotes nearly four pages from that text in *Revolutionary Christianity* (see pp. 127–31).

are roughly equivalent to "structures," by which, in Yoder's words, "psychological and sociological analysts refer to the dimensions of cohesiveness and purposefulness which hold together human affairs beyond the strictly personal level."[44] More specifically, they can be any "'Anities and 'Alities, and 'Ologies and 'Isms," and "'doms and 'hoods," too.[45] In order to help clarify this nebulous definition, causality, fatality, necessity, respectability, fascism, sorcery, moral law, humanism, and Christendom are all provided as examples. And it is precisely these powers that are defeated or subordinated by the cross, resurrection, and ascension of Christ and the outpouring of the Holy Spirit.

But, before the reader gets the sense that the cosmic battle is already finished and Yoder has slipped into some sort of utopian vision of the world, he acknowledges that the world is in a paradoxical state: Jesus Christ is now reigning, yet not all of his enemies have been subjected to him. But they will be at the *parousia*. The new aeon has begun in the person of Jesus and then derivatively in the fellowship of obedient believers, the people pointing forward as the social manifestation of the ultimately triumphant redemptive work of God, or, to use the language of *The Original Revolution*, the people who are participating in Jesus' moral revolution.[46] This kingdom of God is not "within you"; this kingdom of God is unfolding in history.

In the context of this general account of the lordship of Christ in relation to the powers, Yoder then introduces the state—"the fundamental phenomenon that society is organized by the appeal to force as ultimate authority"—as deeply representative of the

---

44. Yoder, *Christian Witness to the State*, 8.

45. Ibid. Later, in a footnote in *Politics of Jesus*, Yoder notes that Paul may have had a precise and technical meaning in mind for each of the terms that he used, but "the best we can do today is to come to some understanding about the general trend of meaning which the total body of thought has for us" (*Politics of Jesus*, 137n2). This principled approach fits Yoder's hermeneutic, and it seems to be his policy in *Christian Witness to the State*, too.

46. In one of the more distracting distinctions Yoder makes in this sometimes amorphous discussion, he designates the "kingdom of the Father" as the not-yet-arrived end of the age and the "kingdom of the Son" as the present period of history. He seems to be pointing to the distinction between the already and the not-yet, and his designation also indicates a qualitative distinction between a time when Jesus is opposed and when there will be no more opposition. See *Christian Witness to the State*, 10.

"world."[47] Specifically, the powers, whether rebellious or submissive, are agents of the "divine economy," agents of God's purpose. Or to restate, as we have seen in the previous chapter, Christ "channels" violence, turning it against itself so as to preserve as much as possible the order that is the "pre-condition for human society and thereby also a vehicle for the work of the church" (i.e., the function of the state is part of the divine plan for the evangelization of the world).[48] And, with that, we finally arrive at a refined definition of the state: the principal incarnation of this channeled evil, especially in its judicial and police functions.[49]

Defining the state, however, is not the same as explaining why or how the Christian witnesses to the state. Or is it? Again, Yoder seems to sense some of the dissonance in equating a definition with a prescription. His footnote addressing this issue is worth reproducing at length:

> It could be argued that the church's knowing of the state's place in history is not yet proof that she should speak to the statesman about it; should she not rather keep this knowledge to herself? There might be something to this if the insights or principles of which we shall speak were disincarnate truths or mysteries; but they are gospel. The putting of the powers in their place is an integral element of the work of Christ. The very fact that this is true is

---

47. Yoder, *Christian Witness to the State*, 12.

48. Ibid., 13. It is important to note that the role of Christ outside the church is not limited to channeling violence. Even though this theme is usually understated in Yoder's own writings during these years, his comments at the Seventh Mennonite World Conference are illuminating (and I want to thank Myles Werntz for bringing this address to my attention): "It is not our business to deny that a communist can be unselfish or a Hindu happy, but to gather every fiber of goodness, whatever the source, every insight, every good intention, just as God wove such pagans as the priest Melchizedek and the harlot Rahab into the fabric of the salvation story. Jesus' words 'apart from me you can do nothing' do not mean that non-Christians can do nothing; if they deal with the subject at all they mean that whatever good any man does, it is not apart from Christ." Yoder, "Lordship of Christ and the Power Struggle," 509.

49. Yoder, *Christian Witness to the State*, 12–13. In *Discipleship as Political Responsibility*, Yoder describes the state's purpose in nearly identical terms: "The divine mandate of the state consists in using evil means to keep evil from getting out of hand" (18), and "The state exists for the purpose of keeping order" (45). It is important to note that Yoder also refuses the invocation of the language of law and grace in this discussion. Rather, he is careful to claim that "both the lordship of Christ over the world and His headship in the church are of grace, though they are distinct" (*Christian Witness to the State*, 12).

necessary and sufficient reason for proclaiming it to *all* men—yea, even to the powers themselves . . . It can, in fact, be argued that the proclamation to the powers is not merely an *announcing* of the victory, but in fact a part of the actualization of that victory.[50]

Here, again, we see Yoder's use of gospel as social revolution and the church carrying on the work of Christ in defeating the powers. This claim seems too rich to be relegated to a footnote! Yet, if this is not enough, Yoder also offers several other, arguably more familiar reasons why the Christian ought to witness to the state: (1) concrete concern for the welfare of the neighbor (Yoder admits that human welfare is not the same as what has been said about the lordship of Christ, but it cannot be in opposition, either); (2) concern for the statesman;[51] and (3) to follow the Old Testament examples of (*a*) denouncing idolatry and (*b*) interpreting what God is doing in history.

These parallel claims are very interesting, not necessarily in themselves, but because of their rough juxtaposition with the systematic description of the rule of Christ. Clearly, as of 1964, Yoder is still working out the ramifications of his theoretical framework of the relationship between the church and the world, and it seems that he has not yet figured out how to narrate these basic "parallel motivations," to use his category, within the language of the rule of Christ. Or has he figured this out?

2. *The Form of the Witness to the State.* Since Yoder has spent so much energy defining the church as a revolutionary moral community, it should surprise no one that his first reflections on the witness to the state appear specifically as "The Church's Existence as a Witness." This is the first of two modes of witness and I will, using Yoder's term, refer to it as the church's implicit witness; I will refer to the second as the church's direct witness.

a. *The Church's Implicit Witness.* Building from the previously noted conclusions that (1) "Christian ethics is for Christians," (2) the

---

50. Yoder, *Christian Witness to the State*, 14n8.

51. More will be said on this shortly. For now, Yoder limits his comments to something like: if the statesman is not a Christian, he ought to be invited to discover a more human, more excellent way than bondage to violence and power; if the statesman is a Christian, "the Christian duty to the 'erring brother' is clear" (*Christian Witness to the State*, 14–15).

church's faithfulness is measured by its own obedience to discipleship, (3) the central meaning of history is borne not by kings and empires but by the church, and (4) the church is a society, Yoder presses forward:[52] "Her very existence, the fraternal relations of her members, their ways of dealing with their differences and their needs are, or rather should be, a demonstration of what love means in social relations."[53]

At this juncture, the language of politics burst into Yoder's corpus in a way that will become definitional for the remainder of his corpus: the church is properly a political entity, a *polis*, and therefore it is, according to the New Testament, best understood as a "deliberative assembly of the body politic." Consequently, and adapting what has been clear from his initial definition of discipleship, the church "is more political (kingdom, Messiah, New Jerusalem, *politeuma*) than cultic." In fact, it is more political—a truer, more properly ordered community—than the state.[54] That said, the politics of the church, even though the world and the church will eventually be "englobed in the same kingdom," cannot be transposed directly into non-Christian society because, as indicated above, the world does not function on the basis of repentance and faith. Therefore, Yoder proposes the mode of "analogy" to articulate how the church witnesses by its very existence: "by analogy certain of its aspects may be instructive as stimuli to the conscience of society."[55] In this way, the order of the church is able to testify to the order of the world concerning the "absolute norm," (*a*) which the church follows, (*b*) which is valid for both, and (*c*) without which the world will never succeed in building a stable temporal order.

---

52. Yoder, *Christian Witness to the State*, 28, 16–17.

53. Ibid., 17.

54. Ibid., 18.

55. Ibid., 17. In framing the relationship as one of "analogy," Yoder is roughly following Barth's distinction between the Christian and the civil community and his suggestion that one can draw certain general lines as to what one can expect from the civil community by analogy. See *Karl Barth and the Problem of War*, 76–77, 115–18. It is important to note, too, that Yoder is not blindly following Barth, as he is also critical of Barth's use of analogy, and of analogy in general: "Analogy is a method which, lending itself to demonstrate almost anything, cannot clearly prove anything" (117).

To illustrate how the "inner life" of the church can provide stimulation and insights to the larger community, Yoder suggests three examples. First, against the hierarchical structures of authority in paganism, the egalitarian thrust of the church casts light beyond the borders of the church. Or, to restate in historical terms, the Christian community's experience of the equal dignity of every member of the congregation laid the groundwork for modern conceptions of human rights.[56] Second, the church community may equally prove instructive through its "sober realism about the temptations of power and the persistence of sin in the life even of the righteous" that demands fraternal admonition and vigilance by the entire congregation. The display of fraternal admonition is most helpful for modeling a democratic and realistic way of exercising supervision of authority entrusted to a few.[57] Third, the gifts of the Holy Spirit are shared by the congregation at large, leading to common study and unforced convinced consensus, true unity.[58] Any secular analogy that presupposes the distribution of creative capacities and authority—such as the town meeting, discussion methods in education, and business management—can be better explained through Christian convictions.[59] In the ensuing years, some form of these examples frequently resurface in the context of the language of sacraments, a development that will be addressed in a subsequent chapter.

Aside from the witness offered analogically through the communal life of the church, Yoder also articulates a second mode of implicit witness that radiates from the church to the world. The difference Yoder is seeking to articulate is that the analogies sketched above are drawn from the "inner life" of the church, while the following "radiating" examples are extensions of the church's service to the world. Whether this distinction between analogy and

---

56. The example indicated here becomes thematized as universal charisma in his later work. Yoder recognized, however, that the world's appropriation of this practice was not unequivocal in his note that this history did take a detour through secular post-Christian humanism. See *Christian Witness to the State*, 18.

57. Yoder, *Christian Witness to the State*, 18–19. This claim evokes his continued concern for the practice of binding and loosing within the faithful community.

58. This third example names the concern for implementing dialogical liberty in the faithful community.

59. Yoder, *Christian Witness to the State*, 19.

radiating is maintained in subsequent years is up for debate. But, for now, it is important to note that Yoder sees these aspects of the church's witness as distinct, even if related. The examples suggested in this "radiating" mode include the building and maintenance of institutions such as schools and hospitals, both of which began as services rendered by the church and then were picked up by the wider society. Further, he adds the examples of Christian voluntary service and international relief work, both of which are now governmental concerns. With a rather high view of the witness of the church, Yoder claims that the church sees (or ought to see) itself as in the business of ministering with a constantly inventive vision for the good of the larger society, constantly willing to move on to new realms when her witness has been grasped at any given point.[60] Third and finally, Yoder also notes the role of the individual in the implicit witness of the church, since the church is made up of laypeople whose primary contact with the world is through earning a living and raising a family in the midst of society. These individuals serve as witnesses by transforming "cases" into persons, by placing community service over profits, by teaching younger generations what really matters, and by being a good neighbor, among other practices. In all of these ways, Christians also serve as a sort of social "leavening" or as a source for "moral osmosis"[61] in a way that leads the world to live according to certain moral values for which it has no spiritual or logical commitment. With these manifold examples of service as witness, Yoder has already outlined a far-reaching account of the Christian witness to the world.[62] But he has said little about witness to the state as the state. For this, one must step beyond the implicit witness of the church.

60. Ibid., 19–20. This claim echoes Yoder's appropriation of the Troeltschian idea that the freedom for social creativity occurs most effectively amongst those in the minority. See "Christ, the Hope of the World," 171–74.

61. See Yoder, "Peace Without Eschatology?" 163, and *Christian Witness to the State*, 20–21.

62. At this point, it is also relevant to note that Yoder follows his usual mode of frequently gesturing to modes of relating to the state that are problematic throughout these particular texts. I have left this part of the conversation out in order to concentrate on the constructive developments and because, by now, I am sure that the reader will have a good idea of what Yoder's criticisms might be.

b. *Direct Witness to the State.* In "Peace Without Eschatology?" Yoder quickly moves past demanding that the church be the church as a form of prophetic witness[63] to the second demand that looks much like a traditional evangelical description of witness. Stating that there is a call to every individual, including the statesman, to be reconciled with God, he continues: "Any social-minded concern that does not have this appeal to personal commitment at its heart is either utopian or a polite form of demagoguery."[64] If the statesman does not want to convert, then the Christian must return to the first Christian confession of faith: Christ is Lord. And, from this position, the statesman is then notified of the requirements of serving God by "encouraging the good and restraining evil."[65]

In *The Christian Witness to the State*, things are not quite as neat. Yoder remains adamant that there is a distinction between those who are Christians and those who are not, and, therefore, individual witness or evangelism is necessary. After all, if this is not necessary, then there would be no separation of church and state, no difference between the ethic of discipleship that is "laid upon every Christian believer by virtue of his very confession of faith" and a vague sort of "social betterment independent of . . . changing men's minds and hearts."[66] But Yoder then continues in a new direction by arguing that there is something deeply questionable about this distinction that restricts the term *gospel* to an invitation addressed to individuals (as it is in contemporary American usage). Here we return to one of the central themes of "The Original Revolution," namely, the conviction that "the kingdom of God has come near!" is a public proclamation about a changed reality. Of course, the proclamation must be answered by each individual. But by no means can this be construed as suggesting that it is merely a personal proclamation. Yoder concludes, pointing in a direction that his corpus would increasingly follow,

---

63. Yoder actually prefers the language of "social critique" to "prophetic witness" since the biblical prophets generally spoke to the people of God and not to the world, which is the audience Yoder intends with this term. This distinction is one more example of his reinforcement of an anti-Constantinian position. See *Christian Witness to the State*, 36.

64. Yoder, "Peace Without Eschatology?" 158.

65. Ibid.

66. Yoder, *Christian Witness to the State*, 23.

with an emphasis on the social dimension of the gospel proclamation: "What was wrong with the 'social gospel' of two generations ago was not that it was social, but that it lacked certain dimensions of the gospel."[67]

Just because Yoder proclaims a social gospel, however, does not mean that the individual becomes irrelevant. In fact, the opposite is the case. One of the major premises in his account of witness is that all communication is addressed to individuals and calls for individual response, even communication through mass media. For this reason, when a Christian speaks to a statesman, the Christian must always remember that he or she is speaking to a person.[68]

Admittedly, all of this is still a sort of preamble because we are not yet at the content of the direct witness. If I may delay one moment more, allow me to note the three criteria Yoder lays out for qualifying the church's witness: (1) the witness to the state must be representative of the church's clear conviction; (2) the witness of the church must be consistent with the church's behavior; and (3) the church should only speak when it has something to say.[69] Now, assuming that these criteria are met, the most complicated aspect of Yoder's position still remains.

As it turns out, direct witness to the state is not exactly direct. Or, to rephrase, direct witness to the state requires a sort of translation simply because the church must speak to the state in terms that are not its own (because, as indicated above, the non-Christian statesman cannot be expected to understand or be able to follow the way of discipleship). This is to say that the church must use language suitable for those "outside the perfection of Christ," yet language that points to the truth that is known only "inside the perfection of Christ." For Yoder, the means to maintain a duality here that does not fall into either a dualism (absolute separation of church and state) or a monism (unity of church and state) is through the selective use of middle axioms

---

67. Ibid.

68. Ibid., 24. See also *Discipleship as Political Responsibility*: "We will not give in to the view that human autonomy is given up when a person becomes part of the state machinery. We will address government officials just as we do other citizens" (45).

69. Yoder, *Christian Witness to the State*, 21.

that mediate "between the norms of faith and the situation conditioned by unbelief."[70]

Stated this way, the middle axiom is the only way that the Christian can "directly" witness to the state. It does not speak the language of a state's self-glorification, self-absolutization, or self-deification. Neither does it speak the true language of the church. Rather, operating on the principle of love, it seeks to speak to the state prophetically "in a corrective way" with "pagan terms" (i.e., liberty, equality, fraternity, education, democracy, human rights) for the purpose of calling the state to the next highest conceivable level of social community. These terms, much like the state itself, have no validity in themselves except as they serve as a projection or reflection of the relevance of the love of Christ, and they find their true culmination only in the conversion of the political leader to Christ.[71]

In *The Christian Witness to the State*, Yoder provides several examples of how the use of middle axioms might play out; I will briefly draw attention to just two. Capital punishment, about which Yoder also had written several years earlier,[72] is one such example. In addressing the question of capital punishment, he begins with the universally approachable assumption that, in a hypothetical ideal state, there would be no need for capital punishment because there would be no crime. (This is not the same as the Christian claim, borrowed from Jean Lasserre, that good governments should follow the Decalogue and, therefore, not take life.[73]) In assuming this belief, Yoder gestures toward a mutual agreement that could serve as the basis for the church's conversation with the state. He then notes—to indicate a link between Christianity and the best governments—that in some

---

70. Ibid., 33n3. The term "middle axiom" is not Yoder's invention. He points to its appearance in the 1948 World Council of Churches' Amsterdam General Assembly preparatory materials, while Cartwright points back to the work of J. H. Oldham for the 1937 Oxford Conference on Life and Work as the source of the term. See Cartwright's "Radical Reform, Radical Catholicity," 17.

71. Yoder, *Christian Witness to the State*, 72–73.

72. See, for example, Yoder's "Capital Punishment and the Bible," *The Christian and Capital Punishment*, and "Capital Punishment."

73. Yoder is borrowing from Lasserre's *War and the Gospel*, which he considered to be the most adequate theological presentation of Christian pacifism at the time.

societies sufficiently influenced by Christian witness, lethal violence has been largely eliminated, and, as a result, the abolishment of capital punishment and the unarming of police officers is an "intelligent and available possibility" because it is within reach. For those societies still on their way to this goal, however, the church must be patient and call for incremental movement towards abolishing capital punishment. Therefore, where there is no rule of law, to begin by attacking the legislative provision for the death penalty "would be to raise the wrong issue first." Of course, Yoder quickly notes that this is not saying that the death penalty is ever justified; this is just saying that it may not be the most offensive thing that the state is doing.[74] And, clearly, he assumes that a significant level of casuistic or prudential reasoning (either individually or communally) must be employed in the use of middle axioms to address this particular issue.

A second, probably more familiar example of Yoder's use of middle axioms is his occasional appropriation of the logic of the just war.[75] As one should expect, Yoder rules out the possibility that there can ever be a just war in the Christian sense of the word—this is the claim that applies to those inside the perfection of Christ. Yet, there are times when the concept of the lesser evil can still be relevant in the elaboration of an ethic for the state. One very helpful way to communicate this is to borrow the Catholic doctrine of the just war because it calls for criteria that delimit the cases in which the use of violence is the least illegitimate.[76] Although Yoder does not use the term "middle axioms" in *When War is Unjust*, the preface to this later text suggests that this is precisely the model he is working within:

---

74. Yoder, *Christian Witness to the State*, 49–50.

75. See, for example, the list of publications by Yoder concerning just war on the final pages of his *When War is Unjust*, 167–68.

76. Yoder, *Christian Witness to the State*, 49. Yoder's appropriation of just war criteria here and its designation as Catholic doctrine can imply one of two things: (1) Catholics have given up the language of the perfection of Christ and settled for an approximation, or (2) Catholics have become incredibly adept at articulating middle axioms to the extent that, in this case, their formalization of middle axioms is a helpful model to draw upon. The former would be a condemnation; the latter would be a compliment. Perhaps he intends a little of both.

> Ecumenical encounter is defined by the recognition that if we differ from fellow-believers in our concrete decisions about action, we probably differ too in the kinds of logical and historical paths whereby we got to these contradictory conclusions.
>
> Respectful dialogue therefore demands the exercise of entering into one's interlocutor's stance and story in search of some common court of appeal before which the clashing claims of the two (or more) holistically opposed positions might be adjudicated, or for some shared experience to which both of us might relate.[77]

As the above indicates, middle axioms need not be limited to a conversation between the Christian and the state since they can also be used between the Christian and any other person who is not Christian (and thus does not share the same Christian language). Over a decade after the publication of *The Christian Witness to the State*, Yoder was still self-consciously working within the basic logic of middle axioms, though the term seems to disappear from the corpus rather quickly. For example, in "The Christian Case for Democracy," originally written in 1977 and significantly revised in 1984, Yoder retained the notion of middle axioms but used the language of semantic frames in its place.[78] On one side, filling the place of "the state," Yoder suggests a semantic frame of "ordinary usage," and, in this later context, this could be specified more accurately as "marketplace semantics" (which Yoder believes, like the common understanding of the state, is deeply indebted to Troeltsch, Max Weber, and the Niebuhrs).[79] On the other end of the communication gap lies the familiar category of "the faith community speaking internally," the distinctive ethic of the Messiah. The "bridge" between the two (clearly a less technical designation than "middle axiom")

---

77. Yoder, *When War is Unjust*, ix. Whether recognized as such or not, it is this sort of exercise that is usually at the root of the claim that Yoder is a conversational writer who begins where the reader is in order to begin the conversation.

78. Craig Hovey has aptly pointed this out in "The Public Ethics of John Howard Yoder and Stanley Hauerwas," 213. Further support for this position can be found in "But We Do See Jesus," where Yoder also points towards an "interworld transformational grammar" (56).

79. Yoder's discussion of this matter is complicated by the fact that he is interested in other matters (i.e., generalizable claims about agency) and seems to presume an understanding of the middle axiom model. See especially the diagram in "The Christian Case for Democracy," 161.

is a pragmatic appropriation of universally understandable language that serves as analogous to the internal language of the faith community, the understandable language "of beneficence whereby the rulers justify themselves and whereby they can be called to greater decency."[80]

Looking back at *The Christian Witness to the State*, it is clear that there are multiple ways in which the Christian witnesses to the world. Yet, there seems to be only one method of speaking directly to the state as a particular manifestation of the world. As we have seen, the application of middle axioms is this method, one that is carried forward in "The Christian Case for Democracy" nearly two decades later. Yet, truth be told, middle axioms were already losing their pride of place in Yoder's corpus with the publication of *The Politics of Jesus*. And, in their demise, the previously relevant distinctions between the other modes of indirect witness slowly begin to disappear, along with the distinction between indirect and direct witness as well. Yoder himself narrates his perspective on the changing shape of the witness to the state as follows. Immediately after summarizing the way in which middle axioms (or the concept of the "bridge") works, he states:

> Still another way to handle the semantic package would be to use what some could call a "Barthian" logic and to say that it is the usage of governmental language within the people of God which is the norm. The governmental logic used within the wider culture is then only a pale reflection, analogy, dilution, perversion of "true politics." Only the politics of Jesus is politics according to the will of God. The politics of the kings and the nations are distorted, fallen, counterfeits of the same. The norms of the kings are dealt with most responsibly when their claim to autonomy and clarity is denied by the church's courageous persistence in using kingdom language first of all within the context of faith, never really granting the propriety of the expropriation of kingdom language by the nations. In a context of catechism, or preaching, or of liturgy, this is the best of the three ways of reasoning. This is what I was doing in calling my book *The Politics of Jesus*.[81]

---

80. Yoder, "The Christian Case for Democracy," 159.

81. Ibid., 163. The "three ways" Yoder refers to at the conclusion of this citation seem to be (1) the Constantinian fusing of the facticity of dominion, the language of legitimation, and the "differentness" of the disciples (157), (2) the middle-axiom model, and (3) the "Barthian" logic of *The Politics of Jesus*.

And so, at last, we arrive at a basic understanding of the way of reasoning displayed in *The Politics of Jesus*.

DISCIPLESHIP AS POLITICS

Taking Yoder's own assessment of what he was doing in *Politics* at face value, it seems that making the "governmental language within the people of God" the norm for explicating reality is, in his estimation, the best way to deal with the "semantic package" of two groups—those within and without the church—using the same terms differently.[82] In truth, he had already taken significant steps in this direction in *The Original Revolution*. But why this self-conscious shift away from the logic of middle axioms? And what does this shift mean for understanding the place of *The Politics of Jesus* within Yoder's corpus?

The problem with middle axioms seems to be rather straightforward (even if Yoder does not fully develop the critique himself): the use of middle axioms grants too much "epistemological sovereignty" to the wider world.[83] Or, to restate, it grants the propriety of the expropriation of the language of true politics (i.e., "kingdom language") to the nations.[84] If Christians have recourse only to the use of middle axioms, they appear to grant that the language of the nations is valid in its own sphere, thereby leaving middle axioms to stand merely as a rhetorical bridge between two autonomous semantic frames. But Yoder is interested in undermining precisely this notion that the wider world is autonomous. Therefore, when

---

Whether or to what extent Yoder is accurate in attributing the semantic logic of *Politics* to Barth is, surprisingly, a question that has received little serious attention or evaluation. Nation's claim that "few have yet to come to grips with Yoder's profound discussion and critique of Barth's views on war" could be stretched to address the entire relationship between Yoder and Barth (Nation, "Editor's Foreword," *Karl Barth and the Problem of War*, xi). Aside from Craig Carter's extensive engagement in *The Politics of the Cross* (61–90), one should also consider Rasmussen, "Politics of Diaspora"; Huebner, "Can a Gift be Commanded?"; and Weaver, "Politics of the Kingdom and Religious Plurality."

82. A form of this logic is also expressed in the later claim: "The truth has come to our side of the ditch." See Yoder, "But We Do See Jesus," 62.

83. It appears that this is one of the concerns that drives Chris Huebner's appropriation of Yoder in *A Precarious Peace* and also the basis around which Christian Early and Ted Grimsrud gathered the essays in Yoder's *A Pacifist Way of Knowing*.

84. Yoder, "The Christian Case for Democracy," 163–64.

one claims that "the Rule of God is the basic category," one introduces a single semantic frame against which all others must be judged.[85]

Second, employing middle axioms always allows the wider world to set the agenda for the conversation to the extent that the faithful community is continually forced to react to the language and claims already existing in the wider world. Therefore, the use of middle axioms, even in the attempt to overcome sectarianism by speaking to "the powers that be," seems to be parasitic upon the value-laden sociological descriptions provided by Troeltsch and the Niebuhrs simply because there are no arguments that can be made by the faithful community that are "independent of the cultural developments of Reformation and Enlightenment."[86]

With this critique in mind, it seems reasonable to suggest that one of the basic tasks of *The Politics of Jesus* (as it has been for much of the corpus) is to challenge the early twentieth-century self-acceptance of a Troeltschian or Niebuhrian realist (i.e., sectarian) definition of and within Anabaptism.[87] Yoder had been arguing in this vein for some time and, occasionally, *The Original Revolution* (both in its language and in its tone) had already latently employed the same sort of semantic logic evident in *Politics*. Yet, in *Politics*, Yoder enlists the support of a new sort of non-Anabaptist, realist academic authority—"biblical realism"—for the purpose of exhorting his revolutionized description of the Anabaptist vision (i.e., faithful Christianity) toward which he had been working for two decades.

Therefore, to state that *The Politics of Jesus* is the maturation of Yoder's early theological developments is, in many cases, accurate. In terms of content, it is an extended argument—loosely rooted in Luke's Gospel[88]—for the normativity of Jesus Christ in Christian ethics. This is, after all, what Yoder had been saying for decades. After the preliminary deconstructive introduction, the constructive argument begins, again, with the political

85. See Yoder, "But We Do See Jesus," 54.

86. Yoder, "The Christian Case for Democracy," 164.

87. To wrest governmental language (including the term "politics") out of its culturally ensconced definitions, *The Politics of Jesus*, understandably, begins polemically. Against the contemporary trends in Christian ethics, Yoder openly challenges what he takes to be modes of thought that marginalize Jesus as non-normative. Positively, he then states his own intended program: the ministry and claims of Jesus are best understood not as presenting the avoidance of politics but as demanding "one particular social-political-ethical option." See Yoder, *Politics of Jesus*, 11.

88. Glen Stassen rightly points out that even though the first part of *The Politics of Jesus* is based on Luke, Yoder does not discuss the "Sermon on the Plain" (Luke 6:20–49). See Stassen, "Politics of Jesus in the Sermon on the Plain," 151.

rendering of Mary's Magnificat, continues with a social reading of Jesus' temptations, and then focuses on Jesus' articulation of the messianic expectation in "the most expressly social terms."[89] As Yoder reads Luke, the opposition to Jesus is not random but organized. And, to this opposition, Jesus responds in kind: "To organized opposition he responds with the formal founding of a new social reality. New teachings are no threat, as long as the teacher stands alone; a movement, extending his personality in both time and space, presenting an alternative to the structures that were there before, challenges the system as no mere words ever could."[90]

This new community chooses neither quietism nor insurrection;[91] this new voluntary community follows the Old Testament lead;[92] this new voluntary community follows a clearly defined lifestyle distinct from the wider world. The distinctness, Yoder notes, is "not a cultic or ritual separation, but rather a nonconformed quality of ('secular') involvement in the life of the world."[93] This lifestyle, because it is political, must then come into contact with competing lifestyles, and, in the case of Jesus' immediate community, this meant suffering and death at the hands of the Jewish and Roman authorities. But Jesus responded in a particular way that Yoder takes to be normative for all the followers of Jesus. Perhaps the most succinct summary of the overall argument of *The Politics of Jesus* is expressed as follows:

> Jesus was, in his divinely mandated (i.e., promised, anointed, messianic) prophethood, priesthood, and kingship, the bearer of a new possibility of human, social, and therefore political relationships. His baptism is the inauguration and his cross is the culmination of

---

89. Yoder, *Politics of Jesus*, 29. In this context, Yoder draws upon Luke's appeal to Isaiah. See Luke 4:18–19 and Isa 61:1–2. Although not appealing directly to the story of Abraham, as he had in several of his earlier writings, Yoder's description of Jesus within this prophetic strand of first-century Judaism again demonstrates the fundamental importance of the Jewishness of Jesus.

90. Ibid., 33.

91. Yoder deconstructs what he takes to be the contemporary binary options further at 103–9, and it is on this basis that Parler and others have praised Yoder's particular genius.

92. That Yoder devotes an entire chapter to Jubilee indicates that he is continually interested in contextualizing Jesus in the story of the Old Testament. See Yoder, *Politics of Jesus*, 60–71.

93. Yoder, *Politics of Jesus*, 39. Note that Yoder is still employing the familiar distinction between the cultic/ritual elements of religion and the "secular" description of social ethics.

that new regime in which his disciples are called to share. Hearers or readers may choose to consider that kingdom as not real, or not relevant, or not possible, or not inviting; but no longer can we come to this choice in the name of systematic theology or honest hermeneutics. *At this one point* there is no difference between the Jesus of *Historie* and the Christ of *Geschichte* . . . No such slicing can avoid his call to an ethic marked by the cross, a cross identified as the punishment of a man who threatens society by creating a new kind of community leading a radically new kind of life.[94]

From this foundation, Yoder then constructs a refined account of the politics of Jesus: (1) by examining and developing the ethical implications of the Jubilee (chapter 3);[95] (2) by sketching the movement from holy war to the possibility of nonviolence for God's chosen people (chapters 4–5);[96] (3) by arguing that Jesus provides a new, formative definition of true humanity that must be imitated at one point and one point alone: in his cross (chapters 6–7);[97] (4) by explaining how the primary social structure through which the gospel works to change other structures is the Christian community (chapter 8);[98] (5) by exhorting his readers to

94. Ibid., 52–53.

95. For a good introduction to Yoder's appropriation of André Trocmé on this theme, see Swartley, "Smelting for Gold," 288–302.

96. Here one finds much that has already been argued in other contexts.

97. Yoder, *Politics of Jesus*, 95. At this juncture, the reader can also sense the narrowing of valid options for the faithful hermeneutic community. What I mean by this is that although there is room for communal specification of the principle, the content of the principle of imitation is fairly rigidly determined by Yoder: "There is but one realm in which the concept of imitation holds—but there it holds in every strand of the New Testament literature and all the more striking by virtue of the absence of parallels in other realms. This is at the point of the concrete social meaning of the cross in its relation to enmity and power. Servanthood replaces dominion, forgiveness absorbs hostility. Thus—and only thus—are we bound by New Testament thought to 'be like Jesus.'" Yoder, *Politics of Jesus*, 131.

It seems to be this kind of reified principle that makes Yoder's scriptural hermeneutic run against itself, and certainly against some of his contemporary interpreters. For example, Peter Ochs has rightly bemoaned that Yoder, at times, appears to freeze the hermeneutic process into "clear-and-distinct, once-and-for-all constructions, articulable in clear sentences and emblems." According to Ochs, this sort of conceptual finality is a form of "secular Western rationalism" that reduced hermeneutics to reason in the first place. See Ochs, *Free Church and Israel's Covenant*, 22–23.

98. It is in this context that Yoder reintroduces Berkhof's reading of the relationship between Christ and the powers. And, although the title of the chapter—"Christ and the Powers"—seems a close semantic complement to Niebuhr's *Christ and Culture*, Yoder is careful to tie the work of Christ to the concrete expression of the church's sociality:

embrace subordination and servanthood as an expression of freedom from the structures of the world (chapter 9);[99] (6) by challenging traditional Protestant thought concerning the separation of one's life into public and private spheres through the process of carefully relativizing the authority of the state and redefining faith as discipleship (chapters 10–11);[100] and, finally, (7) by sketching the cosmic reality, in which a new sort of relevance or effectiveness emerges and against which common understandings in the wider world are shown to be but poor and misunderstood approximations.

Granted, this is but a poor summary of a rich and complex text. Yet, such summaries are not entirely unhelpful because they provide a glimpse into the most basic contours of a text (and it is helpful to remember that most of the detailed arguments in the text are reiterations of previously published arguments). In summarizing this way, however, the importance of the concluding chapter quickly comes into focus. Why? Simply because it finally synthesizes the metaphysical and theological claims that undergird the overarching claim that the politics of Jesus are

---

The Powers have been defeated not by some kind of cosmic hocus-pocus but by the concreteness of the cross; the impact of the cross upon them is not the working of magical words nor the fulfillment of a legal contract calling for the shedding of innocent blood, but the sovereign presence, within the structures of creaturely orderliness, of Jesus the kingly claimant and of the church which is itself a structure and a power in society. Thus the historicity of Jesus retains, in the working of the church as it encounters the other power and value structures of its history, the same kind of relevance that the man Jesus had for those whom he served until they killed him."

Yoder, *Politics of Jesus*, 158.

In this passage, we can see how Yoder positively responds to the state as "structured unbelief"; one can also sense the direction Yoder's thought will take toward "seeing Jesus" as a particular way of living.

99. The mode of exploring this theme through an examination of the *Haustafeln* (household codes) of the New Testament proved rather unpopular, though there were exceptions. On this matter, see Nation, *John Howard Yoder*, 118–19.

100. Certainly, one could object to placing these two chapters together in this way. Yet, by grouping these together here, I am simply suggesting that (other than the consistent critique of traditional "Protestant" theological categories) the theme of obedience ties the two together—the relative obedience to the state in chapter 10 and the obedience required by an understanding of justification as a social phenomenon centered in the reconciliation of different kinds of people through "love made real at the point of its application to the enemy" in chapter 11. See Yoder, *Politics of Jesus*, 225. Whatever the case may be, the deconstructive work accomplished in chapter 10 is logically necessary before the constructive work in the subsequent chapter.

truer than the politics of the wider world. Therefore, to claim that "Jesus is Lord" or that "the Lamb has conquered" is to claim that history is working out and will work out a certain way. As Yoder would later summarize, this means that Jesus provides "a clue to which kinds of causation, which kinds of community-building, which kinds of conflict management, go with the grain of the cosmos." It means that the "wider world"—with its inadequate understandings of relevance, effectiveness, and calculation—is enclosed within, smaller than, and much less true than the sovereignty of the God of the resurrection and ascension.[101]

With this conclusion, it is most evident that *The Politics of Jesus* has accomplished the tasks of (*a*) normatively describing the people of God according to the true politics of the kingdom of God and (*b*) outlining multiple clues as to which kinds of causation and community-building go with the grain of the universe. On some version of these bases, *The Politics of Jesus* gained considerable fame within Yoder's own Mennonite context and also within the larger Christian community. In terms of quantity, it sold over eighty-five thousand English copies in twenty-six years.[102] In terms of quality, the text is considered by some as "a wedge driven into the academic discussion about theological ethics during the last half of the twentieth century."[103] Acknowledging the importance of *Politics* in terms of its reception and appropriation, however, may inadvertently lead to a too-sympathetic reading of the text within Yoder's own corpus. The following comments and questions serve to bring this portion of Yoder's corpus to a tentative conclusion and to indicate why the logic of Yoder's own thought must push beyond the limits of *The Politics of Jesus*.

CONCLUSION

I have already indicated a partial agreement with Zimmerman concerning the place of *Politics* as the maturation of Yoder's early writings. On several levels, it is a logical extension of the theological and ethical convictions present in his early years. Yet, there are several issues that are left

101. Yoder, *Politics of Jesus*, 246.

102. See Nation, *John Howard Yoder*, 110.

103. See Zimmerman, *Practicing the Politics of Jesus*, 173. Stanley Hauerwas and James McClendon are often appealed to as the most favorable advocates of the importance of Yoder's work for twentieth-century theological ethics, but even critics like James Gustafson and Oliver O'Donovan have openly acknowledged the paradigmatic challenge offered by Yoder's *Politics of Jesus*. See Gustafson, *Ethics from a Theocentric Perspective*, 1:75; and O'Donovan, *Desire of the Nations*, 151.

open at the conclusion of *Politics*, issues that deserve further scrutiny and that shape the agenda for the remainder of this book.

First, as Yoder sought to recast discipleship as politics, to what extent had he already translated his position beyond his earlier Anabaptist concerns and descriptions? Much has been made about Yoder's Anabaptist roots, yet neither his twentieth-century mentors nor his sixteenth-century heroes appear in the text; Grebel, Bender, and Hershberger have been replaced by Berkhof, Trocmé, and Cullman. Certainly, a considerable number of Yoder's Mennonite contemporaries recognized *The Politics of Jesus* as an expression of many of their convictions, yet one cannot help wondering why believer's baptism, communal discernment, or any number of other historical marks of the Anabaptist tradition (at least as Yoder understands it) that had been very prevalent in Yoder's thought are minimized in this particular construal of Christian existence. Many of these themes will, of course, return in subsequent years. But they will do so only after they, too, have passed through an initiation into political language. This question is not necessarily a value judgment, but it is an attempt to encourage stepping back and reconsidering whether there can be a simple equation between Anabaptism and the position displayed in *Politics*. Or, to rephrase, does *The Politics of Jesus*—if not intentionally, then in fact—function as a bridge (i.e., a middle axiom) between Anabaptism and the larger world of biblical and theological scholarship? How one answers this question profoundly inflects one's understanding of the place of *Politics* within Yoder's thought as a whole.

Second, and related, I want to note that it is obvious that much good has been gained by the exercise in "fundamental philosophical hermeneutics"[104] that uses governmental language within the people of God as the norm. Yet, by the end of *Politics*, it appears that the only language one can use concerning the people of God is governmental language. On one hand, Yoder's concern to avoid cultic or ritual religion finds an answer in political language; on the other hand, Yoder's concern to avoid the haunting charge of sectarianism also finds its answer in the language of "true politics." There seems to be nothing left to say that is not politics. Jesus is political; conversion is political; salvation is political; interpersonal relations are political; the church is political; the eschaton is political. This may all be true to an extent, but to place a normative priority upon the language of politics for one's description of the entirety

---

104. Yoder, *Politics of Jesus*, x.

of existence seems to indicate a sort of absurd, inverse enslavement to the logic of Troeltsch and the Niebuhrs that does not do justice to the richness of the biblical witness concerning God's relationship to creation, including but not limited to God's chosen people.

Finally, Yoder himself notes that the use of true political language is the best way of reasoning in the context of catechism, preaching, and liturgy.[105] He then continues: "It is misunderstood however in ecumenical and apologetic contexts. Therefore I would not attempt to impose it in a conversation with the children of Troeltsch and Niebuhr, for whom the pagan definitions are semantically prior."[106] If this is the case, however, all that *Politics* has accomplished is a reworking of the in-group conversation that still has to be translated further if it is to be understood by the wider world. Therefore, by Yoder's own description—the Christian community is sent into the world to "communicate a message and gather its hearers into communities"[107]—appropriating the language of politics for the Christian community still leaves incomplete the task of communicating the gospel to the wider world.[108]

As the remaining chapters illustrate, this task exercises Yoder for the rest of his authorship. I propose to separate his search for a methodological solution to this problem into two distinct yet related contexts. First, looking back at the roots of the politics of Jesus, Yoder is forced to come to grips with the relationship between Christianity and Judaism. Second, looking at his contemporary context, he is forced to come to grips with profound differences in ecumenical conversation. In both cases, the conversation must take place through an intermediary bridge of some sort that can no longer function as simply as middle axioms had in his earlier writings. To these we now turn.

---

105. Yoder, "Christian Case for Democracy," 163.

106. Ibid., 163–64.

107. Yoder, *For the Nations*, 7.

108. It appears that Zimmerman has also noticed a shift in emphasis at this point in his corpus. By appealing to David Tracy's distinctions between analogical and dialectical languages, Zimmerman concludes that Yoder's project contains both: it begins with a focus on the dialectical and then it creates new analogies. Although I am sympathetic to Zimmerman's position, I believe that the focus on *Politics* as the fulcrum upon which the language shifts is overstated. See Zimmerman, *Practicing the Politics of Jesus*, 174–77.

FOUR

Reconstructing Jewish Christianity

LATE IN 1972, YODER received a letter—dated September 25—from Rabbi Steven Schwarzschild, a philosophy professor at Washington University in St. Louis. The two had been carrying on a sometimes sedate, sometimes stirring exchange for several years already, and this particular letter addressed *The Politics of Jesus*. After reading a copy of the text, Schwarzschild wrote: "In a general way I have to begin by asserting my Jewish stance. I agree passionately with your ethics, but, bluntly, Jesus offends and bores me. *Ergo* your problems are not my problems." He continues: "Again, you are, I think, substantively and importantly right in identifying imitation with ethical following (discipleship) and the Messiah with the Servant but for neither is—to use the phrase again—Jesus needed (pp. 122, 124); in fact, all of Jewish literature is full of these identifications. In these matters, in other words, I think you are a good Jew and—though you do not like to hear this—a bad Christian."[1] Yet, even after this apparently critical comment, Schwarzschild can also say:

---

1. Letter from S. S. Schwarzschild to J. H. Yoder, Nov. 27, 1971, Box 201, "S.S.S. ztz'l." John H. Yoder Papers, 1947–1997. HM1–48. Mennonite Church USA Archives – Goshen. Goshen, Indiana. Subsequent references to unpublished items from these archives will include only brief author and title information, followed by the box number, folder title, or (where applicable) a page number. In the bibliography, personal letters are grouped and organized under "Correspondence" by box number and folder title; lectures appear alphabetically by title. I would like to acknowledge the generosity of Baylor University's College of Arts and Sciences for providing summer sabbatical funding (2008) that enabled a visit to the Mennonite Church USA Historical Archives in Goshen, Indiana, for the purpose of studying the correspondence between Yoder and Schwarzschild.

"Need I say it? I do love you—and there are few people, of any faith, with whom I seem to be speaking a language so similar as yours."[2]

Yoder, unsurprisingly, almost takes the criticism of being a bad Christian as a compliment, to which Schwarzschild retorts, "OK baby— you're a better Jew than I."[3] But, if Yoder is a bad Christian and a better Jew than a rabbi, what have these terms come to mean for both of the interlocutors, especially when Yoder acknowledged, in 1996, that "I have been taught much by numerous Jewish friends, but by no one else so much as by Steven S. Schwarzschild *ztz'l*, to whose memory [*The Jewish-Christian Schism Revisited*] is dedicated."[4] In 1980, nearly a decade after the publication of *The Politics of Jesus*, Schwarzschild again ruminated about his continued identification with that particular text: "It's still impressive to me how you and I agree. Of course, I do all that, and just like that, without your Christology. I wonder what that proves about your and my methodology and its rationale."[5]

These brief excerpts of a long-running correspondence are enlightening in several ways.[6] First, they indicate that Yoder was in a lengthy and meaningful dialogical conversation with someone beyond what he would refer to as his "in-group."[7] This means, if nothing else, that dialogical communication is possible for Yoder even if he is still far from conclusively thematizing this form of communication. Second, as the letters indicate, it is Schwarzschild, first, who does most of the worrying about why this conversation works so well and why they are speaking such a similar language

---

2. Ibid.

3. Letter from S. S. Schwarzschild to J. H. Yoder, Nov. 8, 1972, Box 132, "Steven Schwarzschild."

4. Yoder, *Jewish-Christian Schism Revisited*, 35. Clearly, Yoder had conversations with other Jewish thinkers such as Pinches Lapide and Michael Berenbaum. Yet, none of these is as important or defining for Yoder as his long-standing relationship with Schwarzschild.

5. Letter from S. S. Schwarzschild to J. H. Yoder, Dec. 11, 1980, Box 201, "S.S.S. Planning Course."

6. Archival evidence indicates the correspondence begins as early as 1968 (with a letter from Yoder dated June 25) and continued sporadically until Schwarzschild's passing in 1986.

7. Michael Cartwright, in the "Editor's Introduction" to *Jewish-Christian Schism Revisited*, notes that the continuity in Yoder's perspective concerning Jewish-Christian relations "can perhaps best be located in Yoder's decades-long conversation with Rabbi Steven S. Schwarzschild." I am in agreement with this claim. See Cartwright, "Editor's Introduction," *Jewish-Christian Schism Revisited*, 12.

even though the importance of Jesus seems indispensable to only one of the interlocutors. Third, and related, the excerpts begin to demand reflection upon what will become Yoder's methodological "bridge" that replaces middle axioms: the new mode of mediation is politics or, to rephrase, the social practices of the faithful community. As I attempt to demonstrate below, theorizing how this communication between himself (a Christian) and Schwarzschild (a Jew) works quickly becomes one of Yoder's primary concerns for the remainder of his corpus.

Late in his life, in the Introduction to *For the Nations*, Yoder noted that the collection of essays gathered under that title could be "described as an analogy to the development of Yiddish."[8] The nod to Yiddish is not merely superfluous. What Yoder is driving at, in the same vein we have seen in the preceding chapters, is the fact that he is attempting to communicate by refusing to adopt the common idiom directly. He explains: "My accepting the 'sectarian' label for myself, for purposes of discussion with American Protestantism, 1950–90, is like the Jew in Babylon in 500 B.C.E. using Chaldean or like Buber, Landau, and Zweig in Germany in 1920 using German; I have usually done it, accepting having no choice but to play by other people's rules. Yet it routinely has led to misunderstanding and misrepresentation. The present book seeks to correct that."[9]

Therefore, Yoder claims that each of the essays in *For the Nations*, in its own way, argues that the "very shape of the people of God in the world is a public witness, or is 'good news' for the world."[10] So, as many nineteenth- and twentieth-century Jews used Yiddish to bridge their Hebraic roots and their Germanic context, so Yoder sought to create, analogically, his own "variant of the common idiom" that is neither his own "ancient in-group language" (read historical Anabaptism) nor the common idiom (read Troeltsch and the Niebuhrs) but that, nonetheless, represents "the

---

8. Yoder, *For the Nations*, 4. Yiddish, at a basic level, is a language that emerged in central Europe among a group of Ashkenazi Jews. It is not linguistically related to Hebrew although it uses the Hebrew alphabet; it is not German although they share a significant amount of vocabulary. In the late nineteenth and early twentieth centuries, Yiddishism (a combination of the language and a cultural movement) emerged as a modern expression of Judaism.

9. Ibid.

10. Ibid., 6. Yoder also makes a point of noting that the essays gathered as *The Royal Priesthood* could be seen as "fitting within a vision of the mission of the Christian community some call 'sectarian' or describe as standing 'against the nations,'" a characterization that he denies and seeks to rectify with *For the Nations*. See *For the Nations*, 5–6.

line of the gospel."[11] This variant of the common idiom turns out to be precisely the means through which Jews and Christians can find a common language and, therefore, communicate with one another.

With this broad claim in the background, the purposes of this chapter are to explore (*a*) the evolution of Yoder's reconstruction of Jewish Christianity after *The Politics of Jesus*;[12] and (*b*) how this reconstruction is dependent upon the normative priority of what Yoder takes to be the original messianic politics of first-century Judaism—his variant of the common idiom. So, to these tasks we now turn.[13]

THE EVOLUTION OF YODER'S JEWISH CHRISTIANITY

As we have seen in the previous chapter, Yoder describes *the* biblical story as beginning with the calling of Abraham.[14] The idea of the prototypical pilgrim people described in "The Original Revolution" is, by Yoder's own admission, intentionally drawn into a critical conversation with "a contemporary perspective drawn from the 'radical reformation' tradition of Christianity" only in the early 1970s in Buenos Aires.[15] Thus began the long series of engagements that, according to Yoder, "articulate one basic alternative perspective" to Jewish-Christian relations and that was posthumously published in 2003 as *The Jewish-Christian Schism Revisited*.

Early Explorations

The first steps in this direction began with an invitation from Rabbi Marshall Meyer and liberation theologian José Miguez Bonino. While in Buenos Aires in the autumn of 1970, Yoder prepared a paper on this

---

11. Yoder, *For the Nations*, 4.

12. The description included in the following pages does not claim to be exhaustive but merely to be sufficiently comprehensive to account for the major developments in this evolution.

13. Although it may tempt one to overdetermine Yoder's interest in Jewish-Christian relations, it is appropriate to note that Yoder's father-in-law was arrested by the Nazis on July 15, 1944, because, as far as I understand it, his son would not join the army. He was sent to Sachsenhausen on September 5, 1944, and then to Buchenwald in February, 1945, where he stayed until American forces arrived at Buchenwald in April, 1945.

14. Paul Doerksen rightly highlights that the story of Babel is, for Yoder, an important backdrop for the calling of Abraham. See Doerksen, *Beyond Suspicion*, 43–45; and Yoder, "Meaning After Babble," 127–30.

15. See Yoder, "What Needs to Change," 34–35.

theme—titled "Minority Christianity and Messianic Judaism"—that was presented at a meeting of Catholic, Protestant, and Jewish theology teachers.[16] The paper's thesis is familiar and yet not quite so: "the predominant Christian understanding of the relation between Jesus and Judaism is fundamentally distorted by the position of cultural establishment from which Christians observe."[17] The simplistic typology Yoder supplied to argue the thesis requires a dualism—both theological and historical—between Lutheranism (where the critique is supplied within the "social framework of established Christendom") and the radical reformation (where the critique focuses "on the issue of the establishment of religion as such").[18] The conclusion plays out as follows: the eventual Constantinian stance of the Christian church was a rejection of the Jewishness of the church precisely because (*a*) the pacifism of the early church was a Jewish pacifism, and (*b*) the trans-ethnic identity of the early church was borne of a Jewish view of God working in history.[19]

A month later, Yoder presented another paper in Buenos Aires to explicate his position further.[20] Rhetorically utilizing a question posed by José Miguez Bonino, Yoder moves to explain not only the possibility of Christian obedience (walking the line between the "Augustinians" who emphasize finitude and sin and the "rabbis" who do not recognize that the possibility of obedience "could only become real if in Jesus and Pentecost the messianic age in fact began"[21]) but also the shape of a possible obedient visible community. To do so, Yoder turns to describe what he refers to as "a social process" that is rooted in *The Schleitheim Confession*. This possible and visible community, echoing Yoder's early theological convictions, is marked (*a*) by following the counter-cultural example of Jesus, (*b*) by being brought together by the Holy Spirit, (*c*) by voluntary entrance into covenant, (*d*) by identifying criteria according to which one is

---

16. The original form of the paper, presented on September 16, 1970, at the Seminario Rabinico of Belgrano, remains unpublished; the ideas first given voice in this early paper eventually grew into a presentation at Notre Dame titled "Tertium Datur," which, in turn, would become revised and published as "It Did Not Have to Be."

17. Yoder, "Minority Christianity and Messianic Judaism," 2.

18. Ibid., 2–4.

19. Ibid.

20. This second paper was presented to the "Lutheran Theological Faculty" in a suburb of Buenos Aires. See "Forms of a Possible Obedience," 129n1.

21. Yoder, "Forms of a Possible Obedience," 123.

ruled outside the community, (*e*) by shared cultic actions, (*f*) by nonconformity to the world, (*g*) by autochthonous leadership, (*h*) by rejection of the sword, and (*i*) by an ethos of trustworthy communication. Of this list, the last seven criteria (*c–i*) are appropriations, in their respective order, of the seven articles found in *The Schleitheim Confession*.

Throughout his construal of this possible community of obedience, Yoder's emphasis is on the shape of the society and not on "dogmatic" convictions. Commenting on nonconformity with the world, Yoder writes: "Every living society has its limits, its *damnamus*. For Anabaptism, the limits are less dogmatic than sociological. They do not condemn heretical doctrinal formulations (as do the Protestant creeds) nor specific personal practices (like the so-called 'pietist ethic'), but rather the expressions of wrong community: apostate worship, alcoholic partying, commitments of bad faith, and violence."[22]

Whether one can, in fact, separate "dogmatic" convictions from expressions of wrong community so easily is debatable—for example, what would apostate worship look like without reference to dogmatic convictions? Yet, before getting caught up entirely in debating what looks much like Yoder's summary description of normative Anabaptism, we must proceed to the end of the paper to discover his point in relation to Judaism: "In a form befitting their century, and within the limits of their capacities and opportunities, the Anabaptists were able to rediscover and realize a functional equivalent of the original messianic Jewish universalism, as of the original Jewish pacifism, which had characterized the earliest churches, which had later been abandoned by both the anti-Judaic Catholicism of 'Christendom' and (to a lesser degree) the defensive Judaism of the Mishnaic codification."[23] With this small paragraph, the semantic framework changes significantly. The primitive Christianity that Yoder has frequently appealed to as normative is, in this quick turn, renamed "the original messianic Jewish" position. The original messianic Jewish position, then, is defined as the center that stands prototypically behind the Radical Reformation and against the later devolutions of Christendom and Judaism.

As is obvious from the above, Schwarzschild had problems with Yoder's Christology. But, on most other points, he was willing to affirm

22. Ibid., 127.
23. Ibid., 129.

Yoder's trajectory. They share a rejection of Maccabean and Zealot expressions of Judaism (including Zionism) and similarly violent Christian parallels; they share an occasionally smug rejection of "classic Christian teachings" (which makes Yoder a "Judaizer" in Schwarzschild's eyes); they share a reading of the politics displayed by Jesus as normative.[24] And, with both Schwarzschild's affirmation and his own piqued interest, Yoder was prepared to cross a vocational threshold beyond which lay the restitution of original Jewish messianism. Yoder hardly had time to settle back in America before embarking on this journey that would concern him for the rest of his life.

Late in 1971, Yoder began to seek out a way to pursue the Jewish-Christian question more intentionally and formally. In a letter to Schwarzschild, he revealed that he was looking ahead to a sabbatical and he was hoping for "a chance to study for a while within the context of some Jewish school."[25] He also sent an inquiry to Rabbi Meyer in Argentina, requesting information on "Jewish funding sources" that might be available for this type of undertaking.[26] Again, one of Yoder's key interests was "arguing that renewal movements within Christendom, of which I take Anabaptism to be paradigmatic, are best interpreted as efforts to restore the Jewishness of normative Christianity."[27] Schwarzschild responded quickly, encouraging the project. Yoder did not keep Rabbi Meyer's response in his files, but nearly a year later, he wrote to Eugene Borowitz and Louis Jacobs—acknowledging their recommendation by Rabbi Meyer—asking for information about either a center for research or funding "for Christians interested in Jewish or inter-faith studies."[28]

Constructing a Concrete Position

In the short term, it looks like these inquiries amounted to very little beyond the connections that Yoder already had at his fingertips, as Yoder

24. In Schwarzschild's terms: "Your reading of Jesus comes, in many ways, close to my—normative—reading of Judaism. In this I rejoice." See Letter from S. S. Schwarzschild to J. H. Yoder, July 9, 1968, Box 201, "S.S.S. ztz'l."

25. Letter from J. H. Yoder to S. S. Schwarzschild, Nov. 18, 1971, Box 201, "S.S.S. ztz'l."

26. Letter from J. H. Yoder to M. Meyer, July 19, 1971, Box 201, "Tantur 74/75 Jewish Pacifism."

27. Ibid.

28. Letter from J. H. Yoder to E. Borowitz and L. Jacobs, Sept. 25, 1972, Box 132, "Jewishness."

ended up spending the 1975–76 academic year at the Tantur Ecumenical Institute for Theological Studies in Jerusalem, which is operated by the University of Notre Dame (where Yoder was teaching by this time). Regardless of the channels Yoder utilized to arrive at Tantur, however, his sabbatical in Israel further reinforced his convictions concerning the centrality of historic messianic Judaism as the way forward in Jewish-Christian relations. To this end, a detailed set of preliminary research conclusions that further developed and explicated Yoder's account of the Jewish-Christian relationship emerged late in 1975. No longer merely arguing the rough sociological parallels between Judaism and Anabaptism, Yoder also highlighted the need to revise the "traditional historiography." He did not abandon the ideas outlined in Buenos Aires—the "minority-Christian" or "radical reformation" perspective is necessary for throwing new light on the issues related to Judaism—but he moved further in questioning the post-Constantinian historical and theological conclusions regarding the New Testament accounts of the emergence of the church between 70 and 150 CE. Particularly, he challenged the account of the "evolution of Church/Christendom as an organically ascending line from Pentecost to Constantine (and onwards)."[29] Ultimately, Yoder's thesis evolved to the point where he was prepared to argue that there is no necessary evolutionary separation between Jews and Christians when freed from the post-Constantinian perspective. Rather, the "gradual reciprocal alienation, concretized in hellenization on the Christian side and withdrawal or babylonianism [sic] on the other, represented *on both sides* a degree of infidelity to the earlier common tradition and vision."[30]

A second research outline—"The Jewish Pacifism of Jesus = A Research Outline"—was also circulated privately late in 1975; a third version—"The Jewishness of Christianity: A Research Program"—was publicly presented late in 1976 at a War/Nation/Church Colloquium in Washington, DC.[31] The conclusion of the late 1975 outline, "The Jewish

---

29. According to Yoder, this ascent means (*a*) hellenization, or leaving provincial Judaism behind, (*b*) Romanization, or the acceptance of the state as a tool of Providence, (*c*) hierarchization, (*d*) the active rejection of Judaism, and (*e*) the projection of later Judaism into the first century. See Yoder, "The Jewish Jesus and the Church/Synagogue Split," 1–2.

30. See Yoder, "The Jewish Jesus and the Church/Synagogue Split," 6–7.

31. Yoder, "War/Nation/Church Colloquium," Box 133, "WANACH 1976." This meeting was held December 3–5, 1976.

Pacifism of Jesus," is worth reiterating in detail, as it succinctly states the summary of Yoder's research at that point:

> VII. The overall outline of the "research program" is here summarized in order to indicate the place of the present outline within it:
>
> A. By "minority Christianity" is meant the stream of culture-critics within Western Christianity, exemplified by Waldenses, Unitas Fratrum, Anabaptism, Quakerism... variously referred to by majority historians as "sectarian," "radical reformation" ... There is reason to expect this perspective to add something to the analysis of Jewish-Christian relationships:
>   1. The sociocultural locus and style of these groups has often been like that of Jewry.
>   2. What they criticize in "Christendom" is often what Jews reject.
>
> B. The "Jewishness" of "radical Christianity" is exemplified:
>   1. By its pacifism (THE PRESENT OUTLINE)
>   2. By its messianic cosmopolitanism or "mission"
>   3. By its non-centralized congregationalism after the model of the diaspora synagogue and the chabourah
>
> C. This orientation will call for restructuring traditional "majority protestant" views in several areas:
>   1. The separation of Church and Synagogue between 70 and 150
>   2. Rehabilitating the concept of "apostasy" [and a] review of the function of scripture in ecumenical conversation.[32]

While still at Tantur, the content of his second outline found its way into several in-house presentations. The first of these—"The Restitution of the Church"—argued that the Christian church could not merely be reformed, but had to be reinstituted, begun anew, so that the "fundamental wrong turn in the past" could be corrected.[33] Historically, the believers churches emerge as the corrective, and they are the corrective at least partially because their perspective is Jewish in that (*a*) they valued the

---

32. See Yoder, "The Jewish Pacifism of Jesus = A Research Outline," Oct. 20, 1975, Box 133, "Tantur JHY."

33. Yoder, "Restitution of the Church," 137. This lecture was described as "an effort to introduce the entire free church or radical reformation vision to an audience with very little background in the area" in a letter to Franklin H. Littell written the following year. See Letter from J. H. Yoder to F. H. Littell, January 10, 1977, Box 133, "Jews/Peace."

particularity of Jesus as the fulcrum for critique, since the most Hebraic way of putting the question is to critique what has come into being in the course of history historically, with the grounds of criteria drawn from the same story; (*b*) they posited a unity of *halakah* and *aggadah*; (*c*) the ethic of Jesus they drew from Scripture was a Jewish ethic (truth-telling, love of enemy, rejection of sword, Jubilee sharing, etc.); and (*d*) their universal acceptance of a prophetic minority position undermined the provincialism of politics and mainstream Western historiography.[34] A second lecture, "The Disavowal of Constantine: An Alternative Perspective on Interfaith Dialogue," was given on February 19, 1976, and later was published in *Ecumenical Institute of Advanced Theological Studies Yearbook: 1975–1976*. The central task of this presentation was to "ask what difference it makes or would make for interfaith dialogue, if instead of seeing every 'religion' as represented by its most powerful 'establishment,' the disavowal of the establishment of religion were restored as part of a specifically Christian witness."[35] In short, the argument of this second presentation in Tantur normatively and methodologically formalizes the historical expressions outlined in the first.

A year later, on October 13, 1977, the ideas germinating during these fertile years blossomed in a rather unlikely venue. At a meeting of the Graduate Theological Union at the University of Notre Dame, Yoder read the first version of "Tertium Datur." He began with significant trepidation, claiming that the material in the presentation was "the hazardous projection of a line of research and a set of hypotheses whose promise lies precisely in their relative originality and untested quality."[36] Despite this caveat, however, Yoder boldly outlines what he understands to be the real issues of the Jewish-Christian schism. Following the lines he had already established in his research agendas, the paper begins with an acknowledgement that the radical reformation perspective initiates and makes possible this particular inquiry, which is to say that the radical reformation provides the possibility for "a point of reference within Christian origins which would permit us to disavow later developments."[37] What Yoder refers to here as "the later developments" are what he took to be the

34. Yoder, "Restitution of the Church," 139–41.

35. See Yoder, "Disavowal of Constantine," 51. Obviously building on his previous writings, this statement resonates deeply with the principled imitation of Jesus in *Politics*.

36. Yoder, "Tertium Datur," 1.

37. Ibid., 6.

"inherited position," which he defined as the assumption that there was a normative Judaism that Jesus and Paul rejected (and vice versa) and that Christianity is defined by these mutual rejections.

Against this position, Yoder then stakes his contrary claims as follows: 1) There is no such thing as normative Judaism in the first century, as this is a projection of later Christianity; 2) Christians did not reject normative Judaism, as (*a*) there was no normative Judaism, and (*b*) what the early Christians were rejecting was a particular set of authorities, or "establishment Judaism";[38] 3) the Jews did not reject Christianity as a belief system, because it is an empirical fact that during the first fifty years of the Christian community one could be both a faithful Jew and a faithful Christian;[39] and 4) at this time there was no normative Christianity, as there were no creeds, no bishops, no occasional synods, and no canon of Scripture.[40]

On the basis of these suggested correctives, Yoder describes the original relationship between Judaism and Christianity in a fashion that radically expands the preliminary narrative found in "The Original Revolution" and—taking up the independent developments of the previous years—becomes normative for all subsequent definitions of the relationship. To begin, he acknowledges that Jews and Christians had differing views concerning Jesus, but this tolerable difference "was a very thin line between degrees or tonalities in the attitude toward the incorporation of Gentiles into the faith of Abraham."[41] Of course, Yoder notes that it is no surprise that the unified plurality within Judaism may be threatened in every city where the new messianic movement came "with some vigor." He continues:

> But even then there is not a basis for creating two movements separate from each other and each united within itself. The Jews at Ephesus or at Corinth or at Berea who have not accepted the messianic message do not thereby acquire a distinctive theological identity and become "normative Judaism." They are defined thus far only at one point, negatively, by their not moving into the next phase into which the messengers of Jesus say that all Jewry is invited. They do not thereby have a rationale or a structure for being

---

38. Ibid., 18.
39. Ibid., 25.
40. Ibid., 32.
41. Ibid., 36.

non-Christian Jews. That rationale and structure will be developed only gradually.[42]

The upshot of this description, however, is that non-messianic Judaism (i.e., those that reject the invitation to move to the next phase to which all Jews are invited), which began with the increasing prominence of the Jamnia school, is "younger than Christianity" and "more marked by its rejection of the messianic Jews' claims than the Christians are marked by rejecting what the other Jews stand *for*."[43]

At this point in Yoder's argument, it becomes impossible to ignore a difficulty that prevails throughout his rethinking of the Jewish-Christian schism: although he claims there is no normative Judaism and no normative Christianity in the first century, his argument rests on the assumption that his account of Jesus' interpretation of Judaism (or, what Yoder will often refer to as messianic Judaism) is, in fact, normative for creating the critical perspective used to deconstruct both "normative Judaism" and "normative Christianity." Only on this assumption can he make the value-laden originary claims against later Judaism and Christianity stated above.[44] Textually, this is most evident early in "Tertium Datur." Immediately after claiming that Christians did not reject normative Judaism, at least partially because there was no normative Judaism, he continues: "Far more than this, what Jesus himself proposed to his listeners was nothing other than what he claimed was the normative vision for Judaism, the proper interpretation of Jewish Scriptures and tradition for the present."[45] We will return to this issue below but, for now, it is important to note that the unity of Judaism and Christianity hinges on this claim since the unified ethical positions held by both "true" Judaism and "true" Christianity (especially pacifism)[46] are not anti-Jewish, but "nothing but Jewish and altogether Jewish"—only in a Jewish context could Jesus' reasons, his attitude toward the enemy, toward violence, toward suffering,

---

42. Ibid.

43. Ibid., 37.

44. This point is also noted by Jewish readers like Daniel Boyarin and Peter Ochs, who, despite considerable sympathy for and solidarity with Yoder, worry that Yoder is not careful enough to avoid ascribing an "essence" to Judaism. See Boyarin, "Judaism as a Free Church," 13; and Ochs' comments in *Jewish-Christian Schism Revisited*, 68, 179–80.

45. Yoder, "Tertium Datur," 13.

46. It is important to note that Schwarzschild is named in this conversation. Yoder, "Tertium Datur," 39.

toward "the ultimate saving purpose of an all powerful God add up to the ethic Jesus teaches."[47] And, to conclude "Tertium Datur," Yoder claims that it is precisely this "Hebrew universality" that is exchanged by the Christian Church for Greek or Roman provincialism (somewhere in the middle of the second century), which becomes "normative Christianity" and which is, like "normative Judaism," a subsequent perversion of Jesus' normative interpretation of Judaism.[48]

In the years following the presentation of "Tertium Datur," Yoder continued to be preoccupied with this argument, and, unsurprisingly, references to Judaism began to emerge in all sorts of places. In February, 1978, Yoder presented a paper—"The Peace Dimension of Medieval Moral Concern"—that highlighted the fundamentally pacifist existence of most "sincere believers in God in the Middle Ages," whether they were Jews or Christians.[49] Later that same year, he responded to a paper by Rolf Rendtorff at the International Theological Symposium on the Holocaust in Philadelphia. In his response, Yoder again asserted his most basic critical claims concerning the Constantinian perversion of Christianity to the extent that he suggested Franklin H. Littell—who chaired the symposium—was critically formed by his early studies of "the Protestant radicals whose 'restitution' call reached back over the Greco-Roman establishment to the Jewishness of the New Testament to condemn the whole triumphal vision."[50]

As the 1970s drew to a close, even the IRS ended up on the receiving end of Yoder's increasing preoccupation. In a letter dated Easter, 1979, Yoder wrote: "I have . . . since 1961 been withholding a token of my IRS obligation, expressing thus my responsibility as a taxpayer to disavow the use made, against my will, against Jewish and Christian morality

---

47. Yoder, "Tertium Datur," 39.

48. An excellent description of Hebrew universality is later provided in "Jesus the Jewish Pacifist": "Only the Jew Jesus, by announcing and accomplishing the fulfillment of God's promises to the Jews, could send out into the world a people of peace open to the Gentiles. Only the Jewish claim that the one true God, known to Abraham's children through their history, was also the Creator and sustainer of the other peoples as well, could enable mission without provincialism, cosmopolitan vision without empire" (75).

49. Yoder, "Christian Attitudes to War/Peace/Revolution: Written Lecture VII," vii–9. A revised version of this paper appears in Yoder, *Christian Attitudes to War, Peace, and Revolution*, 130–36.

50. Yoder, "Response to Rendtorff," Box 132, "Phila Holocaust Conf 1978 Rendtorff."

and against the US constitution, of the moneys gathered by IRS."[51] The Sermon on the Mount and Jesus had been variously present in previous incarnations of this letter, but this seems to be the first time that paying the portion of his tax used for military purposes was described as opposed to Jewish morality.[52]

Refining and Reinforcing a Position

The consistent concentration on the Jewish-Christian schism throughout the 1970s bore considerable fruit in the following decades as Yoder began to refine and propagate his position in a variety of ways. For example, the first draft of "Judaism as a Non-non-Christian Religion" was created in 1981 through the transcription and editing of notes developed for a theology of world mission course at the Associated Mennonite Biblical Seminary in Elkhart, which was offered several times between 1963 and 1973.[53] Drawing from and building on the foundational material contained in "Tertium Datur," these notes attempt to deconstruct Christian anti-Jewish postures and Jewish anti-Christian postures. What emerges positively is a working definition of "true" Judaism, or "committed Judaism: i.e., a discernable people ready thoroughly and sacrificially to order their lives around their convictions as to what constitutes the substance of Torah."[54] Since these notes were originally compiled in the

---

51. See Letter from J. H. Yoder to the Director of Internal Revenue, Box 204, "Income Tax 1960–78." Yoder's challenge concerns "the immoral and illegal use of at least one fourth of my tax dollar for war purposes unrelated to the peace and wellbeing of the citizens of the USA."

52. Uniting the Sermon on the Mount and the Old Testament was also a topic of conversation between Schwarzschild and Yoder, with Schwarzschild happily leaving this problem to Yoder: "I understand what you are saying about the history of Christian polemics about your understanding of the N.T. But this is a Christian problem, not mine—that they misinterpret the Hebrew Bible in order to pit the Sermon on the Mount against it." See Letter from S. S. Schwarzschild to J. H. Yoder, July 9 1968, Box 201, "S.S.S. ztz'l."

53. Although an edited version of this paper was later published in *Jewish-Christian Schism Revisited* under this same title, drafts of the original transcription can be found in various locations in Yoder's papers. See, for example, the copy included with the correspondence with Bruce Hiebert later in 1988: Yoder, "Judaism as Non-non-Christian Religion."

54. Yoder, "Judaism as Non-non-Christian Religion (unpublished)," 8. In the version included in *Jewish-Christian Schism Revisited*, this comment is rendered, "Committed Judaism, i.e., people who visibly order their lives around the Torah," blunting the pathos and possible offense of naming sacrifice as defining committed Judaism ("Judaism as a Non-non-Christian Religion," 154).

context of a course on missions, they end with four conclusions as to how Christian witness should be represented and formulated:

1. Christian witness needs to be repentant, and what Christians must talk about is Jesus Christ and not dogma, religion, or culture, which Jews have already rejected;
2. Judaism is not just "another religion" in the protestant mode of denominational distinctions;
3. Anti-Jewish or non-Jewish Christianity is always ready to sell out to some other younger or older pagan god (i.e., speculative theology, political provincialism, emotional religiosity, etc.);
4. The above constitutes a pro-Jewish commitment that should be addressed to the memory and dignity of historic Judaism through the centuries and to the story of Jews in the recent European experience . . . and not on the westernized Jews of the state of Israel.[55]

Again, in reference to the first point listed above, parsing Jesus Christ from dogma, religion, or culture requires a rendering of Jesus Christ in a moral or political vein that then eschews dogma or religion or culture. Although it seems evident that Yoder means to separate his position from "popular" or "common" understandings of these terms, it is precisely his insistence on this sort of claim that reinforces his early understanding of discipleship as, most basically, ethics.

After working on Jewish-Christian relations for over a decade, Yoder was invited to deliver the Menno Simons Lectures at Bethel College, a Mennonite liberal arts college in Newton, Kansas, in 1982. The title provided for the series was "The Jewish-Christian Division: A Reassessment from a Radical Reformation Perspective," and it consisted of five lectures. The first, "It Did Not Have to Be," was largely a reiteration of the "Tertium Datur" presentation given five years earlier.

The second, "Jesus the Jewish Pacifist," was essentially a developing and fleshing out of the outline created while in Tantur concerning this topic. In this lecture, the basic question is whether there was a clash between Judaism and Christianity "on the level of ethics," and the answer is no.[56] Yoder begins, logically, with the concrete expression, since

55. Yoder, "Judaism as Non-non-Christian Religion (unpublished)," 8–9.
56. Yoder, "Bethel Menno Lecture II," Box 133, "1 AM." See also the revised version of this paper published as "Jesus the Jewish Pacifist," 69.

"*Halakah*, the tradition about specific behavior, is clarified and codified sooner and more firmly than *haggadah*, the reasons why." Or, to rephrase with a slightly different emphasis, the concrete shape of "the culture of faithfulness is more crucial to a people's commonality than is the piety with which it is filled out."[57] It is precisely this commitment to concreteness that makes a peace commitment able to resist selling out to the establishment.

But Yoder then seems to turn around immediately with the claim that it is the Jewishness of Jesus—the particularity of his rootedness in the story of Abraham, Moses, and Jeremiah—that makes his message good news for the whole world. Or, "only the Jew Jesus, by announcing and accomplishing the fulfillment of God's promises to the Jews could send out in the world a People of Peace."[58] So, at the end, one could rightly be confused as to whether the similarity between Judaism and Christianity is (*a*) the concrete expression of ethics (especially since Yoder claims these concretions are "more transculturally translatable, and more definitional for a community's identity") or (*b*) the reasons why a particular ethic makes sense, or (*c*) both.[59]

The third lecture at Bethel (the content of which roughly approximates the second half of the published version of "Jesus the Jewish Pacifist")[60] was titled "Judaism as Historic Peace Church." The purpose of this third lecture is to illuminate and elevate the diaspora nature of Judaism (both in the Old Testament and in the postbiblical era) and the

---

57. Yoder, "Bethel Menno Lecture II"; "Jesus the Jewish Pacifist" in *JCSR*, 74. By framing the relationship this way, Yoder self-consciously opposes the modern fascination with abstract "first principles" from which ethics are subsequently derived. It is interesting that the earlier unity ascribed to *halakah* and *haggadah* is now ordered in this manner. A sympathetic and somewhat Aristotelian reading of what Yoder is driving at is provided by Harry Huebner: "The assumption is that you cannot properly know God and world unless you have been instructed in the art of knowing and living by Christian practices." See Huebner, "Moral Agency as Embodiment," 193.

58. Yoder, "Bethel Menno Lecture II"; Yoder, "Jesus the Jewish Pacifist," 75.

59. Yoder also seems to be aware that his position has some internal instability: "The tilt toward concreteness can be overdone, of course. It has shortcomings in the face of rapid cultural change, or in the face of ecumenical challenge. It can become 'legalism' in the bad sense of the term. It can build a barrier in the way of cross-cultural communication or service. Here however, we are discussing what originally made a commitment to love the enemy and to renounce violence credible and viable in its challenge to the ethos of establishment." Yoder, "Jesus the Jewish Pacifist," 75.

60. Yoder, "Jesus the Jewish Pacifist," 75–87.

Jeremianic nature of rabbinic Judaism. The particular Jeremianic nature Yoder is referring to is found in Jeremiah 29:7: "seek the welfare of the city where I have sent you into exile, and pray to the Lord on its behalf, for in its welfare you will find your welfare." This passage serves, for Yoder, as the quintessential expression of God's call to his people to diaspora, to "the acceptance of a non-sovereign, non-territorial self-definition."[61] With this Jeremianic identification, the pilgrim people—the true children of Abraham—elevated in Yoder's earlier writings are now also called to settle down in the city of the enemy. Evoking the bold claims of "The Original Revolution," Yoder describes the sociological shape or style of Judaism in diaspora:

> In the absence of access to a Temple where proper sacrifices could be celebrated, Jews in diaspora developed a new form of worship . . . [T]he Temple was to be replaced not by another Temple but by a house of prayer, a synagogue, a gathering of believers around the scrolls of Scripture. Thereby a community was created which needed neither priest nor Temple; sociologically speaking perhaps the most fundamental innovation in the history of religion. This change protected the Jews providentially from further evolution in the forms of outward religion, and thereby channeled their energies into forms of community maintenance (one can even ask whether "worship" in the ordinary Gentile sense is the right label) gathered around the Scriptures.[62]

The appropriation of Jeremiah's exhortation to diaspora becomes increasingly prominent later in Yoder's thought and often serves as the instigator for further reflection and debate among his readers.[63] Most emphatically, Yoder is adamant, yet again, that diaspora—in line with the previous lecture—is a social shape, "the *shape* which we later see in the so-called Radical Reformation, Believers Churches, or Peace Churches."[64]

---

61. See Yoder, "To Serve Our God and to Rule the World," 133.

62. Yoder, "Jesus the Jewish Pacifist," 78. See also Yoder, "Original Revolution," 28. The less-than-latent deprecation of sacramentalism and ritual present in this description will be revisited in some detail in the next chapter.

63. For example, A. James Reimer is somewhat critical of Yoder on this point, while Duane K. Friesen and Alain Epp Weaver are much more sympathetic. See Reimer, "Theological Orthodoxy and Jewish Christianity"; Friesen, "Yoder and the Jews"; and Weaver, "On Exile." See also Bourne, *Seek the Peace of the City*; Friesen, *Artists, Citizens, Philosophers*; and Weaver, *States of Exile*.

64. Yoder, "III Judaism as Historic Peace Church," Box 133, "1 PM." A weaker form

The fourth lecture, "Paul the Judaizer," takes up another strand of thought present in "Tertium Datur"—a strand also addressed in its own way in *The Politics of Jesus*—and challenges the familiar Protestant narrative that Paul is the transition figure who made it possible for Christianity to emerge as a prominent and predominantly Gentile religion out of Palestinian culture and the Jewish ghetto. Against this prevailing narrative, Yoder argues that Paul is first and foremost a Jewish writer. Second, Yoder claims that mission to the Gentiles had been going on for generations, and Paul's uniqueness is found only in his place in salvation history, namely, following Jesus' resurrection and ascension, which had initiated the messianic age; the ingathering of the Gentiles is coming true.[65] Therefore, precisely because the messianic age has dawned, Gentiles do not need to become Jews to share in the "glories of the Law-as-Grace," and because Jesus is the Messiah of the Jews, Jews do not need to renounce their identity, either. This, in sum, is what Paul preaches, and this sharing of the messianic age is what Yoder refers to as "the most authentic interpretation of classical Judaism," making Paul the great Judaizer of Hellenistic culture.[66]

The final lecture—"The Jewishness of Anabaptism"—funnels all of this material back to the identity of the primarily Mennonite audience. Repeating much of what has been outlined already, Yoder affirms that Anabaptism—as the code reference for "renewal within Christianity in general"—shares with Judaism the perspective of "God in correlation with historical change and criticism rather than with sanctifying the present."[67]

At the conclusion of the Menno Simons Lecture at Bethel College, Yoder energetically continued to march forward, pressing for avenues and venues in which to study and spread his quickly crystallizing message about the possible ethical unity between Jews and Christians. One year later, while presenting a series of lectures on nonviolence in Warsaw, Poland, he included a lecture explaining how the group of stories of divine salvation in the Old Testament is the narrative and theological thread that

---

of this statement is produced in the published version. See Yoder, "Jesus the Jewish Pacifist," 81.

65. Yoder, "Paul the Judaizer," 95–96.

66. Ibid., 95.

67. See Yoder, "New File 31 Dec JUDSMH Last Newton Lecture," Box 133, "Newton 1982." The heart of this lecture can also be found in "Jewishness of the Free Church Vision," 108–10.

leads to Jesus. Once again, rather than acknowledging a disjunction between Jesus (peaceful) and the Old Testament (violent), Yoder attempts to describe how Jesus' pacifism is truly Jewish in that it represents "the culmination of the prophetic critique" that redefined Jews as a community without king or national sovereignty. And, again, Jeremiah's charge to the Jews of the Babylonian diaspora emerges as normative.[68]

To conclude 1983, Yoder made a strong push to revitalize and renew the research program revealed in "Tertium Datur." To do so, he applied to both the Rockefeller Foundation and the Guggenheim Memorial Foundation for research funding. The proposals submitted to each foundation were identical: "The Jewishness of Apostolic Christianity and the Renewal of Western Christendom." Essentially, the research agenda is described by Yoder himself as one of "updating and synthesis," and there is not much new in his proposal except perhaps the increased focus on drawing from the years between 50 and 150 CE to provide new models of intellectual adjustment and institutional articulation for the post-Holocaust upheavals in both the Christian and Jewish worlds.[69]

68. Again, see *Nonviolence*, 73–84. The passage he returns to most frequently here is Jeremiah's call to "seek the peace of the city where I have sent you into exile" (Jer 29:7).

Also in 1983, Yoder collected and semi-unofficially published *Christian Attitudes to War, Peace, and Revolution: A Companion to Bainton*. Attempting to "converse" with Bainton's seminal text—*Christian Attitudes to War and Peace*—Yoder critically engages Bainton by drawing attention to issues, eras, and questions emerging from class discussions and Yoder's own research. For our purposes here, it is important to note the inclusion of a chapter entirely devoted to the nonviolence of rabbinic Judaism (aptly titled "The Nonviolence of Rabbinic Judaism"), complemented by a supplement consisting of quotations describing rabbinic pacifism collected and circulated by Yizhad Tal (Tel Aviv) in 1976. See Yoder, *Christian Attitudes to War, Peace, and Revolution*, 130–43. In the revised version of Yoder's *Christian Attitudes*, the supplement containing the quotations has been elided.

69. See Yoder, "The Jewishness of Apostolic Christianity and the Renewal of Western Christendom," Box 132, "Rockef Oct 83" and "Guggenh Oct 83." There were still other occasions for revisiting this theme in subsequent years. At a workshop at the National Workshop on Christian-Jewish Relations in St. Louis, Yoder presented a brief paper on "War and Peace in the Traditions." Again returning to the task of revising Christian perceptions of Judaism, Yoder, in this context, argued that Zionism is not truly Jewish, but rooted in modern Western nationalism, which is borrowed from "the Christians." See Yoder, "NCCJ St. Louis National Workshop," 2. Further, at a meeting convened by the Anti-Defamation League of B'nai B'rith and the Lilly Foundation in Bloomington, Indiana, Yoder presented "Earthly Jerusalem and Heavenly Jerusalem: A Mis-located Dualism," which struck at the heart of the dualism present in much Christian thought, the dualism that reinforced the spiritual supremacy of Christianity over a superseded, worldly Judaism.

In 1985, merely two years later, Yoder once again revisited the status of his thinking through another series of lectures presented at Earlham College in Richmond, Indiana. The three lectures titled "It Did Not Have to Be," "Judaism as the Original Peace Church," and "The Jewishness of the Free Church Vision" essentially revisit and repackage what Yoder had already argued except that this time Yoder sought to engage an audience attentive to Quaker sensitivities. It appears that by this time, Yoder had essentially settled on his revised account of the Jewish-Christian schism and the nuances of the historical and contemporary relationship between Jews and Christians. And, by this date, his correspondence with Schwarzschild had also trickled to a stop. Yes, more letters were exchanged with Jewish colleagues in the ensuing years, but the issue had essentially been decided and codified. Perhaps nothing indicates this more explicitly than the compilation and circulation of a series of papers in 1991, the series that eventually became the heart of *The Jewish-Christian Schism Revisited*. In a prefatory memo to the package circulated privately to colleagues in 1991, Yoder stated:

> Ever since the lectures in Bethel and Earlham . . . I have considered the prospect of a major effort in this area to be unlikely . . . even though I am sure there is a message to be worked on. But I have been moved to reopen the file by the coinciding of several considerations:
>
> 1. the fact that after twenty years some of [this material] needs to be said;
> 2. the recent expression of interest by several brethren;
> 3. the awareness provoked by aging and accident that I need to be more careful in contemplating what I might still get done in the next few years of scholarship;
> 4. a certain flowing together of this concern with other (missiology, history of pacifism, radical reformation, ethical methodology) in which I am interested.[70]

Therefore, in 1991, and again in 1994, Yoder "reopened" his files for his friends so that he could circulate a consolidated form of what had already been argued in a multitude of venues. During these years, a new, short section on "The Pacifism of Rabbinic Monotheism" was inserted into the revised version of *Nevertheless* (1992), arguing the by-now-familiar refrain that the pacifist characteristics of first-century Judaism were

---

70. See Yoder, *Jewish-Christian Schism Revisited*, 37n25.

taken over unquestioningly by the first Christians, as well as the corollary claim that "none [of the characteristics] is specific to Christian faith; all of them continued to characterize non-messianic Jewish thought as well."[71]

In a fitting culmination of his thinking, Yoder presented "See How They Go with Their Face to the Sun" in 1995 and included it in *For the Nations*, the final collection of essays published before his death.[72] In this final exposition of the relationship between Judaism and Christianity, Yoder once again highlights the diaspora nature, the cosmopolitan homelessness, of Jewish and Christian existence. In line with the trajectory begun already back in 1971, the sociological shape of central theological categories—the sacraments, obedience to God, grace, and vocation—is elevated to the extent that the sociological description, the ethos, becomes normatively definitive. And, true to form, the theological reasons that may be given to support or undergird the sociological description are essentially Jewish, "unimpeachably Jewish."[73]

THE PRIORITY OF POLITICS AS THE MEANS OF REVISITING THE JEWISH-CHRISTIAN SCHISM

Glancing back at this lengthy survey, it is clear that the issue of Jewish-Christian relations permeated Yoder's thought for two and a half decades. Certainly, Yoder was exercised by other questions and other issues during these years. But, after 1971, he steadfastly continued to attend carefully—both publicly and privately—to this particular issue. Although the above narrative has not been entirely exhaustive, it provides a fairly in-depth summary of the individual components of Yoder's position and a suggestive timeline of their development. Despite the richness of his analysis, it is crystal clear that several general features of his construal of Jewish-Christian relations remain relatively stable. The first feature is the antiestablishment—whether as pilgrim or, later, diaspora—shape that both true Judaism and true Christianity share (and this is necessary for both critical and constructive projects); the second is the peaceful nature of this antiestablishment existence; the third feature is the shared theological assertions concerning the messianic age and the providence of a monotheistic God throughout history. Concerning the latter, however,

---

71. Yoder, *Nevertheless*, 122–25.
72. This essay also serves as the final chapter of *Jewish-Christian Schism Revisited*.
73. Yoder, "See How They Go with Their Face to the Sun," 69.

Yoder is clear that the concrete shape of existence is the most important. To use his own words, "the culture of faithfulness is more crucial to a people's commonality than is the piety with which it is filled out."[74] Here Yoder's appropriation of an analog to Yiddish resurfaces (although perhaps he appeals as much to Yiddishism as to Yiddish itself because his concern is less language and more social style). For example, the shape of existence that emerges in Yoder's analysis is antiestablishment (as Yiddishism challenged the centrality of the synagogue and the church), anti-Constantinian (as Yiddishism challenged the aspirations of Zionists and German nationals), and antiauthoritarian (as Yiddishism challenged the dominance of Hebrew among Jews). To this extent, Yoder's variant of the common idiom appears to be an apt analog to Yiddish or Yiddishism.

Yet, the neatness of the identification of a common messianic style that need not have separated into Judaism and Christianity appears to make even Schwarzschild a bit nervous. Writing in 1979, he cryptically comments: "Of course, you, as you'd have to and always do, you being what you are, do these things always using (your understanding of) Christianity as the standard—so that authentic Judaism turns out, in your view, to be the best instantiation of Christianity, but this is only fair: after all, I regard you (and yours) as very good approximations of Judaism (as I've often told you). So, we're even. Until you become a Jew . . ."[75]

But, what are we to make of this "Until you become a Jew . . ."? Schwarzschild does not fully disclose his own position on these matters for several years, a position that I believe still poses a challenge to Yoder and his readers. Before turning directly to the clear revelation of Schwarzschild's position, however, a slight biographical diversion is needed.

Late in 1979, at the end of a handwritten note to Yoder, Schwarzschild refers to the "skeleton" of Yoder's account of Judaism, and suggests that it could be "fleshed out" in a bibliography. He continues: "But this is a pretty big job. Get me a (research) semester at Notre Dame, and I'll do it for you (and especially for me)."[76] In the spring semester of 1981, this research semester at Notre Dame became a reality—sort of. In actuality, Schwarzschild offered a graduate course on Jewish Peace Ethics, and he also provided a significant bibliography for the course, a bibliography that

74. Yoder, "Jesus the Jewish Pacifist," 74.

75. See Letter from S. S. Schwarzschild to J. H. Yoder, Sept. 26, 1979, Box 201, "S.S.S. Planning Course."

76. Ibid.

occupied numerous letters until it was finalized. The increased energy devoted to the mundane details of Schwarzschild's visit to Notre Dame also reenergized the central issue of their original conversations, namely, their shared similarities despite their differences.

In one of these letters, Schwarzschild revisits the question in an indirect way with reference to a forthcoming article—"Shalom"—that he had just completed.[77] "Shalom" begins with a single, unapologetic statement: "Peace is the highest value in Judaism."[78] The remainder of the article attempts to demonstrate precisely how the "best reading of classical Jewish culture can thus be seen to be the absolute, unqualified injunction to act peacefully."[79] Schwarzschild, in the letter to Yoder, then forces the methodological question. And, almost apologizing for the article, he writes: "[A]s you may have gathered in the past, I am really a philosopher, basically, not a theologian, or, at best (or worst) a philosophical theologian, and you, for one, might well take theological offense at what I do, or rather how I do it. Then again, what the hell?"[80]

Once again, Schwarzschild's honesty, if not his sensitivity, is refreshing. These comments, written right before visiting Notre Dame, set the stage for the final chapter of their correspondence. It is unclear how much time and energy Yoder and Schwarzschild had for each other during their shared time at Notre Dame. By all indications, it was less than expected, and certainly less than hoped. Yoder, although apologetic that further conversation did not occur, indicates that more time together may not actually have furthered the conversation anyway.[81] Underneath and through the difficulties of interpersonal engagement at Notre Dame, the question of methodology finally takes center stage.

Flowing from the conversation at the close of the final seminar, Yoder's last archived letter to Schwarzschild finally asks the methodological question that has been lurking in the background of this chapter throughout. Yoder iterates a series of perceptive questions pertaining to

---

77. Schwarzschild, "Shalom," 166–76. Yoder had a draft of this article enclosed in his files of the Bethel Lectures.

78. Ibid., 166.

79. Ibid., 173.

80. Letter from S. S. Schwarzschild to J. H. Yoder, Dec. 10, 1980, Box 201, "S.S.S. Planning Course."

81. Letter from J. H. Yoder to S. S. Schwarzschild, May 11, 1981, Box 132, "Steven Schwarzschild."

hermeneutic flexibility that he has wrestled with in his own reading of the biblical text:

> Does great flexibility mean total flexibility? All that we got said in the seminar session was that the only answer to the presence of a debatable issue is the ongoing process of debate according to the rules. In the face of a traditional orthodoxy this looks unsettling: but is it *utterly* unsettling? Or is it the case that within that "ongoing debate according to the rules" there is still some inner criterion, which is more than just the comparison of the relative skills in semantic ping-pong brought to the various sides of the table by the people beholden to the various interests and parties?[82]

As this is the longest letter written by Yoder in the Schwarzschild correspondence, it appears that his interest in these methodological questions is finally piqued. And, the issue is very close to his heart, as he is probing Schwarzschild for his thoughts about the "inner criterion" of his Judaism, for an answer to what makes him similar to Yoder and different from his Zionist "confreres" who have the same texts at their disposal.

Schwarzschild's response is complex, and it is worth quoting at length:

> Now, you raise again, as you did in my last class-session, and you raise rightly, the meta-criteria question in the employment of the criteria "Torah from Heaven" and learning. Here again I still think that "theology" leaves you, i.e., everyone, in the lurch. Here "philosophy" has to enter and does. I.e., reason, as Kantianly understood, that is to say, "pure reason" and, therefore, "the primacy of practical reason" = ethical values, must be and is the ultimate meta-criterion. This entire concatenation of reason is how I (and, indeed, Kant himself) unpack "the holy spirit." Such unpacking removes all subjectivity, enthusiastic claims, etc. from "the holy spirit." Hermann Cohen, in a number of places, especially in an essay under this very title, stresses that "the holy spirit" is *ru'ach hakodesh*—i.e., really "the spirit of holiness" [it isn't that "the spirit" *is* holy but that it, as it were, transmits holiness] and "holiness" is, as also Kant defines it, morality as God practices it, i.e., perfectly.[83]

The neo-Kantian background of Schwarzschild's method is finally brought to the center of the conversation: ethical value must be the ultimate meta-criterion for reading the Torah. But, as we have seen throughout this

82. Ibid.

83. Letter from S. S. Schwarzschild to J. H. Yoder, May 20, 1981, Box 132, "Steven Schwarzschild."

chapter, a reading of the biblical texts is also intimately linked with a right reading of this history of God's chosen people. Schwarzschild, turning to address this question, continues very quickly:

> The right basic answer to this question is, I think, a combination of Kant and Marx. Kant: all teleology is always regulative, not descriptive; i.e., there is no "meaning" in history but we put it there (this is one dimension of "the Copernican revolution" of Kant's), and thus we are back with "the primacy of practical reason" *supra*. (This is where Hegel's Christian incarnationalism becomes so invidious: if the *logos* is *in* the world, then the world, at least insofar as the *logos* is in it, is "rational" = good!) Now, of course, there is a very complex dialectic, according to Kant, between theoretical = descriptive and practical = ethical = regulative reason, i.e., between empirical evidence, in this case history, and norms; therefore, Marx: you have to take history with the same infinite seriousness and study it as devotedly as you do literary texts . . . but, again, *sub specie* "the primacy of (pure) practical reason." In this way the history of Israel is, I think and think increasingly, a classical case for "Marxist analysis." But, again, no "wax-nose" here, it seems to me.[84]

Though more substantive, this account is neither qualitatively different from that offered in "Shalom" nor different from the popularized account offered by Schwarzschild in his introduction to *Roots of Jewish Nonviolence*, where he argued that the chief problem of a criterion of selection and interpretation of historical events turns out to be messianic fulfillment. As in any rational system, the end determines the means, and since it is universally agreed that the state of peace, justice, and truth are constitutive of messianic fulfillment, practical reason is all that is needed to make this teleological orientation regulative.[85] In this way, ethical value (in Schwarzschild's case, the highest ethical value is peace) is the ultimate "meta-criterion" for interpreting the Scriptures, and "holiness" is ethical action as God practices it. This is the content that "puts meaning into history," the "primacy of practical reason" that occupies the formally Marxist interpretation of history.

With this final step into a methodological debate, the archived correspondence between Yoder and Schwarzschild dries up. What we have

---

84. Ibid.
85. Schwarzschild, "Introduction" to *Roots of Jewish Nonviolence*, 5.

been left with here, however, is incredibly illuminating and provoking at the same time. Whether Yoder agreed with Schwarzschild is doubtful, as it would be hard to imagine Yoder self-consciously subscribing to a neo-Kantian methodology. That said—and recognizing that Schwarzschild suspected he may have offended Yoder with an explicitly philosophical rendering of his method—the similarities between the two should give Yoder's readers pause: both read their respective authoritative texts with ethical value as the meta-criterion (whether in the form of discipleship or practical reason); both construe their ethics teleologically as culminating in the fulfillment of the messianic age to come; both assume that ethical means are determined by ends; both assume the priority of action over explanation; both assume that an antiestablishment nonviolent stance is the highest value in their respective accounts of Judaism;[86] both seek to support their ethical claims with reference to history.[87] In fact, several of their similarities can be seen on the final pages of *The Politics of Jesus*:

> The secularistic and the Marxist criticism of the vision of marching to Zion claims that the promise of "pie in the sky bye and bye" cuts the nerve of action today. The expectation of "fairer worlds on high" is supposed to detach the present from that which is promised.
>
> This may well have been the case when in recent centuries the beneficiaries of the social system appealed to a future world to encourage their subjects to remain docile. But our interest is not in asking whether eighteenth-century religion could be the opiate of the people, but rather understanding the function of the apocalyptic vision in the first-century church, whose seers were not on any drug.
>
> In the worldview of that time the gap between the present and the promise was not fundamental. What we are doing now is what leads to where we are going ... The unforeseeable future is farther along in the same direction as the foreseeable future for which we are responsible.
>
> ... [I]f one does not begin by assuming the unbridgeable gap between here and there, then this proclamation of a meaningful

---

86. In his recommendation comments in support of Yoder's Guggenheim Fellowship (which Schwarzschild forwarded to Yoder), Schwarzschild openly states, in concert with Yoder's proposal, that "'minority' commitments and diaspora existence are of the very essence of 'religion.'" See Box 132, "GUGGENH Oct 83."

87. And, it seems to be more than accidental that Yoder sought to return to a historical analysis of the years between 50 and 150 CE in the years subsequent to this final exchange, as evidenced by his Rockefeller Fellowship application.

future cannot possibly have the sense of turning away from the present. They are statements of the same promising future, throwing light back upon the present imperative, for which precisely recent "secular theology" has been looking.

The future that the seer of Patmos sees ahead is a universe—that is, a single system—in which God acts and we act, with our respective actions relating to each other. The spiritual and providential laws which we expect to see at work in this system are as solid for the believer as are the laws of dialectical materialism for the Marxist.[88]

Of course, in *The Politics of Jesus* and elsewhere, Yoder argues for the unique role of Jesus in constituting and defining the Christian community. Yet, the question of whether select ethical principles stand behind and define Yoder's rendering of Jesus must be raised, principles that are fundamentally rooted in the "single system" with laws—the grain of the universe, if you will—that are "as solid for the believer as the laws of dialectical materialism for the Marxist."[89] When forced to engage Judaism, the role of Jesus becomes slightly more complicated for those who conclude simply that "Jesus is the bearer of a new possibility for human, social, and political relationships."[90] The elevation of the Jeremianic community to the approximate instantiation of the messianic community (and, in the same way, to the paradigmatic precursor to the Anabaptist restitution) is one example that suggests that the politics of Jesus may have been both available and possible within Judaism before Jesus, thereby implying that Jesus merely restores a right expression of normative Judaism to its central place in the history of Israel. The reduction of Jesus to the role of reinforcing and validating the Jewish "ethos" of not being in charge and not considering any local state structure to be the primary bearer of the movement of history is another way to restate this same difficulty.[91] Both of these examples are developed through Yoder's articulation of Jewish-Christian relations. When pressed, contra Schwarzschild, Yoder is always

---

88. Yoder, *Politics of Jesus*, 241–42.

89. Travis Kroeker has most aptly stated that Yoder presents a "messianic ethic rooted in a providential ordering of history and a theology of creation that is discerned Christologically." See Kroeker, "Is a Messianic Political Ethic Possible," 149. The status of the last qualifier—whether familiarity with Christ is required to discern or live according to the ordering of history—is what becomes less clear in the later writings.

90. See Zimmerman, *Practicing the Politics of Jesus*, 185.

91. Yoder, "See How They Go with Their Face to the Sun," 69.

willing to maintain the language of Jesus' lordship and messiahship. Yet, in Yoder's resistance to dogmatic claims and the misguided metaphysical questions asked by Christian orthodoxy, these terms turn out to be little more than terms that express a certain ethical or political stance that is completely understandable, to Schwarzschild at least, within the categories of Judaism and without specific reference to Jesus as fulfilling the categories.

A TENTATIVE CONCLUSION

But perhaps Schwarzschild is wrong about all of this and, therefore, worrying about his similarities with Yoder leads us down the wrong path. After all, there is little agreement amongst Jewish scholars with his conclusions.[92] Indirectly rebutting Schwarzschild's affirmation of Yoder, Ochs rejects the absoluteness of Yoder's Jeremianic definition of Judaism. Ruefully commenting on "See How They Go with Their Face to the Sun," Ochs notes that "it is an ethically moving yet late-modern effort to overgeneralize one chapter of Jeremiah's long prophecy, as if it were the only alternative to what remains Israel's late-modern practice of landedness." He then concludes that it is, "in that sense, not prophetic."[93]

But, if Schwarzschild is wrong about Judaism, what has been gained in the reconstruction of Jewish-Christian relations through Yoder's politicization of Christianity? Granted, many of Yoder's readers appreciate the patience of his dialogical engagement with both Jews and other "outsiders."[94] Yet, Yoder's entire project of revisiting the Jewish-Christian schism is contingent on the ethical unity shared in the normative vision of what he considers original messianic Judaism. Or, to restate, if either Jews or Christians reject the politics Yoder attributes to this first-century community,[95] the possibility of bridging the established divide between Judaism and Christianity is undermined or negated. In this context, the

---

92. Schwarzschild tells Yoder as much when he writes that he is "not exactly *persona gratissima* in [Jewish] establishment circles." See Letter from S. S. Schwarzschild to J. H. Yoder, Nov. 27, 1971, Box 201, "S.S.S. ztz'l."

93. *The Jewish-Christian Schism Revisited*, 204.

94. See, for example, Boyarin, "Judaism as a Free Church," 1; and Coles, "The Wild Patience of John Howard Yoder," 217.

95. Yoder himself acknowledges that he has described these in "sociological terms" and then also acknowledges that if you would have asked the people involved at the time, they would have provided theological answers. See "See How They Go with Their Face to the Sun," 67.

question of determining whether Yoder is right or not about the politics of the first century is not the issue. Rather, my point here is simply to argue that it is precisely Yoder's construal of the politics of Jesus—thereby reducing Jesus to his messianic politics—that creates the possibility of a shared language with Schwarzschild.

By the conclusion of Yoder's reconstruction of Jewish-Christian relations, it appears that the fullness of the Jeremianic definition of Judaism is paradigmatic for messianic Judaism, and it is only because of this particular paradigmatic shape that the separation between Judaism and Christianity "did not have to be."[96] Cartwright is right to acknowledge that "there is a sense in which Yoder and Schwarzschild came closer to agreeing about the embodiment of a common messianic vocation for Christians and Jews than they could ever come to agreeing about the content of the covenants involved."[97] Yet, this is precisely the point at which Schwarzschild challenges the readers of John Howard Yoder. What he indirectly suggests (whether Yoder says so or not) is that the contents of the covenants involved are, in fact, secondary issues for Yoder; the embodiment of a vocation is primary. In this way, we are forced to ask whether Yoder—even if couched in the familiar language of discipleship—operated with the assumption of the primacy of practical reason, with the assumption that ethics is the "ultimate meta-criterion" by which one should interpret Christianity.

Despite his extensive research and writing on the theme, the conversation between Jews and Christians was not Yoder's only concern in the years following the publication of *Politics*. As is already evident in his earliest writings, Yoder is also deeply concerned with ecumenical relations, with the relations between varieties of Christians. Before pushing further toward a conclusion concerning Yoder's methodology employed in bridging the Jewish-Christian schism, we must also consider the methodology employed in bridging the various ongoing Christian-Christian schisms. To this we turn in the next chapter.

---

96. "It Did Not Have to Be" ended up as the title in *Jewish-Christian Schism Revisited* for what was essentially the heart of the 1977 University of Notre Dame presentation, then "Tertium Datur."

97. Cartwright, "Editor's Introduction," in *Jewish-Christian Schism Revisited*, 19.

FIVE

The New Shape of Ecumenism

THE NINE YEARS THAT John Howard Yoder spent in France following 1949 were exceptionally formative for his thinking, including his thinking about ecumenism. During these years, he became convinced that ecumenical conversation ought to be carried out in a particular manner, a manner that still drew heavily on the construal of Anabaptism he distilled during this period.

In 1957, Yoder published a series of articles in a Mennonite periodical—*The Gospel Herald*—on the topic of ecumenism, a series that was gathered and published under the title of *The Ecumenical Movement and the Faithful Church* the following year. Nation has argued that this pamphlet presents the heart of Yoder's views on ecumenism and, even further, that these views remain substantially unaltered for the next four decades.[1] In the following pages, I intend to demonstrate that *The Ecumenical Movement and the Faithful Church* represents the foundation for Yoder's views on ecumenism—as already suggested in chapter 2—that then develop and evolve as the years go by. In a manner similar to Yoder's reconstruction of Jewish-Christian relations, Yoder increasingly formalizes the appeal to sociological expressions of ethical action in order to describe the way in which Christians must become united. Eventually, this trajectory culminates in a radical rethinking of Christian worship and sacraments.

The previous chapter sought to indicate how particular messianic political perspectives and actions serve to bridge what Yoder believes is the divide between Christianity and Judaism. To push the conversation

---

1. Nation, *John Howard Yoder*, 78.

beyond the familiar confines usually assumed in that discussion, I allowed Schwarzschild to serve as a provocateur throughout. Yet, the tentative conclusions of that chapter are quite possibly merely selectively anecdotal or, at best, suggestive without confirmation drawn from Yoder's own theorizing about how particular social actions become the most basic defining feature of messianic Christianity and how they replace middle axioms as the best mode of communication between an "in-group" and outsiders. The purpose of this chapter is to fill that gap by examining Yoder's own evolving description of the role of sacraments in bridging intra-Christian relations.

The argument of this chapter traces three interlocking steps in the development of Yoder's thinking concerning ecumenism. First, the argument begins with a selective review of Yoder's account of how and why the church must take a particular shape.[2] Or, to put it more directly, it outlines how Yoder determines what the faithful church—the church that claims Jesus is Lord—looks like vis-à-vis both the rest of the world and the unfaithful church. The second step of the argument illuminates the need for a particular set of tools that Yoder will then use to build unity between Christians—the kinds of tools that build "catholicity," a catholicity that begins from the bottom up and that avoids the pitfalls ascribed to the unfaithful church. Lastly, the chapter turns to the third and final step of critically examining the evolving use of sacraments as the means by which Yoder articulates how the ecumenical church both becomes united and addresses the world. In conclusion, this chapter also argues that ecumenism is no narrow or discrete element in Yoder's thought. Rather, it ambitiously and broadly binds the worship, sacraments, and mission of the church together in its practices. And, to that extent, it also defines the faithful church.

DISCERNING THE FAITHFUL CHURCH

In *The Priestly Kingdom*, published twelve years after *The Politics of Jesus*, Yoder provides a sort of "state of my life and authorship" introduction. Despite his refusal to "clarify, explicate, and defend" himself openly, he subtly attempts to situate the new text in relation to *The Politics of Jesus*, experiences in his life, and the larger horizons in which he was working. One of the experiences he highlights is his participation in what he refers

---

2. Some of this section will revisit previously addressed material in a new vein.

to as the "conciliar" form of ecumenical relations. He goes on to note his attendance at the World Council of Churches commissions and assemblies at Bossey, Montreal, Uppsala, Nairobi, Melbourne, and Vancouver.[3] This list of locations, if nothing else, indicates that Yoder was already an experienced ecumenist of sorts by the mid-1980s.

There is, of course, more to the story. At least since his move to Europe, Yoder seemed to have a clear understanding that there must be more to worldwide Christianity than merely his American Mennonite background. His note, near the beginning of *The Ecumenical Movement*, bears this out: "Since Mennonites and other evangelicals of the Anabaptist-Free Church tradition have never taken the position that they are the only Christians, they cannot honestly be content with the same indifference or the self-righteousness with which an organization claiming to be 'the only true church' can face the ecumenical movement."[4]

This statement of concern about the relationship between the churches in the Anabaptist tradition and the rest of the Christian family cuts both ways. Positively, it recognizes that people belonging to other churches are Christians. Yet, at the same time, its description of other churches is already laden with negative designations such as indifference and self-righteousness, not to mention the latent critique within the scare quotes. Yoder's critique may or may not be on target here, but whatever the case may be, it is important to recognize that there cannot be a faithful church without an unfaithful church—otherwise the adjective would be redundant.

For Yoder, the faithful church requires ecumenism since the New Testament and the witness of the Anabaptists agree "that it is the duty of the evangelical Christian to establish and maintain brotherly relationships with anyone who confesses Christ."[5] For Yoder, unity is found in Christ,

---

3. Yoder, *Priestly Kingdom*, 1–2.

4. Yoder, *The Ecumenical Movement*, 1–2.

5. Ibid., 35. It is worth noting that Yoder believed that ecumenism was already present in the New Testament, as the early church was broken up into various denominations. Citing Acts 6, Yoder understands the Hellenists to be a denomination (naming) in the literal sense of the word. And, citing 1 Corinthians 1:12, he describes the various groups named after Paul, Peter, and Apollos as denominations. Other examples could be brought forward here as well. Nonetheless, the key, for Yoder, is that although there was division of a denominational sort in the New Testament, both Paul and Jesus point to the reality that the "essence of discipleship is to follow Christ in the humility which enables unity." See *Ecumenical Movement*, 19–24.

which has a particular meaning relative to discipleship and not necessarily to dogmatic or confessional agreement. Yoder expresses the heart of his ecumenical conviction in this way: "it means that we lay upon him the claims which Christ lays upon those who confess his name."[6] Stating the meaning of unity and ecumenical agreement in this way, Yoder can then claim that *"Christian unity is not to be created, but to be obeyed."*[7] This early pamphlet is, admittedly, a paper written by a Mennonite for a Mennonite audience, and Yoder does not go to any lengths to mollify his description of other churches.[8] In the end, he calls for increased ecumenism but his call seems to tend toward construing the conversation as a refracted monologue. What I mean is that, in concluding *The Ecumenical Movement*, Yoder calls for a conversation in the following way: "The question is whether, following the example of the New Testament and the Anabaptists, we will give to misinformed and seeking believers the help they are looking for and which only the heirs of the Anabaptist tradition can give; and whether we will seek, as this tradition itself demands, whatever correction, admonition, and instruction may be received from the encounter with fellow confessors of the Lord's name under the norm of Scripture and the guidance of his Spirit."[9]

Nation suggests that these last lines convey the spirit of the pamphlet as a whole, and I believe he is correct in this assessment. Within these lines, Yoder manages to remain deeply devoted to his own tradition while providing a point of contact for engaging other Christians. In his mid-century context and among his peers, this position may have been rather forward-looking. To put it bluntly, however, this early position is very limited: Yoder is open to ecumenical engagement as long as it occurs according to his criteria, or as long as other Christians agree with Anabaptists in their reading of the New Testament that (1) the key is obedience to Christ; (2) obedience to Christ entails biblical baptism, separation from the world, and the rest of what the gospel implies (by which we ought to read at least pacifism); and (3) they—the Anabaptists—will welcome correction, admonition, and instruction from other Christians

6. Ibid., 36. See also the discussion in chapter 2.

7. Ibid., 21.

8. It is important to note that Yoder will not claim that his own church is the faithful church. Rather, he notes that perfect sanctification is the goal and the standard of God's fellowship and not its prerequisite. See ibid., 17–18.

9. Ibid., 43.

that reinforce (1) and (2). Sketched this way, Yoder's ecumenism is still relatively self-referential and monolingual (i.e., it operates solely according to its own in-group language).

Shortly thereafter, however, Yoder provides a complementary approach that highlights the importance of visible church practices. In 1960, Yoder's "The Otherness of the Church" provided a more ambitious attempt to qualify the faithful church as a visible church. In one of his early volleys against Constantinianism, Yoder argues that, for the early Christians, church and world were visibly distinct even though they affirmed a faith that the Lord was ruler over both. As the Lord was ruler over both, Yoder also maintained that the center of the meaning of history "is in the work of the church."[10]

But, what does this have to do with ecumenism? Simply put, the recognition of the church as a unique sociological entity allows Yoder to sharpen the definition of the faithful church that reveals the meaning of history. In "Let the Church Be the Church," Yoder spells it out clearly: "For us to say with the current ecumenical fashion that the church is a witnessing body, a serving body, and a body fellowshipping voluntarily and visibly, is to identify her thrice as not being the same things as the total surrounding society. This definition demands for the church an existence, a structure, a sociology of her own, independent of the other structures of society."[11] Therefore, the unity of the church that was previously assumed to be "one, holy, catholic, and apostolic," or "where the sacraments are properly administered and the Word of God is properly preached," is found with new clarity in the church's relationship to the world, in the church's "sociology of her own."[12]

To begin defining this unique Christian sociology of the church, Yoder clarifies what it is not. Taking this logic to its anti-Constantinian conclusion, Yoder also takes aim at those churches that have accepted the fusing of the visible church with the world, a transformation that uses the name of Constantine "as a label" and that "began before AD 200 and took over 200 years."[13] According to Yoder, this transformation gave rise to an increasingly problematic trajectory for the existence of the church,

---

10. Yoder, "Otherness of the Church," 60.
11. Yoder, "Let the Church Be the Church," 108.
12. Ibid.
13. Yoder, "Otherness of the Church," 57.

beginning with the doctrine of the invisible church (Augustine), the subsequent and necessary fusion of pagan and Christian ethics (Ambrose), the renewal of *Corpus Christianum* in the embrace of the secular vocation (Luther), and then its culmination in the politically motivated struggle between Christian peoples (Thirty Years' War).[14] Despite the significant historical issues opened by this claim, Yoder's claim is singular: "Obviously, the composition of the church changed."[15]

Affirming what we have seen as a central tenet of the call to diaspora, the basic normative stance of the church, for Yoder, is that of a minority. This is enough to begin the deconstruction of the unfaithful church. As we have already seen, Yoder's first use of the church's weakness is to dismantle the magisterial, the established, the Constantinian stance that has been pervasive in the church since before Constantine. If the composition of the church had changed so much, if only the Anabaptists saw this change, and if only the Anabaptists understood the answer to this change, one can see how Yoder's earlier comments concerning the uniqueness and necessity of the Anabaptist voice in ecumenical conversation were justified. But, with this formulation, it just may be that instead of building ecumenical relations, Yoder has merely renewed lines of division, or worse, created new nomenclature for denunciation. Yoder himself is not ignorant of the difficulty he has now placed himself in, and his solution turns on the same categories as his critique, namely, the church's own sociology.

THE NEED FOR TOOLS TO BUILD UNITY

When Yoder suggests that the unity of the church is located in its sociological expression, he recognizes the wide-ranging consequences of his claim. In "Let the Church Be the Church," he boldly claims:

> The old yardsticks for knowing what constitutes a church used to be called the "marks" (*notae*) of the church. They pointed almost exclusively to characteristics which could be measured by looking right at the management of the church's liturgy or her business. They had to do with theological affirmations, with the qualification of the clergy, and the meaning of the sacraments. But today

---

14. Ibid., 57–61. There are other steps in this trajectory, but these are the most significant in Yoder's account of the devolution of the church. There are other variations of this narrative in Yoder's corpus. For example, see "Constantinian Sources of Western Social Ethics," 135–47; "Racial Revolution in Theological Perspective," 103–8.

15. Yoder, "Constantinian Sources of Western Social Ethics," 135.

> increasingly it is coming to be recognized that the real tests of whether the church is the church call for measurements to be taken not in the meeting nor in the administrative structure but at the point of the relation of church and world.[16]

In one simple revaluation, Yoder has wiped clean much of the history of ecumenical dialogue in positing the "real" test for the true church. Viewed from one perspective, this is a refreshing opening for further conversation, conversation that can go beyond all the obtuse debates of the last two thousand years. Viewed from another perspective, Yoder's grand stroke elides what many have taken as central to the definition and practice of the church, an action that Yoder's halfhearted retraction by rhetorically softening his stance—"Unity in ethical commitment was for the apostolic church no less central than unity in faith and worship"—cannot undo.[17] After all, his claim that the relation of the church to the world is the "real" test of the true church simply disallows an easy return to equality with theological affirmations, clergy qualifications, or the practice of sacraments.

In fact, Yoder embraces the ramifications of his position as he willingly condemns any church that identifies itself with the wider society regardless of its theological stance. For example, using the medieval church as a representative of the unfaithful church, he claims, "it must be said that the identification of the church with a given society, for which the church-state marriage of the Middle Ages was a sign and a safeguard, is wrong."[18] Even a casual observer will note, however, that more than the medieval church is challenged here. Essentially, Yoder is challenging all forms of the church that he also labels as Constantinian or "establishment" churches, a label that covers Catholic, Eastern Orthodox, sixteenth-century Protestant, post-Enlightenment American Protestant, nationalist-oriented Marxist, and future-looking neo-Marxist churches. All of these—and any other—forms of the church commit the "basic error" of failing to see that the church and the world must be visibly distinct.[19] Echoing the previous appeal to the unique Anabaptist voice, he reframes the debate in much simpler terms:

---

16. Yoder, "Let the Church Be the Church," 110.
17. Yoder, "Nature of the Unity We Seek," 228.
18. Yoder, "Let the Church Be the Church," 111.
19. Yoder, "Constantinian Sources of Western Social Ethics," 141–43.

> If the locus of our unity is Jesus Christ, it would seem that the only feasible solution to the problem of authority would be to declare inadmissible the attribution of authoritative character to any particular historical development and to recognize, as the only legitimate judge *Christ himself* as he is made known through Scripture to the congregation of those who seek to know him and his will . . . Neither what the modern mind can accept, nor what the medieval mind could accept, nor what one of the Councils of Constantinople could accept, would have the right to stand above, or beside, or even authoritatively under Christ and the Scripture.[20]

The simplicity of this appeal, however, is a façade. What Yoder hides in this claim is that his own reading of the Bible, his own approach to reading the Bible, his own framing of the question, and even the claim that historical development ought not to have authority is a historical development rooted, by Yoder's own admission, in sixteenth-century Anabaptist thought. Obliquely acknowledging this challenge, Yoder later shifts the tenor of his criteria: "The clash is not tradition versus Scripture but faithful tradition versus irresponsible tradition."[21] This later slightly sophisticated framing of the question is still, in essence, the same either/or as the earlier construal of Christ versus historical developments. In "The Authority of Tradition," Yoder continues: "So the issue—if there be a genuine issue—is not tradition versus Scripture, nor Scripture versus some one fragment of the rest of tradition, nor . . . the scriptural fraction of tradition versus some other one of many traditions. The issue is (as Jesus said it) the traditions of men versus the commandment of God . . . Not all varieties of vision—or of ethics—can fit together within a tolerant pluralism. What we need are tools to identify and denounce error, while welcoming variety and celebrating complementarity."[22]

After years of grasping in various directions, Yoder finally settles on some of the "tools to identify and denounce error" that also welcome variety and complementarity. These tools are the social practices of the church. At this point, the politics of Jesus (both the social practices and

---

20. Yoder, "Nature of the Unity We Seek," 225. Or, to restate in a potentially problematic way, Yoder defines the criteria for testing prophecy and proclamations concerning the kingdom of God as follows: "Our criteria must be not merely 'Christological' in some vague, cosmic sense, but 'jesulogical.'" See Yoder, "Discerning the Kingdom of God in the Struggles of the World," 241.

21. Yoder, "Authority of Tradition," 69.

22. Ibid., 76.

the text by that title) naturally fits within Yoder's vision of the church, especially his claim that following Jesus only holds "at the point of the concrete social meaning of the cross in its relation to enmity and power. Servanthood replaces dominion, forgiveness absorbs hostility."[23] Thus—and only thus—are we bound by New Testament thought to "be like Jesus."

As Yoder moved beyond *The Politics of Jesus*, he remained committed to this perspective, and he again returned to the question of how this is communicated communally by the church. Having already articulated that the church is social and distinct from society and that true politics is best displayed in the church, Yoder then moves to exploring how the church expresses the claim that Jesus is Lord:

> The duality of church and world is not a slice separating the religious from the profane, nor the ecclesiastical from the civil, nor the spiritual from the material. It is the divide on this side of which there are those who confess Jesus as Lord, who in so doing are both secular and profane, both spiritual and physical, both ecclesiastical and civil, both individual and organized, in their relationships to one another and to others. The difference as to whether Christ is confessed as Lord is a difference on the level of real history and personal choices; not a difference of realm or levels or even dimensions.[24]

This passage is an example of an element of Yoder's thought that has given considerable impetus to a theme currently in vogue in Christian ethics, namely, overcoming the problematic modern dualisms that have constrained the available options (i.e., ethics vs. worship, beauty vs. good, subjective vs. objective, internal vs. external, public vs. private, etc.).[25] Branson Parler understands Yoder's methodological subversion of modern binaries as "expansionist." The term is intended to convey that Yoder is "trying to expand our view so we can see why the logic of the debate does not make sense biblically and theologically in the first place."[26] This much is absolutely clear and indisputable. Yet, an appeal to the "real" sneaks into Yoder's description as well. In response to the illegitimate options that have assumed priority in the popular and academic discourse, Yoder posits a new dualism that severely limits whatever expansion might

---

23. Yoder, *Politics of Jesus*, 131.
24. Yoder, "Why Ecclesiology Is Social Ethics," 108–9.
25. See, for example, Hauerwas and Wells, *The Blackwell Companion*, 4–7.
26. Parler, "Spinning the Liturgical Turn," 181.

have been gained in the rejection of the problematic dualisms; in their place, he firmly if quietly positions a new criterion: the difference on the level of "real history and personal choices." In a manner completely consistent with all he has said about following Jesus and the faithful church, a new dualism is then implicitly posited: true politics vs. false politics. Only a difference in "real history and personal decisions" can serve as the singularly appropriate criterion for confessing Jesus as Lord.

In considering Yoder's very early "The Anabaptist Dissent," we saw that Yoder articulated ethics as the basic definition and, therefore, criterion for determining true discipleship. Worship and other familiar elements of Christianity were not dismissed entirely but granted a secondary status.[27] As he continues to return to this theme, however, the role of worship slowly insinuates itself back into the discussion as a worthy participant. For example, Yoder will also claim that "every meeting of the church is a meeting for worship" (although he is sure to clarify that "worship" is not a ceremonial procedure, not the result of hierarchical unification, but the fulfillment of the promise of the presence of the Spirit).[28] As Yoder presses forward, worship becomes increasingly important; it is united with social ethics. For example, in "The Hermeneutics of Peoplehood," Yoder defines worship as "the communal cultivation of an alternative construction of society and of history."[29] In this process of cultivating an alternative society and history, the particular tools Yoder uses most often in his later writings are the sacraments.

WORSHIP AND SACRAMENTS IN SERVICE OF ECUMENISM

In the initial sections of this chapter, I have attempted to concentrate on Yoder's texts as they build towards *The Priestly Kingdom*, as they build toward the identification of social ethics as gospel; in the remaining pages of this chapter, I intend to illuminate Yoder's development of the sacraments. Furthermore, I will retain a more rigid chronological order of texts than I have thus far with the intention of specifying the movement that is built on the general foundation already sketched (diachronically cycling through almost the same years that were covered in the previous chapter).

---

27. Yoder, "Anabaptist Dissent," 29.
28. Yoder, "Free Church Ecumenical Style," 240.
29. Yoder, "Hermeneutics of Peoplehood," 43.

Once an examination of the role of the sacraments is complete, we can return to the issues tentatively posed in the conclusion of chapter 4.

At first blush, my claim that the sacraments are the key to Yoder's ecumenism might sound a little far-fetched or overstated. Granted, the sacraments were not always so central to Yoder's ecumenism. Yet, as the corpus progresses, they take on an increasingly important role. To distinguish the basic progression of Yoder's thought, the remainder of this chapter attends to the three basic developments of Yoder's ecumenical sacramentalism.[30]

Discerning the Body

In *Revolutionary Christianity*, the posthumously published collection of lectures Yoder presented in South America in 1966, Yoder titled the first series "The Believers Church." The first three lectures in this series are loosely organized around ecclesial activities that eventually become known as sacraments: baptism, binding and loosing, and the Lord's Supper, respectively. Yoder treats all three in a similar manner, but, because of the familiarity of the Eucharist as a Catholic sacrament (remembering that these lectures were presented in Buenos Aires), his comments on this activity are carefully and polemically developed against traditional understandings of the Eucharist and, therefore, most effectively illustrate his early thought.

As one might expect, Yoder provides a brief historical narration of the devolution of the Lord's Supper, which, in Catholic thought, became a "quasi-magical understanding of the mass as an assuredly efficacious transaction whenever the proper words are spoken by a properly qualified officiant."[31] The Reformers fair as poorly in his evaluation, as they were so consumed with rejecting certain aspects of Catholic practice that they were willing to agree with "the assumption that the mass was a ritual distinct from the rest of life," thereby failing to restore "the reality of

---

30. In a previous incarnation of this argument, I suggested that these basic developments roughly corresponded to dates of published correspondence. These dates were never meant to delineate radical eruptions in Yoder's thought, and I have dropped them in this context because they occasionally distracted readers from the logic of the developments that they were meant to illuminate. See Martens, "Problematic Development of the Sacraments in the Thought of John Howard Yoder."

31. Yoder, *Revolutionary Christianity*, 26..

communion."[32] To respond to these problematic practices, Yoder appeals, again, to *The Schleitheim Confession* and argues:

> It is appropriate that communion be thought of, primarily, as the name for the group and not merely the sacrament.
>
> Therefore, unity can only be celebrated when it exists. The unity of the congregation and the proper belonging of each member within it are prerequisites for and not results of the celebration. Thus, not only the conditions of the individual membership are related to the communion celebration but the disciplined life of the congregation has as its goal this genuine unity that can permit the common breaking of bread to be genuine.[33]

The bearer of the meaning of communion, according to Yoder's reading of the New Testament, is not the bread but the body, the church. Therefore, Paul's exhortation to "discern the body"[34] before participating in communion is a directive concerning the failure to share the table with everyone in the same church in Corinth. It was precisely the "reality of communion," the unity of the sacrament with the daily life of the church, that was shattered by the evolution of sacramentalism.[35] Therefore, foreshadowing much of what Yoder will argue for the next thirty years, the response to sacramentalism is to return to the true meaning of the Eucharist:

> Let a cell of that body be recreated in every place, composed of believers whose life together proclaims the Lord's death until he comes. Let this death be proclaimed, and let the universality of that communion be visible in every place in the reality of persons whose lives are wholly shared with one another and not by a definition in words or in ordination. Let us be freed from our capacity to separate the action and its meaning until our eating together truly means that our life is real communion.
>
> Then forces of social renewal, like those unleashed in the first Christian centuries, may well go out from this table.[36]

This, for Yoder, is the missionary posture of the church as communion, and it neatly displays the church's implicit witness described in *Christian*

---

32. Ibid.
33. Ibid., 28–29.
34. See 1 Corinthians 11:28.
35. See Yoder, *Revolutionary Christianity*, 30.
36. Ibid., 31.

Witness to the State. The same is reinforced in his treatment of baptism and binding and loosing.[37]

In two issues of *Concern* that followed in the late 1960s—"Binding and Loosing" (1967) and "The Fullness of Christ" (1969)—Yoder returned to expand important internal church issues that also stand as the foundation for ecumenical engagement.[38] The first of these essays clarifies the question of church discipline by focusing on Matthew 18:15–20. Yoder's primary concern is to intertwine forgiveness and moral discernment, presupposing and including both in the practice of binding and loosing.[39] He goes on to claim that this is the central work of the church and that the Holy Spirit is promised only to the church that practices binding and loosing appropriately. Following the Reformers, he also refers to binding and loosing as "the rule of Christ."[40] At the conclusion of the essay, Yoder suggests that wider implications of this practice might include the following: (1) the witness of the church always includes and may center upon the quality of personal relationships that even the outsider may observe; (2) we should not be surprised to discover that Christian duty, in this sense, is also secular good sense; and (3) forgiveness is not a generally accessible human possibility but the miraculous fruit of God's own bearing of the cost of human rebellion.[41] Two years later, "The Fullness of Christ" appeared, making explicit the anti-hierarchical, anti-specialist sentiments latent in "Binding and Loosing." To make his case for the universality of ministry—the priesthood of all believers—Yoder appeals to a wide variety of texts within the Pauline corpus. In essence, he argues that all members of the congregation are gifted by the Holy Spirit, and, on this basis, all should minister according to the specific grace they have been given. Taking a cue from the business world, he notes that if division of

---

37. A representative comment (both in content and vigor) might be: "In the ages before Constantine, the churches grew not because they were able to preach in public or to argue people into recognition of their guilt; it was the demonstration of the quality of life in the community that made others see their need and the power of God." See Yoder, *Revolutionary Christianity*, 21.

38. This recognition was also implied by Michael Cartwright when he included "Binding and Loosing" under the heading of "Radical Catholicity" in *Royal Priesthood*.

39. Yoder, "Binding and Loosing," 4–7.

40. Ibid., 15.

41. Ibid., 30.

labor is at the heart of the efficiency of business, why should it not be realistic in the congregation?[42]

Following the popular treatments in the 1966 lectures, these two definitional essays carefully develop Yoder's early position on what he will later thematize as sacraments in his own way. Although each essay addresses a single theme—binding and loosing and the individual gifting by the Holy Spirit, respectively—Yoder draws no attention to their relationship. Their formal similarities, however, are striking in that practices demanded by both ordinances are (*a*) biblical, (*b*) interpersonal, (*c*) enabled by the Holy Spirit, (*d*) internal to the church yet observable by those outside, (*e*) missional, (*f*) critical correctives to historical and contemporary practices, (*g*) individualizing in the service of the covenant community, and, in short, (*h*) absolutely necessary for the church to be the church. Given Yoder's definition of the church as an assembly of people for "deliberation and for public pronouncement,"[43] it should not surprise his readers that these two initial ordinances are identified neither as worship nor as sacramental.

At the 1979 Society of Christian Ethics annual meeting, Paul Ramsey presented a paper titled "Liturgy and Ethics." One year later, an entire issue of the *Journal of Religious Ethics* was devoted to this topic with Ramsey's paper headlining the issue.[44] These scholarly provocations challenged Yoder to reassess his own understanding of worship. Ramsey, acknowledging that the Christian church believes that *lex orandi lex credendi*—the order of prayer is the order of believing—pushes beyond the relationship between liturgy and belief. Not mincing words (neither Latin nor English), Ramsey simply claims that the church ought to claim *lex orandi lex credendi lex bene operandi*: the order of prayer is the order of believing is the order of doing well, a statement that is also reversible.[45] Yoder quickly took steps to appropriate this formulation in his own way, and he wrote several different articles attempting to address the relationship between liturgy

---

42. Yoder, "Fullness of Christ," 91. See also the later revision and expansion of this article published as *The Fullness of Christ: Paul's Vision of Universal Ministry*, 102. Yoder, in the preface to the revised volume, clearly places this topic within the discussion of ecumenism. Yoder, *Fullness of Christ*, iii.

43. See Yoder, "Binding and Loosing," 9.

44. Ramsey, "Liturgy and Ethics," 139–71.

45. Ibid., 139.

and ethics in the following years. In these articles, Yoder revises his earlier denunciation of sacramentality.

Worship as Social Construction

In answering Ramsey's challenge, Yoder began to graft concerns for worship explicitly to work already in progress. This is most evident in "The Hermeneutics of Peoplehood," written in 1982, where he makes two advances upon his earlier position and supplies a further entrenchment. First, Yoder articulates an account of practical moral reasoning that provides the appropriate context and constraints for binding and loosing and the universality of charisma. Yoder refers to this process—in which every prophetic voice is heard and every witness evaluated, as suggested in 1 Corinthians 14—as "dialogical liberty."[46] Logically and practically, binding and loosing and the expression of the individual gifts of the Holy Spirit occur only under the assumption of the practice of dialogical liberty, communal discourse that is not prematurely censured or restricted.[47]

The second tentative advance Yoder makes is relating these church processes to worship. He is nervous that Ramsey's claim may still be hindered by establishment assumptions in one's understanding of church, a concern he addresses with the claim that "neither in the New Testament documents nor in radical Protestantism is there a discretely identifiable function called 'priesthood' or a specific activity called 'worship.'" Continuing the anti-hierarchical, anti-specialist trajectory of his earlier writings, he continues: "What we call 'worship' is hard to locate as the task of one officer. Breaking bread in the solemn memory of the Lord's suffering and the joyous acclamation of his presence and promised return was one of the things both the early Christians and the radical Protestants did regularly, but they needed no special officers for that. It was no more such action that constituted them as 'church' than were the sending out of missionaries, the collection of famine relief moneys, or practical moral reasoning."[48]

Therefore, although Yoder affirms the unity of worship and morality, worship and practical moral reasoning, etc., he goes further and

---

46. Yoder, "Hermeneutics of Peoplehood," 22.

47. Sider has generously expanded these overlapping practices in *To See History Doxologically*, 161–94, while drawing primarily from this era of Yoder's authorship.

48. Yoder, "Hermeneutics of Peoplehood," 31–32.

disciplines the term in a manner consistent with his practice of defining theological terms as, most basically, ethics: "Worship is the communal cultivation of an alternative construction of society and history."[49] This step is substantial in that it opens the door for all the activities described thus far—tools to be used in the "alternative constructions of society"—to be included under the broad umbrella of worship. And, finally, the further entrenchment of these activities as visible phenomena significantly aids their integration into the task of worship.[50]

Two years later, in 1984, Yoder introduces two more significant developments: (*a*) he applies the notion of sacramentality to binding and loosing, and (*b*) he places binding and loosing alongside baptism and the Eucharist, thereby overtly recognizing the parallels that have been present since the beginning. In "The Kingdom as Social Ethics," Yoder—leaning heavily on Barth—claims that the church as an alternative community has a modeling mission. Continuing a theme from his earlier writings, Yoder refers to the church as a "firstfruit" of the kingdom. As a "firstfruit" of the kingdom, the church exemplifies sacramentality, which Yoder cryptically describes by stating that "meanings which make sense on an ordinary level make more of the same kind of sense when they are embedded in the particular history of the witness of faith."[51] This claim is followed with an affirmation that the church is a sacrament because the empowerment undergirding her witness and presence in the midst of society is not accessible in the same way to the wider society.[52] This is probably as close as Yoder comes to the traditional understanding of sacraments as visible signs of the invisible grace of God.[53] His point—which resonates with so much of his thought—is that the specific practices of the sacraments suggest what the world can and should be. For example, baptism could

49. Ibid., 43.

50. Although Yoder recognizes that Ramsey initiates this discussion by linking the terms *ethics* and *liturgy*, he always reverts to framing the question as the relation between *ethics* and *worship*. Liturgy appears to be a less helpful term than worship because of its ritualism, its association with a hierarchy (or at least a single specialist), its insinuation of mystery, and its resistance to public expression.

51. Yoder, "Kingdom as Social Ethic," 93.

52. Ibid.

53. The logic of Yoder's claims becomes even more convoluted when he claims that "sometimes this sacramental quality is read in the direction of saying about the church what one says about the rest of society." Yoder, "Kingdom as Social Ethic," 93. This sort of claim again illuminates how confident Yoder is in both (*a*) the grain of the universe and (*b*) the rule of God outside the church.

again become the basis of Christian egalitarianism as it was in the New Testament (i.e., its true meaning), and the Lord's Supper could again become an expression of sharing bread between those who have and those who have not.[54]

While Yoder mentions only baptism, the Lord's Supper, and binding and loosing in "The Kingdom as Social Ethics," this essay truly prefigures the position that solidifies later. Before moving to the late elevation of five sacraments, however, please allow a brief pause to consider a return to the three original ordinances as they were discussed in 1990. In a lecture in honor of James McClendon's retirement—"Catholicity in Search of Location"—Yoder articulates the marks of catholicity.[55] Although this, again, looks like a list of the marks of the faithful church, and although the term sacrament is not used here, Yoder clearly brings the two together: it is clear that the authority of the Holy Spirit would be functionally discernable where every member would know herself as a bearer of a particular charismatic empowerment (universal charisma) and where everyone would have the authority to take the floor in a meeting (dialogical liberty). In addition, he affirms that the Holy Spirit is working wherever the church practices binding and loosing. Here, locally, is where catholicity—or one might say ecumenism—is located.[56]

In sum, Ramsey's instigation in 1979 produced an important initial response from Yoder that then bears fruit in the subsequent decade. By this time, all five sacraments have been examined even though Yoder has not yet sorted out their formal similarities. And, although the sacraments are communal phenomena that signal what the world can and should become, some confusion still exists about whether they are fully understandable only by those in the faithful church or whether they make sense in a way discernable by the unfaithful and those in the wider world. The question of communication is placed in the middle of the conversation in the next years.

Communicating Civil Imperatives

In "Sacrament as Social Process," Yoder returns to the alternative responses to Ramsey's reflection on liturgy and ethics that emerged in the

---

54. Yoder, "Kingdom as Social Ethic," 93.
55. See Yoder, "Catholicity in Search of Location," 316–18.
56. Ibid., 318.

intervening years.[57] Challenging all the options, he states: "What these varied efforts have in common is that they begin with the problem of the qualitative distance between the two realms of liturgy and ethics and maintain that a bridge of some kind needs to be built. With gratitude and great respect for those efforts, but not satisfied by them, I propose to set beside them a simpler account."[58]

With that, Yoder launches into a description of the commonality underlying all five practices already discussed—baptism, the Eucharist, binding and loosing, universal charisma, and dialogical liberty—as concerned with both the internal activities of the gathered Christian congregation and the ways the church interacts with the world.

Over the next three years, Yoder wrote on the sacraments several more times. The following observations are drawn from "Firstfruits: The Paradigmatic Role of God's People," which serves as an excellent representative of this stage in his thought.[59] Before turning to "Firstfruits," however, I would like to introduce a perceptive observation offered by Gordon Kaufman. In a review of Yoder's *The Priestly Kingdom*, Kaufman noted the following: "What is important for Yoder's program, in my opinion, is not so much that Jesus be taken as an 'authority' who is to be 'obeyed,' but rather that the story of Jesus be taken as the fundamental 'paradigm' (as Yoder also suggests, p. 118) on the basis of which the moral norms ordering human life are developed."

And he continues: "It need not be the case that it is 'The Rule of God [which] is the basic category' (54), and that Christian morality must be understood primarily in terms of the sovereign 'lordship' of Christ (a metaphor that appears repeatedly throughout the book). The important thing, rather, is that we 'see Jesus,' and thus are enabled in our freedom to turn toward a mode of human existence and action which is truly redemptive in and for this world."

And he concludes: "Though one must criticize the vestiges which remain here of the more traditional authoritarian piety which originally

---

57. Yoder, "Sacrament as Social Process," 33–44.

58. Ibid., 33.

59. The chapter was initially presented in 1992 and published in 1997. Other relevant late writings are *Body Politics* (1992), which presents five sample ways (the "good news") in which the church is called to operate as a polis in ordinary human language, and "The New Humanity as Pulpit and Paradigm," which expresses the functional necessity of the church speaking paradigmatically, that is, through pattern recognition.

nurtured this way of thinking about Christian faith and morality, one can hope and expect that Yoder will continue to develop his views in a way which will make them accessible to a wide circle of Christians."[60]

Whether one agrees with Kaufman's sharp opposition between authority and the usefulness of paradigmatic display in Yoder's corpus, his review puts a finger on some of the competing themes and articulations of the faithful church that were the subject of this book. With Yoder's near complete repression of the language of obedience in favor of paradigm in this late stage, one might begin to wonder whether Kaufman's hope may be on its way to realization.

In the previous pages, I have attempted to demonstrate that Yoder builds incrementally upon the previous with each progressive stage in his development of the sacraments. In this last stage, how the church models and communicates what the world can and should become turns out to be the critical issue. Yoder's justification for this focus is rooted in the theological claim that Jesus Christ is Lord not only of the church but of the whole cosmos.[61] In the face of this claim, the self-imposed challenge Yoder attempts to meet is to purify, clarify, and simplify the church's witness so that the world can perceive it to be good news without having to learn a foreign language.[62]

Before moving to the content of "Firstfruits," a few comments concerning its rhetorical brilliance are in order. In short, I read "Firstfruits" as Yoder's constructive appropriation of the logic of Niebuhr's *Christ and Culture*. After the preliminary destabilizing of the terms of the debate concerning "the public good," Yoder begins again. The first "baseline" approach he presents is the "Christendom" or "royal" approach that includes the Renaissance, the Enlightenment, and, of course, Christendom.[63] The second approach is the "Puritan" approach (rooted in but also transcending the Reformation) that is an advance on the first to the extent that it was concerned with the Scriptures, it assumed a congregational structure, and it recognized no provincial boundaries.[64] The remaining three approaches are "extrapolations" from the Puritan posture.

60. Kaufman, "Review of *The Priestly Kingdom*," 79–80.
61. Yoder, "Firstfruits," 24.
62. Ibid.
63. Ibid., 19.
64. Ibid., 20.

The first of the final three approaches is that offered by H. Richard Niebuhr in "The Social Gospel and the Mind of Jesus." The fourfold strategy of Jesus, according to Niebuhr, calls for repentance, faith, forgiveness and nonresistance, and innocent suffering.[65] Yoder continues: "What matters for our present search is that Niebuhr describes this reading as a 'strategy,' not a spirituality or a speculative theology or a theodicy (though it is also all of those), nor as a tactic that might or might not promise to be effective for getting institutionally from here to there. He describes 'the way things work' in social-process terms accessible to any observer."[66]

Yoder then turns to Karl Barth for a fourth approach. Working from *Church Dogmatics* IV/2, Yoder highlights Barth's convictions that true church law "is the pattern for the formation and administration of human law generally"[67] and that "the faith community and the human community are connatural; each is human, historical, social."[68] Yoder then provides a list of six publicly demonstrable examples of how the faith community speaks the prophetic word and is itself the beginning of the transformation of the cosmos:

1. it is a grace-driven order of servanthood;
2. the grace of Jesus Christ is the qualification for being the subject of divine ordering;
3. its authority is trust;
4. its members commit themselves totally;
5. every member is seen as a person, as an equal;
6. its law (i.e., church law) may be a model that is continuously flowing from the worse to the better.

Again, as with Niebuhr, none of these qualities is "esoteric or mystical, subjective or arbitrary, private or sectarian."[69]

And, with that, Yoder paves the way for the fifth and final approach, which, without claiming to be so explicitly, stands above all of the previous. His own words are worth reiterating: "Between H. Richard Niebuhr's list of four marks and Karl Barth's of six, let me close with my own list of

---

65. Ibid., 22.
66. Ibid., 23.
67. Ibid., 24.
68. Ibid., 27.
69. Ibid., 28.

five. This list differs from the others in that it is derived straightforwardly, inductively, from the experience of the first Christians, and in that it makes still more evident the unity between medium and message."[70]

This is the "simpler" way forward—the unity of medium and message. With an indirect nod to Marshall McLuhan, the turn to the church as paradigm is the step that finally renders middle axioms obsolete. In "The New Humanity as Pulpit and Paradigm," Yoder explains further that ethics is more than ethics; "actions proclaim."[71] Or: "*What* God is doing is bringing into existence a new historic reality, a community constituted by the flowing together of two histories, one with the law and one without. *How* God is doing it is not distinguishable from *what* God is doing, and *how the world can know* about it is again the same thing."[72]

This is the new order of redemption in which "social/ethical/sacramental practices" are rooted.[73] There are no longer two languages that need a bridge; there is one language: pattern recognition. Why? Because most communication works "not by projecting and then reassembling a maximum number of atoms of information, nor of axioms and maxims."[74] And, returning to the categories of *The Christian Witness to the State*, if middle axioms are rejected, the implicit witness of the church is, in turn, elevated to direct witness.

Therefore, although the sacraments are first introduced in "Firstfruits" as "marks of the church" that make evident the unity of the message and medium of the first Christians,[75] by the time he is finished, the sacraments

---

70. Ibid., 29.
71. Yoder, "New Humanity as Pulpit and Paradigm," 41.
72. Ibid.
73. This is a phrase Yoder uses in "Sacrament as Social Process," 42.
74. Yoder, "New Humanity as Pulpit and Paradigm," 43.
75. Yoder, "Firstfruits," 29. In "New Humanity as Pulpit and Paradigm," he refers to these as "phenomena which are all part of our common apostolic heritage" (43). This list of the "marks of the church" looks different from some of the earlier accounts Yoder provides. See, for example, the list provided in chapter 2, 41–52, and "A People in the World" (1969): (1) holy living; (2) brotherly and sisterly love; (3) witness; and (4) the cross. And, one does not see the early Yoder's complete and utter unconcern for offense: "The preacher who tailors his or her message to what the people will understand is not simply making a practical mistake of 'not moving fast enough'; he or she is failing by the very structure of his or her approach to communicate one particular thing, namely, that his or her loyalty to Christ is the sole absolute." See Yoder, "A People in the World," 89. One must note that at least the rhetoric concerning the need for clear communication has changed, if not more.

are no longer merely marks or attributes of the church but "sample civil imperatives": baptism has become egalitarianism; the Eucharist has become socialism; binding and loosing has become forgiveness; dialogical liberty has become the open meeting; and universal charisma has become the universality of giftedness.[76] In short, Yoder's initial description of the real sacraments—which were already translations from their description in Mennonite Confessions of Faith at the time[77]—have become further translated into secular terms. Let me illustrate with at least one transition or, perhaps, translation.

In this context, Yoder does not begin to discuss baptism as "a sign of [a believer's] cleansing from sin" or as "a pledge before the church of [a believer's] covenant with God to walk in the way of Jesus Christ through the power of the Holy Spirit," as one might expect from a Mennonite theologian.[78] Rather, he starts to describe baptism as the reconciliation between Jew and Gentile, male and female, and so forth. This, he claims, is the early Christian root of egalitarianism. Of course, to claim that reconciliation in the body of Christ is unrelated to baptism would be very difficult, but it is not traditionally where Mennonites began. Yoder then goes on to refer to baptism as trans-ethnic inclusivism. He completes the translation as follows: "Our world still needs to learn that the reason every person and every kind of person must be seen with equal respect is not that their culture is equally healthy, or that they have earned equal treatment, but that equal dignity is ascribed by virtue of a divine bias in favor of the Other."[79]

For the practice of the sacrament to "seem natural, it helps to have gone through an exodus or a Pentecost together, but neither the substance nor the pertinence of the vision is dependent on a particular faith."[80]

---

76. Yoder, "Firstfruits," 33.

77. In this instance, one ought to be aware that Yoder's "internal" definitions of the sacraments as ordinances or marks of the church are already redescriptions of what would commonly be held in a Mennonite church.

78. These are parts of the first two sentences in the *Confession of Faith in a Mennonite Perspective*, 46, published jointly by the General Board of the General Conference Mennonite Church and the Mennonite Church General Board. This particular confession was written three years after "Firstfruits" was presented and two years before it was published in *For the Nations*.

79. Yoder, "Firstfruits," 30.

80. Ibid., 32. Yoder uses this particular phrase in the context of his discussion of the Eucharist, but it is certainly applicable to all other sacraments. This is a significant shift from his earlier construals.

Nothing stands in the way of the sharing of bread being a model for Social Security and negative income tax, or dialogical liberty explaining why the Japanese make better cars than Detroit, or dialogue under the Holy Spirit functioning as the ground floor of democracy.[81]

Throughout all four texts on this theme in this stage, Yoder tirelessly reduces the sacraments to social processes that he hopes will avoid Catholic sacramentalistic and Zwinglian symbolic/rationalistic temptations.[82] The former is simply unbiblical and useless for social ethics; the latter is too individualizing and explains symbolic, not concrete, social behavior. Yoder applies the notion of paradigm as a means to circumvent these false options. Language and text are rejected or severely circumscribed in their social usefulness; empirical and sociological practices remain the only possible means of uninhibited communication. The expected result, therefore, is that they can be communicated without the wider world having to learn a foreign language (i.e., Christian theology or the Christian narrative) but simply by recognizing the obvious efficiencies and values of the form of the church's social community as polis. There is nothing "esoteric" or opaquely ritualistic about the sacraments; "they lend themselves to being observed, imitated, and extrapolated."[83] And, repeating an old refrain within what I consider a significantly altered framework, Yoder again reiterates his position as messianic: "Because the risen Messiah is at once head of the church and *kyrios of the kosmos*, sovereign of the universe, what is given to the church through him is in substance no different from what is offered to the world. The believing community is the new world on the way."[84] In this way Yoder cleanly and effectively concludes his development of the notion of sacraments in his later years.

In ways that sometimes pain me, I have argued that the sacraments have become the means of uniting the nature and mission of the faithful church both internally and in the face of the unfaithful church and the wider world. In *Body Politics*, Yoder states, "The difference between

---

81. Yoder, *Body Politics*, 77–78.
82. See Yoder, "Sacrament as Social Process," 36–37.
83. Yoder, *Body Politics*, 75.
84. Yoder, "New Humanity as Pulpit and Paradigm," 50. It is also important to note that in this same chapter, Yoder provides an ethical summary of what he means by christological specificity (a "threefold cord of christological specificity"): servanthood, enemy love, and forgiveness. He continues: "if we are interested in making sense to our unbelieving and otherwise-believing neighbors, let this threefold cord be the test case" (48).

church and state or between a faithful and an unfaithful church is not that one is political and the other no, but that they are political in different ways."[85] This, as indicated earlier, is the new dualism proposed by Yoder. His reflections on the social processes of the church, therefore, are essential for understanding his ecumenical vision for the church. And, in this way, Yoder creates his own idiosyncratic ecumenical vision, a vision that begins at the bottom and that he believes is the only hopeful way forward: "Our agenda is ecumenical, not in the modern organizational sense of arranging conversations among denominational agencies, or in the sense of comparing and contrasting the foundational documents of conflicting confessions, but in the simpler sense of being relevant to all kinds of Christians."[86]

CONCLUSION

From his very earliest writings, Yoder is concerned with ecumenism. His concern entails both a desire to define the faithful church and to critique the unfaithful church. These definitions and the critiques they entail require Yoder to find a new way forward in ecumenical conversation, a way that begins with the practices of the faithful church, a way that ties together the church's worship, morality, and mission. Over time, the sacraments become the vehicle through which all of these issues find their meaning and unity.

Looking back, one can make several observations concerning Yoder's uses of the sacraments. First, these social processes highlight the communal nature of the church, the social nature of humans, and the reality that redemption includes human interdependency. In a very real sense, the sacraments provide the communal means for understanding the claim, found in the closing paragraphs of *The Politics of Jesus*, that "the future that the seer of Patmos sees ahead is a universe—that is, a single system—in which God acts and we act, with our respective actions relating to each other."[87] Second, even though he had long rejected derogatory definitions of passive or apolitical sectarianism, the sectarian charge haunts Yoder to the end to the extent that relevance and communicability become overriding and, at times, obsessive. By embracing the sacraments as the tools for

85. Yoder, *Body Politics*, ix.
86. Ibid., x.
87. Yoder, *Politics of Jesus*, 242.

building the kingdom, Yoder desires to demonstrate that these social processes are not only for the church itself but for the wider world in the most direct way. In this way, the anti-Hauerwasian title of *For the Nations* barely scratches the surface of the difference between the two prolific Protestant pacifists. Scratching further, however, is reserved for the next chapter.

SIX

Conclusion: The Heterodox Yoder

IN THE MIDST OF "The Otherness of the Church," Yoder offers the following assessment of the result of the Reformation's embrace of Constantinianism: "Fully to accept the Constantinian synthesis is to explode it. The Reformers created modern secularism; not, as the liberalism of two generations ago boasted, intentionally, by glorifying the individual, but unintentionally, through the inner contradictions of their conservatism."[1] The explosion, as Yoder understands it, is not an explosion that separates church and state in a return to pre-Constantinianism. Rather, the explosion means, for Yoder, the complete disintegration of the value or role of the church so that all that is left after the Reformation is the secular power of the state.

To turn Yoder's thought on itself, I wonder if the logic expressed in the above assessment also applies to Yoder's own method. Throughout his corpus, Yoder has sought to unite the gospel with a social style, with a particular politics.[2] But perhaps it is also true that to accept fully the synthesis offered as "the politics of Jesus" is also to explode the sought-after unity of Jesus' gospel with a particular politics. However he phrases it—whether as the unity between medium and message, deeds that "say," "gospel" as a secular term,[3] practices that a social scientist could recommend, or any

---

1. Yoder, "Otherness of the Church," 61.

2. To restate this in a slightly different way, theology and sociology "*are not two distinct and different things, but two aspects of the same thing.*" See Parler, "Spinning the Liturgical Turn," 179–80.

3. See Yoder, "Original Revolution," 15.

other form of this same principle—the culmination of Yoder's decades of theological and ethical reflection appears to be the same: Yoder seems to leave us with a Jesus who has become merely an ethico-political paradigm that opens the door for a supersessive secular ethic. The "social blueprint"[4] of the politics of Jesus becomes a minority ethic that seeks the peace of the city;[5] the meaning of the believer's cross becomes suffering as the "key" to understanding the social problems of the world;[6] sacraments become secular social processes; the spiritual and providential laws of the single universe become, "with a turn of the hand," the province of good social science "without any change to [their] inner structure."[7] Whether the secularization of the gospel was intended or not, Yoder's attempt to distill and therefore rehabilitate what he understood as original messianic Judaism through the creation of his own analog of Yiddish seems to have the same result as Yiddishism itself—namely, it robbed modern Jews of the "sustaining power of the religious regimen and religious symbolism" that "was, for many, merely a stepping stone to assimilation."[8]

To the extent that Yoder seeks to discipline and bend theological terms and categories systematically toward an ethical end (a process that begins as early as his determination of discipleship as, most basically, ethics), I take him to fit within the modern trajectory of theologians—including but not limited to Kant, Hegel, Harnack, Ritschl, and Rauschenbusch—with formally similar agendas. This is the root of my disagreement with Nation and Carter, because they appear to assume that the theological language employed by Yoder functions within the same categories and with the same referents as evangelical, traditional, or orthodox theology.

---

4. Yoder, *Politics of Jesus*, 58.

5. See also Daniel Barber's claim that "perhaps the most 'perfect' overcoming of the cultic operation is lived by Jesus himself." See Barber, "The Particularity of Jesus and the Time of the Kingdom," 76.

6. In *Politics of Jesus*, Yoder claims that "the believer's cross is no longer any and every kind of suffering, sickness, or tension, the bearing of which is demanded. The believer's cross is, like that of Jesus, the price of social nonconformity" (96). Later, in *Nonviolence*, he writes that Tolstoy discovered the "key" to the Scripture message: "the cure for evil is suffering" (21). He goes further in "The Paradigmatic Public Role of God's People," where he claims that the oppressed are the bearers of the meaning of history (and this is a matter of "serious social science") (35).

7. This is precisely the language that Yoder uses to describe Reformation trust in the order of creation. See Yoder, "Otherness of the Church," 60.

8. See Goldsmith, "Yiddishism and Judaism," 11.

Therefore, as I see it, the problem with Yoder's gospel is not that it entails social processes, civil imperatives, social ethics, politics, or whatever term might be most appropriate. The problem lies in what it excludes or, at best, renders irrelevant.

For years, Anabaptist scholars have wondered whether Yoder reduces theology to ethics. A. James Reimer and Tom Finger have been two of the most vocal critics in this regard, the former arguing that Yoder essentially ignored "theological orthodoxy" and the latter arguing that Yoder almost uniformly elides any form of the transcendent from his theology.[9] It appears that both have a case, because the systematic nature of these exclusions is deeply rooted in Yoder's constructive project in at least two ways: (1) Yoder's new politics cannot appropriate the theological support structure of the old politics, and (2) Yoder's delimitation of the "real" to ethical actions expressed in history undermines any appeal to other realities.[10] Allow me to explain further.

With respect to the first claim, it is obvious from the start that the ethic of Jesus—understood through a principled reading of the Scriptures—is taken as normative for true Christianity, whether described as the early church, the original messianic or Jeremianic Judaism, or in its restituted sixteenth-century form as Anabaptism. According to Yoder's narration, in none of these contexts were the creeds, the sacraments (as traditionally understood), mysticism, or any number of the Constantinian church's excesses present or necessary. Only after the "fall of the church" did these elements become a part of Christian history. Yoder can be very sympathetic to the reasons why they came to be (as we saw in relation to the creation of the creeds). Yet, none of these accretions is sufficiently representative of true Christianity to undermine the Constantinian synthesis of the church, and, in fact, many are used to mollify or even support it. Therefore, the assertion of the pre- and post-Constantinian politics of Jesus does not require any of these developments (e.g., creeds) and, at times, must reject some (e.g., hierarchy and sacerdotalism) in order to maintain the required voluntary, minority, communal, ethical, jesulogical politics.[11]

---

9. See Reimer, "Theological Orthodoxy and Jewish Christianity"; Finger, "Did Yoder Reduce Theology to Ethics?"

10. At this point, one can see that the neo-Kantian similarities suggested between Yoder and Schwarzschild at the conclusion of chapter 4 become much more evident.

11. J. Denny Weaver has taken this position one step further by adopting the position that "Mennonites as a peace church should develop that distinctiveness into a particular

144   THE HETERODOX YODER

With respect to the second claim, in the attempt to overcome the dualisms of twentieth-century Christian ethics that foreclosed the possibility of following Jesus, Yoder appeals to a new criterion for determining appropriate ethics, namely, "real history." As we have seen, this is the arena of social ethics, of practices, of politics. All other "realms," "levels," or "dimensions" are irrelevant when one wants to claim that Christ is Lord.[12] Whether this claim is anything more than a functional or ethico-political claim is unclear. And, if Jesus' lordship can be summarized *in toto* as such, then there seems to be little need to retain any ties to the particularities of Jesus once the function of his paradigmatic politics is understood. If this position is expansionist, it is expansionist only in the sense that all other considerations (e.g., emotions, matters of the soul, spiritual development, divine mystery, propositional confessions of faith, etc.) are as important as wrapping paper (which is, to continue Yoder's metaphor, thrown away once the package itself is opened).[13]

At the end of the day, therefore, I think that the term *heterodox* may best describe Yoder's theological position, a designation that he may have been comfortable with.[14] Clearly, he is openly critical of "orthodoxy," and he works hard to differentiate himself from its concerns and claims. On the other hand, to claim that Yoder is heretical is not straightforward either, as his open contradictions of orthodoxy are limited to critiques of what he understands as its political practices, thereby leaving his assertions that orthodoxy is simply misguided or asking the wrong questions as relatively weak criteria for determining direct contradiction of the creeds. So, as ambiguous as it may be, I have come to the conclusion that heterodox may simply be the best available option, recognizing, of

---

theology for the peace church which, rather than building on classic orthodoxy, will pose important alternatives to it." Weaver, *Anabaptist Theology in Face of Postmodernity*, 26. In an alternate vein, recent Anabaptist anthologies have made historical appeals to diverse voices within the tradition that do not follow the same trajectory as Yoder. See, for example, Snyder, *Following in the Footsteps of Christ*; Liechty, *Early Anabaptist Spirituality*.

12. See Yoder, "Why Ecclesiology Is Social Ethics," 109.

13. See Yoder, "Original Revolution," 32. This is, unfortunately, where I most strongly disagree with Parler's attempt to rehabilitate Yoder's treatment of the sacraments.

14. I have chosen this term as most appropriate because it acknowledges Yoder's Christian context while also indicating the unorthodox manner in what he construes as authoritative in defining true Christianity. There are times when reduction or secularizing may be appropriate, but I think neither of these terms captures the complexity and occasional ambiguity in Yoder's thought.

course, that there will be readers of Yoder who will fall on both sides of this conclusion. Whatever the case may be, it is clear that this determination cannot be decided merely by appeals to Yoder's position vis-à-vis the creeds; this determination must consider the larger movements in Yoder's thought that lead to his idiosyncratic assessment of the creeds.

Throughout this book, I have sought to illuminate how this position only solidifies in Yoder's later years. This implies, therefore, that there may be internal means of destabilizing the final conclusions stated above from within the corpus. Throughout this book, I have sought to illuminate the development of central theological themes in Yoder's work. Repeatedly, I have brought forward varying examinations of Yoder's account of discipleship, the church, and the relationship between the church and the wider world. There are any number of shifts—both in terms and emphases—over the years. Yet, there are two critical shifts that, in my estimation, determine Yoder's final conclusions. The first shift occurs in the mid-1960s and becomes codified in *The Politics of Jesus*, namely, the appropriation of governmental language (the language of politics and the description of the church as polis) as normative for the church.[15] With this shift, two accomplishments result: (1) the internal language of the church becomes constrained by the limits of the language of politics, and (2) a perspective is established that allows the church to judge and to witness to the wider world, which does not understand that its own politics is merely a shadow of true politics (i.e., the practices of the church). I take the first accomplishment to be problematic, and I also believe the second could be accomplished without Christianity becoming colonized by political language.

Even with this shift, however, the die is not irrevocably cast. The second significant shift in Yoder's thought that leads to his final position can be stated in two ways: either the disposal of middle axioms or the idiosyncratic embrace of paradigmatic language.[16] However one wants to construe this late shift, it is this methodological move that elides so many of the differences between the church and world that Yoder had argued so vehemently for in his early years. Describing the social practices of the church as completely accessible and understandable in the world without passing through the Exodus or Pentecost is the final step needed

15. This move is spelled out in chapter 3. In this shift, it is evident that the new "true politics" is, in many ways, still indebted to Yoder's understanding of common politics.

16. This shift is displayed in chapters 4 and 5.

to transpose Christ's lordship over the world into a form of secular social ethics that, in "real history," yields a particular sociological or political position that is in no way particularly Christian.[17]

※

As I indicated in the introduction, because Yoder has become such a pivotally important figure in the field of Christian ethics (not to mention his role in representing a form of Anabaptism to the wider world), no defense is needed to justify a critical engagement with his thought. Yet, I have no doubt that many of us grew up hearing a version of the phrase, "If you cannot say anything positive, don't say anything at all." In truth, I have been conflicted about publishing this volume for quite some time because I fear that it will be received as not saying anything positive. To preempt some of these criticisms, first, and most simply, I admit that my conclusion is an overall critical assessment of the trajectory of Yoder's corpus. To say there is nothing to be learned from Yoder or that I have not learned much myself, however, would be dissembling, at best.

That said, my hope is that a tentative critical assessment of Yoder's trajectory will have a positive effect on contemporary debates in Christian ethics and, by extension, within the church. To that end, I offer this text in order to stimulate further conversation about Yoder's place in a critically important ongoing discussion. Over the last years, I have come to the conclusion that Yoder serves many Christians—both academics and non-academics—in a particular and limited sense. Please allow a few words by Hauerwas concerning Anabaptism, words I believe also apply particularly to Yoder:[18] "I am often accused of romanticizing both Catholicism and Anabaptism, and no doubt that is a danger. But the reason I am so attracted to those traditions is that they have managed to keep some practices in place that provide resources for resistance against the loss of Christian presence in modernity. For that is the heart of the matter—

17. Unless, of course, Christianity is defined as a particular politics alone, in which case all expressions of that particular politics would be Christian.

18. I have no intention of diving into the "compare and contrast" conversation surrounding Hauerwas and Yoder. If one is interested in that debate, one might best begin with Gerald Schlabach's "Continuity and Sacrament," Craig Hovey's "The Public Ethics of John Howard Yoder and Stanley Hauerwas," and Paul Doerksen's "Share the House: Yoder and Hauerwas Among the Nations."

namely, practices. Practices make the church the embodiment of Christ for the world."[19]

And, a little later: "In a Christendom world it took conviction to be a pagan or an Anabaptist, but given the world in which we are now living it is hard to distinguish pagans from Anabaptists. That is why I emphasize the importance of practices, which may of course involve 'doctrine' as well as 'called membership,' since practices provide the material specifications that help us resist the endemic character of modernity, bent as it is on turning faith into just another idea."[20]

What these comments indicate is that Yoder—and perhaps Yoder as representative for Anabaptism—frequently provides Christians with an account of the importance of practices as constitutive of the church. Against the modern temptation to turn faith into just another idea, Yoder appears to provide rich resources for resistance. From Hauerwas' autobiographical perspective—a Methodist who had "all the experience and self-understanding [he] could use for a lifetime" by the time he was fifteen[21]—this makes a whole lot of sense. Yet, what I think Hauerwas wrongly implies in his conclusion is that there is only *one* temptation within modernity. As I see it, the temptation to turn faith into just another idea has a dialectical opposite that is equally as problematic, namely, the powerful temptation to turn faith into just another form of ethics or series of practices. From my own autobiographical experience within the Anabaptist tradition, I have seen how this latter temptation can cripple and corrupt Christianity in very troubling ways.[22] I hope this book demonstrates—through an examination of Yoder's corpus—that turning to practices or politics as the sole normative language for reinforcing Christianity against the temptations of modernity may not, in fact, free the church from the grip of modernity. Therefore, I hope it is clear that this book is, alongside the current trend of constructive appropriations of Yoder, a helpful diagnosis; it is a caution against letting a contemporary challenge, whether it be sectarianism, Christendom, or perhaps even one's Methodist upbringing, overwhelmingly dictate one's corrective articulation of Christianity.

19. Hauerwas, *In Good Company*, 67–68.

20. Ibid., 73.

21. Ibid., 75.

22. For this reason, I have always been sympathetic to Steve Dintaman's "The Spiritual Poverty of the Anabaptist Vision," despite its flaws.

Bibliography

PUBLISHED WORKS BY YODER

Yoder, John Howard. *Anabaptism and Reformation in Switzerland: An Historical and Theological Analysis of the Dialogues Between Anabaptists and Reformers*. Edited by C. Arnold Snyder. Translated by David Carl Stassen. Kitchener, ON: Pandora, 2004.

———. "The Anabaptist Dissent." In *The Roots of Concern: Writings on Anabaptist Renewal, 1952–1957*, edited by Virgil Vogt, 29–43. Eugene, OR: Cascade Books, 2009.

———. "The Authority of the Canon." In *Essays on Biblical Interpretation: Anabaptist-Mennonite Perspectives*, edited by Willard Swartley, 265–90. Elkhart, IN: Institute of Mennonite Studies, 1984.

———, and David A. Shank. "Biblicism and the Church." In *The Roots of Concern: Writings on Anabaptist Renewal, 1952–1957*, edited by Virgil Vogt, 67–101. Eugene, OR: Cascade Books, 2009.

———. "Binding and Loosing." *Concern* 14 (1967) 2–32.

———. *Body Politics: Five Practices of the Christian Community Before the Watching World*. Scottdale, PA: Herald, 1992.

———. "But We Do See Jesus: The Particularity of the Incarnation and the Universality of Truth." In *The Priestly Kingdom: Social Ethics as Gospel*, 46–62. Notre Dame: University of Notre Dame Press, 1984.

———. "Caesar and the Meidung." *Mennonite Quarterly Review* 29 (1949) 76–98.

———. "Capital Punishment." *The Mennonite*, 11 June 1963, 390–94.

———. "Capital Punishment and the Bible." *Christianity Today*, February 1960, 3–6.

———. "Catholicity in Search of Location." In *The Royal Priesthood: Essays Ecclesiological and Ecumenical*, edited by Michael G. Cartwright, 300–20. Grand Rapids: Eerdmans, 1994.

———. "Christ, the Hope of the World." In *The Original Revolution*, 148–84. Scottdale, PA: Herald, 1971.

———. *The Christian and Capital Punishment*. Newton, KS: Faith and Life Press, 1961.

———. *Christian Attitudes to War, Peace, and Revolution*. Edited by Theodore J. Koontz and Andy Alexis-Baker. Grand Rapids: Brazos, 2009.

———. "The Christian Case for Democracy." In *The Priestly Kingdom: Social Ethics as Gospel*, 151–71. Notre Dame: University of Notre Dame Press, 1984.

———. *The Christian Witness to the State*. Newton, KS: Faith and Life Press, 1964.

———. *Confession of Faith in a Mennonite Perspective*. Scottdale, PA: Herald, 1995.

———. "The Constantinian Sources of Western Social Ethics." In *The Priestly Kingdom: Social Ethics as Gospel*, 135–47. Notre Dame: University of Notre Dame Press, 1984.

———. "The Disavowal of Constantine: An Alternative Perspective on Interfaith Dialogue." In *Aspects of Interfaith Dialogue: Ecumenical Institute for Advanced Theological Studies Yearbook: 1975–1976*, edited by W. Wegner and W. Harrelson, 47–68. Tantur/Jerusalem: Ecumenical Institute for Advanced Theological Studies, 1979.

———. "Discerning the Kingdom of God in the Struggles of the World." In *For the Nations: Essays Public and Evangelical*, 237–45. Grand Rapids: Eerdmans, 1997.

———. *Discipleship as Political Responsibility*. Translated by Timothy J. Geddert. Scottdale, PA: Herald, 2003.

———. "Earthly Jerusalem and Heavenly Jerusalem: A Mis-Located Dualism." In *The Jewish-Christian Schism Revisited*, edited by Michael G. Cartwright and Peter Ochs, 160–66. Grand Rapids: Eerdmans, 2003.

———. *The Ecumenical Movement and the Faithful Church*. Focal Pamphlet Series 3. Scottdale, PA: Mennonite Publishing House, 1958.

———. "Firstfruits: The Paradigmatic Public Role of God's People." In *For the Nations: Essays Public and Evangelical*, 15–36. Grand Rapids: Eerdmans, 1997.

———. *For the Nations: Essays Public and Evangelical*. Grand Rapids: Eerdmans, 1997.

———. "The Forms of a Possible Obedience." In *The Jewish-Christian Schism Revisited*, edited by Michael G. Cartwright and Peter Ochs, 121–31. Grand Rapids: Eerdmans, 2003.

———. "The Free Church Ecumenical Style." In *The Royal Priesthood: Essays Ecclesiological and Ecumenical*, edited by Michael G. Cartwright, 231–41. Grand Rapids: Eerdmans, 1994.

———. "The Fullness of Christ." *Concern* 17 (1969) 33–93.

———. *The Fullness of Christ: Paul's Vision of Universal Ministry*. Elgin, IL: Brethren Press, 1987.

———. "The Hermeneutics of the Anabaptists." *Mennonite Quarterly Review* 41 (1967) 291–308.

———. "The Hermeneutics of Peoplehood: A Protestant Perspective." In *The Priestly Kingdom: Social Ethics as Gospel*, 15–45. Notre Dame: University of Notre Dame Press, 1984.

———. "If Abraham Is Our Father." In *The Original Revolution*, 91–111. Scottdale, PA: Herald, 1971.

———. "It Did Not Have to Be." In *The Jewish-Christian Schism Revisited*, edited by Michael G. Cartwright and Peter Ochs, 43–66. Grand Rapids: Eerdmans, 2003.

———. "Jesus the Jewish Pacifist." In *The Jewish-Christian Schism Revisited*, edited by Michael G. Cartwright and Peter Ochs, 69–89. Grand Rapids: Eerdmans, 2003.

———. *The Jewish-Christian Schism Revisited*. Edited by Michael G. Cartwright and Peter Ochs. Grand Rapids: Eerdmans, 2003.

———. "The Jewish Jesus and the Church/Synagogue Split," December 1975. Box 133, "Tantur JHY." John H. Yoder Papers, 1947–1997. HM1–48. Mennonite Church USA Archives – Goshen. Goshen, Indiana.

———. "The Jewishness of the Free Church Vision." In *The Jewish-Christian Schism Revisited*, edited by Michael G. Cartwright and Peter Ochs, 105–19. Grand Rapids: Eerdmans, 2003.

———. "Judaism as a Non-non-Christian Religion." In *The Jewish-Christian Schism Revisited*, edited by Michael G. Cartwright and Peter Ochs, 147–58. Grand Rapids: Eerdmans, 2003.

———. *Karl Barth and the Problem of War and Other Essays on Barth*. Edited by Mark Thiessen Nation. Eugene, OR: Cascade Books, 2003.

———. "The Kingdom as Social Ethic." In *The Priestly Kingdom: Social Ethics as Gospel*, 80–101. Notre Dame: University of Notre Dame Press, 1984.

———. "Let the Church Be the Church." In *The Original Revolution*, 113–31. Scottdale, PA: Herald, 1971.

———. "A Light to the Nations." *Concern* 9 (1961) 14–18.

———. "The Lordship of Christ and the Power Struggle." In *The Lordship of Christ: Proceedings of the Seventh Mennonite World Conference, August 1–7, 1962, Kitchener, Ontario*, 507–12. Elkhart, IN: Mennonite Publishing House, 1962.

———. "Meaning After Babble: With Jeffrey Stout beyond Relativism." *Journal of Religious Ethics* 24:1 (1996) 125–39.

———. "The Nature of the Unity We Seek: A Historic Free Church View." In *The Royal Priesthood: Essays Ecclesiological and Ecumenical*, edited by Michael G. Cartwright, 221–30. Grand Rapids: Eerdmans, 1994.

———. *Nevertheless: The Varieties and Shortcomings of Religious Pacifism*. Rev. ed. Scottdale, PA: Herald, 1992.

———. "The New Humanity as Pulpit and Paradigm." In *For the Nations: Essays Public and Evangelical*, 37–50. Grand Rapids: Eerdmans, 1997.

———. *Nonviolence: A Brief History: The Warsaw Lectures*. Edited by Paul Martens, Matthew Porter, and Myles Werntz. Waco, TX: Baylor University Press, 2010.

———. "On the Meaning of Christmas." *Concern* 16 (1968) 14–19.

———. "The Original Revolution." In *The Original Revolution*, 13–33. Scottdale, PA: Herald, 1971.

———. *The Original Revolution*. Scottdale, PA: Herald, 1971.

———. "The Otherness of the Church." In *The Royal Priesthood: Essays Ecclesiological and Ecumenical*, edited by Michael G. Cartwright, 53–64. Grand Rapids: Eerdmans, 1994.

———. *A Pacifist Way of Knowing: John Howard Yoder's Nonviolent Epistemology*. Edited by Christian E. Early and Ted Grimsrud. Eugene, OR: Wipf & Stock, 2010.

———. "Paul the Judaizer." In *The Jewish-Christian Schism Revisited*, edited by Michael G. Cartwright and Peter Ochs, 93–101. Grand Rapids: Eerdmans, 2003.

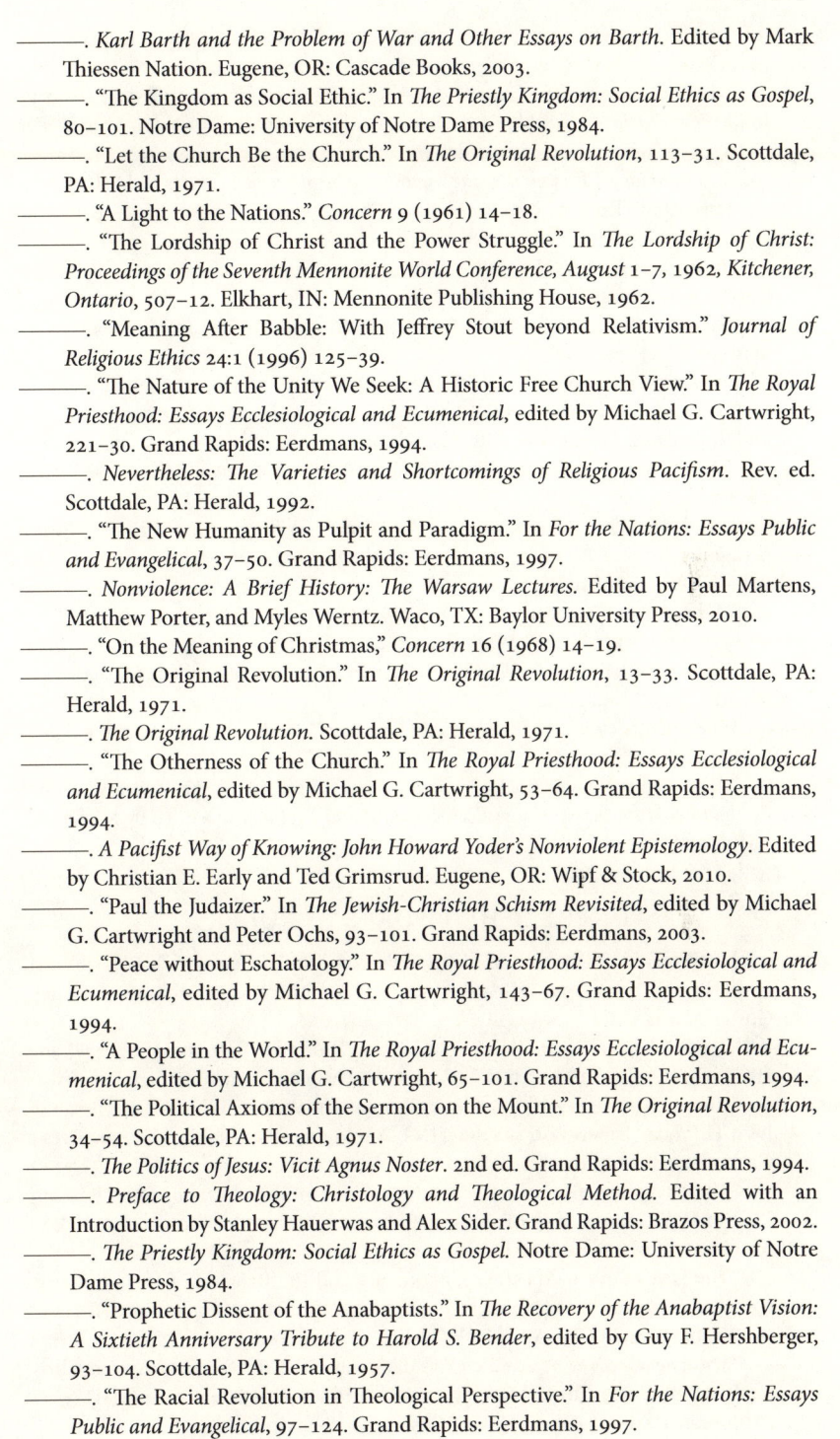

———. "Peace without Eschatology." In *The Royal Priesthood: Essays Ecclesiological and Ecumenical*, edited by Michael G. Cartwright, 143–67. Grand Rapids: Eerdmans, 1994.

———. "A People in the World." In *The Royal Priesthood: Essays Ecclesiological and Ecumenical*, edited by Michael G. Cartwright, 65–101. Grand Rapids: Eerdmans, 1994.

———. "The Political Axioms of the Sermon on the Mount." In *The Original Revolution*, 34–54. Scottdale, PA: Herald, 1971.

———. *The Politics of Jesus: Vicit Agnus Noster*. 2nd ed. Grand Rapids: Eerdmans, 1994.

———. *Preface to Theology: Christology and Theological Method*. Edited with an Introduction by Stanley Hauerwas and Alex Sider. Grand Rapids: Brazos Press, 2002.

———. *The Priestly Kingdom: Social Ethics as Gospel*. Notre Dame: University of Notre Dame Press, 1984.

———. "Prophetic Dissent of the Anabaptists." In *The Recovery of the Anabaptist Vision: A Sixtieth Anniversary Tribute to Harold S. Bender*, edited by Guy F. Hershberger, 93–104. Scottdale, PA: Herald, 1957.

———. "The Racial Revolution in Theological Perspective." In *For the Nations: Essays Public and Evangelical*, 97–124. Grand Rapids: Eerdmans, 1997.

---. "Reinhold Niebuhr and Christian Pacifism." *Mennonite Quarterly Review* 29 (1955) 101–17.

---. "The Restitution of the Church: An Alternate Perspective on Christian History." In *The Jewish-Christian Schism Revisited*, edited by Michael G. Cartwright and Peter Ochs, 133–43. Grand Rapids: Eerdmans, 2003.

---. *Revolutionary Christianity: The 1966 South American Lectures*. Edited by Paul Martens, Mark Thiessen Nation, Matthew Porter, and Myles Werntz. Eugene, OR: Cascade Books, 2012.

---. *The Royal Priesthood: Essays Ecclesiological and Ecumenical*. Edited by Michael G. Cartwright. Grand Rapids: Eerdmans, 1994.

---. "Sacrament as Social Process: Christ the Transformer of Culture." *Theology Today* 48:1 (1991) 33–44.

---, translator and editor. *The Schleitheim Confession*. Scottdale, PA: Herald, 1973.

---. "'See How They Go with Their Face to the Sun.'" In *For the Nations: Essays Public and Evangelical*, 51–78. Grand Rapids: Eerdmans, 1997.

---. "The Turning Point in the Zwinglian Reformation." *Mennonite Quarterly Review* 32 (1958) 128–40.

---. "To Serve Our God and to Rule the World." In *The Royal Priesthood: Essays Ecclesiological and Ecumenical*, edited by Michael G. Cartwright, 127–40. Grand Rapids: Eerdmans, 1994.

---. "What Are Our Concerns?" In *The Roots of Concern: Writings on Anabaptist Renewal 1952–1957*, edited by Virgil Vogt, 164–76. Eugene, OR: Cascade Books, 2009.

---. *What Would You Do? A Serious Answer to a Standard Question*, Expanded ed. Scottdale, PA: Herald, 1983.

---. *When War is Unjust: Being Honest in Just-War Thinking*. Rev. ed. Maryknoll, NY: Orbis, 1996.

---. "Why Ecclesiology is Social Ethics: Gospel Ethics Versus the Wider Wisdom." In *The Royal Priesthood: Essays Ecclesiological and Ecumenical*, edited by Michael G. Cartwright, 102–26. Grand Rapids: Eerdmans, 1994.

UNPUBLISHED WORKS BY YODER

Yoder, John Howard. "III Judaism as Historic Peace Church." Box 133, "1 PM." John H. Yoder Papers, 1947–1997. HM1–48. Mennonite Church USA Archives – Goshen. Goshen, Indiana.

---. "Bethel Menno Lecture II." Box 133, "1 AM." John H. Yoder Papers, 1947–1997. HM1–48. Mennonite Church USA Archives – Goshen. Goshen, Indiana.

---. "Christian Attitudes to War/Peace/Revolution: Written Lecture VII." Box 132. John H. Yoder Papers, 1947–1997. HM1–48. Mennonite Church USA Archives – Goshen. Goshen, Indiana.

---. "The Jewish Pacifism of Jesus = A Research Outline," Oct. 20, 1975. Box 133, "Tantur JHY." John H. Yoder Papers, 1947–1997. HM1–48. Mennonite Church USA Archives – Goshen. Goshen, Indiana.

---. "The Jewishness of Apostolic Christianity and the Renewal of Western Christendom." Box 132, "Guggenh Oct 83." John H. Yoder Papers, 1947–1997. HM1–48. Mennonite Church USA Archives – Goshen. Goshen, Indiana.

---. "The Jewishness of Apostolic Christianity and the Renewal of Western Christendom." Box 132, "Rockef Oct 83." John H. Yoder Papers, 1947–1997. HM1–48. Mennonite Church USA Archives – Goshen. Goshen, Indiana.

---. "Judaism as Non-non-Christian Religion." Box 133, "Hiebert 1988." John H. Yoder Papers, 1947–1997. HM1–48. Mennonite Church USA Archives – Goshen. Goshen, Indiana.

---. "Minimal Prospectus for a Research Project." Box 132, "GUGGENH Oct 83." John H. Yoder Papers, 1947–1997. HM1–48. Mennonite Church USA Archives – Goshen. Goshen, Indiana.

---. "Minority Christianity and Messianic Judaism." Box 201, "Buenos Aires." John H. Yoder Papers, 1947–1997. HM1–48. Mennonite Church USA Archives – Goshen. Goshen, Indiana.

---. "NCCJ St. Louis National Workshop." Box 132, "8th National Workshop on Christian-Jewish Relations Folder." John H. Yoder Papers, 1947–1997. HM1–48. Mennonite Church USA Archives – Goshen. Goshen, Indiana.

---. "New File 31 Dec JUDSMH Last Newton Lecture." Box 133, "Newton 1982." John H. Yoder Papers, 1947–1997. HM1–48. Mennonite Church USA Archives – Goshen. Goshen, Indiana.

---. "The Politics of Jesus Revisited." Lecture presented at Toronto Mennonite Studies Center, unpublished, March 1997.

---. "Response to Rendtorff." Box 132, "Phila Holocaust Conf 1978 Rendtorff." John H. Yoder Papers, 1947–1997. HM1–48. Mennonite Church USA Archives – Goshen. Goshen, Indiana.

---. "A Study in the Doctrine of the Work of Christ." Unpublished paper presented at Domburg Seminar, April 27, 1954.

---. "Tertium Datur: Refocusing the Jewish-Christian Schism," Oct. 13, 1977. Box 133, "Tertium Datur 1977." John H. Yoder Papers, 1947–1997. HM1–48. Mennonite Church USA Archives – Goshen. Goshen, Indiana.

---. "War/Nation/Church Colloquium." Box 133, "WANACH 1976." John H. Yoder Papers, 1947–1997. HM1–48. Mennonite Church USA Archives – Goshen. Goshen, Indiana.

---. "The Wrath of God and the Love of God." Unpublished paper presented in September, 1956, at a Historic Peace Churches and International Fellowship of Reconciliation Conference in England.

CORRESPONDENCE

Box 132, "GUGGENH Oct 83." John H. Yoder Papers, 1947–1997. HM1–48. Mennonite Church USA Archives – Goshen. Goshen, Indiana.

Box 132, "Jewishness." John H. Yoder Papers, 1947–1997. HM1–48. Mennonite Church USA Archives – Goshen. Goshen, Indiana.

Box 132, "S.S.S. ztz'l." John H. Yoder Papers, 1947–1997. HM1–48. Mennonite Church USA Archives – Goshen. Goshen, Indiana.

Box 132, "Steven Schwarzschild." John H. Yoder Papers, 1947–1997. HM1–48. Mennonite Church USA Archives – Goshen. Goshen, Indiana.

Box 133, "Jews/Peace." John H. Yoder Papers, 1947–1997. HM1–48. Mennonite Church USA Archives – Goshen. Goshen, Indiana.

Box 201, "S.S.S. Planning Course." John H. Yoder Papers, 1947–1997. HM1–48. Mennonite Church USA Archives – Goshen. Goshen, Indiana.

Box 201, "S.S.S. ztz'l." John H. Yoder Papers, 1947–1997. HM1–48. Mennonite Church USA Archives – Goshen. Goshen, Indiana.

Box 201, "Tantur 74/75 Jewish Pacifism." John H. Yoder Papers, 1947–1997. HM1–48. Mennonite Church USA Archives – Goshen. Goshen, Indiana.

Box 204, "Income Tax 1960–78." John H. Yoder Papers, 1947–1997. HM1–48. Mennonite Church USA Archives – Goshen. Goshen, Indiana.

OTHER WORKS

Bainton, Roland H. *Christian Attitudes Toward War and Peace: A Historical Survey and Critical Re-evalution.* Nashville: Abingdon, 1979.

Barber, Daniel. "The Particularity of Jesus and the Time of the Kingdom: Philosophy and Theology in Yoder." *Modern Theology* 23:1 (2007) 63–89.

Bender, Harold S. "The Anabaptist Theology of Discipleship." *Mennonite Quarterly Review* 24 (1950) 25–32.

———. *The Anabaptist Vision.* Scottdale, PA: Herald, 1944.

Bergen, Jeremy, and Anthony G. Siegrist, editors. *Power and Practices: Engaging the Work of John Howard Yoder.* Scottdale, PA: Herald, 2009.

Berkhof, Hendrik. *Christ and the Powers.* Translated by John Howard Yoder. Scottdale, PA: Herald, 1962.

Bourne, Richard. *Seek the Peace of the City: Christian Political Criticism as Public, Realist, and Transformative.* Eugene, OR: Cascade Books, 2009.

Boyarin, Daniel. "Judaism as a Free Church: Footnotes to John Howard Yoder's *The Jewish-Christian Schism Revisited*." In *The New Yoder*, edited by Peter Dula and Chris K. Huebner, 1–17. Eugene, OR: Cascade Books, 2010.

Carter, Craig A. *The Politics of the Cross: The Theology and Social Ethics of John Howard Yoder.* Grand Rapids: Brazos, 2001.

Cartwright, Michael G. "Radical Reform, Radical Catholicity: John Howard Yoder's Vision of the Faithful Church." Introduction to *The Royal Priesthood: Essays Ecclesiological and Ecumenical*, by John Howard Yoder, 1–49. Grand Rapids: Eerdmans, 1994.

Coles, Romand. "The Wild Patience of John Howard Yoder: 'Outsiders' and the 'Otherness of the Church.'" In *The New Yoder*, edited by Peter Dula and Chris K. Huebner, 216–52. Eugene, OR: Cascade Books, 2010.

Cullman, Oscar. *The Christology of the New Testament.* Revised, edited, and translated by Shirley C. Guthrie and Charles A. M. Hall. Philadelphia: Westminster, 1963.

Dintaman, Stephen F. "The Spiritual Poverty of the Anabaptist Vision." *Conrad Grebel Review* 10:2 (1992) 205–8.

Doerksen, Paul. *Beyond Suspicion: Post-Christian Protestant Political Theology in John Howard Yoder and Oliver O'Donovan.* Eugene, OR: Wipf & Stock, 2009.

———. "Share the House: Yoder and Hauerwas Among the Nations." In *A Mind Patient and Untamed: Assessing John Howard Yoder's Contributions to Theology, Ethics, and Peacemaking*, edited by Ben C. Ollenburger and Gayle Gerber Koontz, 187–204. Telford, PA: Cascadia, 2004.

Dula, Peter, and Chris K. Huebner, editors. *The New Yoder.* Eugene, OR: Cascade Books, 2010.

Finger, Tom. "Did Yoder Reduce Theology to Ethics?" In *A Mind Patient and Untamed: Assessing John Howard Yoder's Contributions to Theology, Ethics, and Peacemaking*, edited by Ben C. Ollenburger and Gayle Gerber Koontz, 318–39. Telford, PA: Cascadia, 2004.

Friesen, Duane K. *Artists, Citizens, Philosophers: Seeking the Peace of the City: An Anabaptist Theology of Culture.* Scottdale, PA: Herald, 2000.

———."Yoder and the Jews: Cosmopolitan Homelessness as Ecclesial Model." In *A Mind Patient and Untamed: Assessing John Howard Yoder's Contributions to Theology, Ethics, and Peacemaking,* edited by Ben C. Ollenburger and Gayle Gerber Koontz, 145–60. Telford, PA: Cascadia, 2004.

Goldsmith, Emanuel. "Yiddishism and Judaism." In *Politics of Yiddish: Studies in Language, Literature and Society,* edited by Dov-Ber Kerler, 11–22. Walnut Creek, CA: AltaMira, 1998.

Gustafson, James. *Ethics from a Theocentric Perspective.* Vol. 1. Chicago: University of Chicago Press, 1981.

———. "The Sectarian Temptation: Reflections on Theology, the Church, and the University." *Catholic Theological Society of America Proceedings* 40 (1985) 83–94.

Hauerwas, Stanley. *A Better Hope: Resources for a Church Confronting Capitalism, Democracy, and Postmodernity.* Grand Rapids: Brazos, 2000.

———, and Chris K. Huebner. "History, Theory, and Anabaptism: A Conversation on Theology after John Howard Yoder." In *The Wisdom of the Cross: Essays in Honor of John Howard Yoder,* edited by Stanley Hauerwas, Chris K. Huebner, Harry J. Huebner, and Mark Thiessen Nation, 391–408. Grand Rapids: Eerdmans, 1999.

———. *In Good Company: The Church as Polis.* Notre Dame: University of Notre Dame Press, 1995.

———, and Michael Broadway. "The Irony of Reinhold Niebuhr: The Ideological Character of 'Christian Realism.'" In *Wilderness Wanderings: Probing Twentieth-Century Theology and Philosophy,* 48–61. Boulder, CO: Westview, 1997.

———. "When the Politics of Jesus Makes a Difference." *The Christian Century* (October 13, 1993): 982–87.

Hauerwas, Stanley, and Samuel Wells, editors. *The Blackwell Companion to Christian Ethics.* Malden, MA: Blackwell, 2004.

Hauerwas, Stanley, Chris K. Huebner, Harry J. Huebner, and Mark Thiessen Nation, editors. *The Wisdom of the Cross: Essays in Honor of John Howard Yoder.* Grand Rapids: Eerdmans, 1999.

Heilke, Thomas. "Yoder's Idea of Constantinianism: An Analytical Framework Toward Conversation." In *A Mind Patient and Untamed: Assessing John Howard Yoder's Contributions to Theology, Ethics, and Peacemaking,* edited by Ben C. Ollenburger and Gayle Gerber Koontz, 89–125. Telford, PA: Cascadia, 2004.

Hovey, Craig. "The Public Ethics of John Howard Yoder and Stanley Hauerwas: Difference or Disagreement?" In *A Mind Patient and Untamed: Assessing John Howard Yoder's Contributions to Theology, Ethics, and Peacemaking,* edited by Ben C. Ollenburger and Gayle Gerber Koontz, 205–20. Telford, PA: Cascadia, 2004.

Huebner, Chris K. "Can a Gift be Commanded? Theological Ethics Without Theory by Way of Barth, Milbank, and Yoder." *Scottish Journal of Theology* 53:4 (2000) 472–89.

———. *A Precarious Peace: Yoderian Explorations on Theology, Knowledge, and Identity.* Scottdale, PA: Herald, 2006.

Huebner, Harry. "The Christian Life as Gift and Patience: Why Yoder Has Trouble with Method." In *A Mind Patient and Untamed: Assessing John Howard Yoder's Contributions to Theology, Ethics, and Peacemaking,* edited by Ben C. Ollenburger and Gayle Gerber Koontz, 23–38. Telford, PA: Cascadia, 2004.

———. "Moral Agency as Embodiment: How the Church Acts." In *A Mind Patient and Untamed: Assessing John Howard Yoder's Contributions to Theology, Ethics, and Peacemaking,* edited by Ben C. Ollenburger and Gayle Gerber Koontz, 189–212. Telford, PA: Cascadia, 2004.

Hunter, James Davison. *To Change the World: The Irony, Tragedy, and Possibility of Christianity in the Late Modern World*. Oxford: Oxford University Press, 2010.

Kaufman, Gordon. Review of *The Priestly Kingdom*, by John Howard Yoder. *Conrad Grebel Review* 4:1 (1986) 79–80.

Kerr, Nathan T. *Christ, History, and Apocalyptic: The Politics of Christian Mission*. London: SCM, 2008.

Klassen, William. "Jesus and the Zealot Option." In *The Wisdom of the Cross: Essays in Honor of John Howard Yoder*, edited by Chris K. Huebner, Harry J. Huebner, and Mark Thiessen Nation, 131–49. Grand Rapids: Eerdmans, 1999.

Kroeker, P. Travis. "Is a Messianic Political Ethic Possible? Recent Work by and about John Howard Yoder." *Journal of Religious Ethics* 33:1 (2005) 141–74.

Lasserre, Jean. *War and the Gospel*. Scottdale, PA: Herald, 1962.

Leithart, Peter J. *Defending Constantine: The Twilight of an Empire and the Dawn of Christendom*. Downer's Grove, IL: IVP Academic, 2010.

Liechty, Daniel. *Early Anabaptist Spirituality: Selected Writings*. New York: Paulist, 1994.

Martens, Paul. "The Problematic Development of the Sacraments in the Thought of John Howard Yoder." *Conrad Grebel Review* 24:3 (Fall 2006) 65–77.

Miller, John W. "In the Footsteps of Marcion: Notes Toward an Understanding of John Yoder's Theology." *Conrad Grebel Review* 16:2 (1998) 82–92.

Mouw, Richard J. Foreword to *The Royal Priesthood: Essays Ecclesiological and Ecumenical*, edited by Michael G. Cartwright, vii–ix. Scottdale, PA: Herald, 1998.

Murphy, Nancy. "John Howard Yoder's Systematic Defense of Christian Pacifism." In *The Wisdom of the Cross: Essays in Honor of John Howard Yoder*, edited by Stanley Hauerwas et al., 45–68. Grand Rapids: Eerdmans, 1999.

Nation, Mark Thiessen. "The 'Ecumenical' and 'Cosmopolitan' Yoder: A Critical Engagement with Nonviolence—A Brief History and Its Editors." *Conrad Grebel Review* 29:3 (2011) 73–87.

———. *John Howard Yoder: Mennonite Patience, Evangelical Witness, Catholic Convictions*. Grand Rapids: Eerdmans, 2006.

Niebuhr, H. Richard. *Christ and Culture*. New York: Harper & Row, 1956.

———. "The Social Gospel and the Mind of Jesus." *Journal of Religious Ethics* 16:1 (1988) 115–27.

Niebuhr, Reinhold. *An Interpretation of Christian Ethics*. New York: HarperCollins, 1963.

Ochs, Peter. *The Free Church and Israel's Covenant*. Winnipeg: CMBC Publications, 2010.

O'Donovan, Oliver. *The Desire of the Nations: Rediscovering the Roots of Political Theology*. Cambridge: Cambridge University Press, 1996.

Ollenburger, Ben C., and Gayle Gerber Koontz, editors. *A Mind Patient and Untamed: Assessing John Howard Yoder's Contributions to Theology, Ethics, and Peacemaking*. Telford, PA: Cascadia, 2004.

Parler, Branson. "Spinning the Liturgical Turn: Why John Howard Yoder Is Not an Ethicist." In *Radical Ecumenicity: Pursuing Unity and Continuity after John Howard Yoder*, edited by John C. Nugent, 173–91. Abilene, TX: Abilene Christian University Press, 2010.

Pinches, Charles. "Christian Pacifism and Theodicy: The Free Will Defense in the Thought of John H. Yoder." *Modern Theology* 5:3 (1989) 239–55.

Ramsey, Paul. "Liturgy and Ethics." *Journal of Religious Ethics* 7 (1979) 139–71.

Rasmussen, Arne. "The Politics of Diaspora: The Post-Christendom Theologies of Karl Barth and John Howard Yoder." In *God, Truth, and Witness: Engaging Stanley Hauerwas*, edited by L. Gregory Jones, Reinhard Hütter, and C. Rosalee Velloso Ewell, 88–111. Grand Rapids: Brazos, 2005.

Reimer, A. James. *Mennonites and Classical Theology: Dogmatic Foundations for Christian Ethics*. Kitchener, ON: Pandora, 2001.

———. "Mennonites, Christ, and Culture: The Yoder Legacy." *Conrad Grebel Review* 16:2 (1988) 5–14.

———. "Theological Orthodoxy and Jewish Christianity: A Personal Tribute to John Howard Yoder." In *The Wisdom of the Cross: Essays in Honor of John Howard Yoder*, edited by Stanley Hauerwas, Chris K. Huebner, Harry J. Huebner, and Mark Thiessen Nation, 430–48. Grand Rapids: Eerdmans, 1999.

Schlabach, Gerald. "Continuity and Sacrament, or not: Hauerwas, Yoder, and Their Deep Difference." *Journal of the Society of Christian Ethics* 27:2 (2007) 171–207.

Schwarzschild, Steven S. Introduction to *Roots of Jewish Nonviolence*, edited by Allan Solomonow, 4–5. Nyack, NY: Jewish Peace Fellowship, 1981.

———."Shalom." *Confrontation* 21 (1981) 166–76.

Shank, David A., and John Howard Yoder. "Biblicism and the Church." In *The Roots of Concern: Writings on Anabaptist Renewal, 1952–1957*, edited by Virgil Vogt, 67–101. Eugene, OR: Cascade Books, 2009.

Sider, J. Alexander. "Constantinianism Before and After Nicea: Issues in Restitutionist Historiography." In *A Mind Patient and Untamed: Assessing John Howard Yoder's Contributions to Theology, Ethics, and Peacemaking*, edited by Ben C. Ollenburger and Gayle Gerber Koontz, 126–44. Telford, PA: Cascadia, 2004.

———. *To See History Doxologically: History and Holiness in John Howard Yoder's Ecclesiology*. Grand Rapids: Eerdmans, 2011.

Snyder, C. Arnold. *Following in the Footsteps of Christ: The Anabaptist Tradition*. Maryknoll, NY: Orbis, 2004.

Stassen, Glen H. "The Politics of Jesus in the Sermon on the Plain." In *The Wisdom of the Cross: Essays in Honor of John Howard Yoder*, edited by Stanley Hauerwas, Chris K. Huebner, Harry J. Huebner, and Mark Thiessen Nation, 50–67. Grand Rapids: Eerdmans, 1999.

Stauffer, Ethelbert. "The Anabaptist Theology of Martyrdom." *Mennonite Quarterly Review* 19 (1945) 179–214.

Stoltzfus, Philip E. "Nonviolent Jesus, Violent God? A Critique of John Howard Yoder's Approach to Theological Construction." In *Power and Practices: Engaging the Work of John Howard Yoder*, edited by Jeremy M. Bergen and Anthony G. Siegrist, 29–46. Scottdale, PA: Herald, 2009.

Swartley, Willard M. "Smelting for Gold: Jesus and Jubilee in John H. Yoder's *Politics of Jesus*." In *A Mind Patient and Untamed: Assessing John Howard Yoder's Contributions to Theology, Ethics, and Peacemaking*, edited by Ben C. Ollenburger and Gayle Gerber Koontz, 288–302. Telford, PA: Cascadia, 2004.

Taylor, Rachel Reesor. "Yoder's Mischievous Contribution to Mennonite Views on Anselmian Atonement." In *A Mind Patient and Untamed: Assessing John Howard Yoder's Contributions to Theology, Ethics, and Peacemaking*, edited by Ben C. Ollenburger and Gayle Gerber Koontz, 303–17. Telford, PA: Cascadia, 2004.

Weaver, Alain Epp. "Missionary Christology: John Howard Yoder and the Creeds." *Mennonite Quarterly Review* 74:3 (2000) 423–39.

———. "On Exile: Yoder, Said, and a Politics of Land and Return." In *The New Yoder*, edited by Peter Dula and Chris K. Huebner, 142–65. Eugene, OR: Cascade Books, 2010.

———. "Politics of the Kingdom and Religious Plurality: With Barth and Yoder Toward a Nonresistant Public Theology." *Mennonite Quarterly Review* 72:3 (1998) 411–40.

———. *States of Exile: Visions of Diaspora, Witness, and Return.* Scottdale, PA: Herald, 2008.

Weaver, J. Denny. *Anabaptist Theology in Face of Postmodernity: A Proposal for the Third Millennium.* Telford, PA: Pandora, 2000.

Wogaman, J. Philip. *Christian Ethics: A Historical Introduction.* Louisville: Westminster John Knox, 1993.

Wright, Nigel Goring. *Disavowing Constantine: Mission, Church and the Social Order in the Theologies of John Howard Yoder and Jürgen Moltmann.* Carlisle: Paternoster, 2000.

Zimmerman, Earl. *Practicing the Politics of Jesus: The Origin and Significance of John Howard Yoder's Social Ethics.* Telford, PA: Cascadia, 2007.

Name Index

Abraham, 56–58, 61n26, 63, 81n89, 90, 97, 99n48, 102–3
Ambrose, 121
Anselm, 26, 28, 30–31
Apollos, 118n5
Augustine, 22n7, 26, 91, 121
Aquinas, Thomas, 26

Bainton, Roland H., 105n68
Barber, Daniel, 142n5
Barth, Karl, 23, 70n55, 78–79, 131, 135
Bender, Harold S., 11–12, 15, 21, 31, 42, 85
Berenbaum, Michael, 88n4
Berkhof, Hendrik, 33n43, 66n43, 82n98, 85
Bonino, José Miguez, 90–91
Borowitz, Eugene, 93
Bourne, Richard, x, 103n63
Boyarin, Daniel, 98n44, 114n94
Buber, Martin, 89

Carter, Craig A., 6, 8n21, 9, 15–17, 23n13, 26n20, 36n54, 79n81, 142
Cartwright, Michael G., 8n22, 75n70, 88n7, 115, 128n38
Cohen, Hermann, 110
Coles, Romand, 114n94
Collier, Charlie, 3n4

Constantine, 26–27, 57n11, 94, 96, 120–21, 128n37
See also Constantinianism
Constantius, 26
Cullman, Oscar, 23, 29n30, 36n55, 85

Dintaman, Stephen F., 61n23, 147n22
Doerksen, Paul, 90n14, 146n18
Dula, Peter, 8n22

Finger, Tom, 143
Friesen, Duane K., 103n63

Gideon, 58, 63
Goldsmith, Emanuel, 142n8
Grebel, Conrad, 85
Gustafson, James, 11n35, 84n103

Harnack, Adolf von, 142
Hauerwas, Stanley, 7–8, 23–24, 35n49, 38–39, 54n1, 77n78, 84n103, 124n25, 140, 146–47
Hegel, G. W. F., 111, 142
Heilke, Thomas, 47n90
Hershberger, Guy F., 85
Hezekiah, 58n14
Hiebert, Bruce, 100n53
Hovey, Craig, 77n78, 146n18
Huebner, Chris K., 8n22, 14n41, 35n49, 79

Name Index

Huebner, Harry J., 102n57
Hunter, James Davison, 11n34

Jacobs, Louis, 93
Jehoshaphat, 58n14
Jeremiah, 56, 63n35, 102–3, 105, 113–15, 143
John (the Baptist), 60–61

Kant, Immanuel, 110–12, 142–43
Kaufman, Gordon, 133–34
Kerr, Nathan T., 39n65, 63n36
Klassen, William, 57n9
Kroeker, P. Travis, 5n10, 113n89

Landau, Yehezkel, 89
Lapide, Pinches, 88n4
Lasserre, Jean, 75
Leithart, Peter J., 22n7, 46n90, 56n8
Liechty, Daniel, 144n11
Littell, Franklin H., 95n33, 99
Luther, Martin, 25–26, 31, 41, 91, 121

Marcion, 36n53
Martens, Paul, 126n30
Marx, Karl, 111–13, 122
Mary, 60n20, 81
McClendon, James, 6, 38, 84n103, 132
McLuhan, Marshall, 136
Melchizedek, 68n48
Meyer, Marshall, 90, 93
Miller, John W., 36n53
Moses, 57–58, 63, 102
Mouw, Richard J., 5n10
Murphy, Nancy, 7–8, 10

Nation, Mark Thiessen, xii, 4n6, 6, 15, 17, 21n5, 52n114, 79n81, 83–84, 116, 119, 142
Niebuhr, H. Richard, 11, 45n83, 77, 80, 82n98, 86, 89, 134–35

Niebuhr, Rienhold, 11–12, 20, 22–23, 49n100, 50n104, 77, 80, 86, 89

Ochs, Peter, 82n97, 98n44, 114
O'Donovan, Oliver, 84n103

Parler, Branson, xii, 4, 81n91, 124, 141n2, 144n13
Paul, 12n38, 23, 30, 35, 66–67, 97, 104, 118n5, 127–29
Peter, 35, 118n5
Pinches, Charles, 31–32

Rahab, 68n48
Ramsey, Paul, 129–32
Rasmussen, Arne, 79n81
Rauschenbusch, Walter, 142
Reimer, A. James, 8n21, 19n2, 26n20, 103n63, 143
Rendtorff, Rolf, 99
Ritschl, Albrecht, 142

Samuel, 58, 63
Schlabach, Gerald, 146n18
Schwarzschild, Steven S., 87–88, 92–93, 98n46, 100n52, 106, 108–15, 117, 143n10
Shank, David A., 34–38
Sider, J. Alexander, x, 47n90, 130n47
Snyder, C. Arnold, 144n11
Stassen, Glen H., xii, 80n88
Stauffer, Ethelbert, 21n4
Stoltzfus, Philip E., 30n32
Swartley, Willard M., 82n95

Taylor, Rachel Reesor, 28n25
Theodosius, 26
Tracy, David, 86n108
Trocmé, André, 82n95, 85
Troeltsch, Ernst, 11, 72n60, 77, 80, 86, 89

Weaver, Alain Epp, 26–27, 79n81, 103n63
Weaver, J. Denny, 26–27, 143n11
Weber, Max, 77
Wells, Samuel, 124n25
Werntz, Myles, 68n48
Wogaman, J. Philip, 38–39
Wright, Nigel Goring, 22n8

Zimmerman, Earl, 6–7, 15, 19–21, 23, 56, 84, 86n108, 113n90
Zweig, Stefan, 89
Zwingli, Ulrich, 52n115, 138

Subject Index

aeons, 46–48, 58n15, 65–67
agape, 32–33
aggadah, 96, 102
Amish, 39–40
antinomianism, 22n7
apocalyptic, 63n36, 112
apostles, 34
Ascension, 67, 84, 104
Associated Mennonite Biblical
    Seminary, 100
atonement, 25, 28, 30–31

baptism, 15–16, 52, 85, 119, 126,
    128, 131–33, 137
    infant, 41
    Jesus', 29n30, 81
Bethel College, 101–2, 104, 106,
    109n77
Bible, 23, 27–28, 31, 34–36, 38,
    42–43, 53, 57, 66, 123
    biblicism, 31, 34–35, 38, 40
    New Testament, 10, 24–25,
        29–30, 33–38, 54, 56, 59n16,
        66, 70, 82–83, 94, 99, 118–19,
        124, 127, 130, 132
    Old Testament, 56–59, 61, 63, 69,
        81, 100n52, 102, 104–5
binding and loosing, 71n57, 126,
    128–33, 137

capital punishment, 75–76

Catholic, 21, 26, 34, 40, 76, 91–92,
    122, 126, 138, 146
    anti-, 22n7
    catholic, 120
    catholicity, 117, 132
Christendom, 14n42, 28, 36, 44, 67,
    91–95, 105, 134, 147
Christology, 17, 26, 63n36, 88, 92
church
    believers, 15, 27n23, 95, 103, 126
    early, 3, 28, 36n53, 46, 49n101,
        91, 118n5, 143
    ekklesia, 64n38
    free, 2, 5, 17, 26, 33, 35n51,
        39n64, 51–53, 59, 95n33, 106,
        118
    qahal, 64n38
Communion, 28–30, 127
    See also Eucharist
Concern Group, 20n2, 40
Concern, 24, 39, 128
Constantinian(ism), 2, 26–28,
    32–33, 42, 45–47, 56, 73n63,
    78n81, 91, 99, 120–22, 141,
    143
    anti-, 73n63, 108, 120
    post-, 94, 143
    pre-, 141, 143
Corpus Christianum, 121
    See also Christendom
cosmos, 10, 66, 84, 134–35, 138
creed(s), 2, 26–30, 92, 97, 143–45
    Nicene, 26–27, 29

Subject Index

cross, 4n6, 23, 29n30, 33, 46, 51, 67, 81–83, 124, 136n75, 142

dialogical liberty, 71n58, 130, 132–33, 137–38
diaspora, 17, 95, 102–3, 105, 107, 112n86, 121
Docetism, 22n7, 29n30

Earlham College, 106
Eastern Orthodox, 122
ecclesiology, 17, 27, 39–40, 53, 59, 64
    See also church
Enlightenment, 31, 80, 134
    post-, 122
eschatology, 26, 44, 47, 65
Eucharist, 41, 126–27, 131, 133, 137
euangelion. *See* gospel
evil, 31–33, 44–49, 58, 68, 73, 76, 142n6
exodus, 137, 145
exousiai. *See* powers

faith, 30, 38, 41–42, 45n86, 58n14, 70, 73, 75, 77–78, 83, 88, 97, 107, 120, 122, 131, 134–35, 137, 144, 147
    bad, 92
    inter-, 93, 96
forgiveness, 12n38, 24, 33n43, 62, 82n97, 124, 128, 135, 137–38
fundamentalism, 40, 43

Gentile, 61, 97, 99, 103–4, 137
Goshen Biblical Seminary, 55
Goshen College, 19, 21
gospel, 35–36, 41n70, 48, 52, 59–61, 68–69, 73–75, 82, 86, 90, 119, 125, 141–43
Greek
    provincialism, 99
    thought, 29

Guggenheim Fellowship, 14n42, 105, 112n86

halakah, 96, 102
Hebrew
    language, 89n8, 108
    mind, 27n23
    people, 58
    universality, 99
Hellenism, 4n6
Holocaust, 99, 105

Incarnation, 29n30, 35, 57n11, 111
Institute of Mennonite Studies, 8, 66

Jubilee, 81–82, 96

kosmos. *See* cosmos
kyrios, 138

liberalism, 40–41, 43, 141
liberation, 58n14, 90
Lord's Supper, 126, 132
    See also Eucharist
lordship (of Christ), 9–11, 48, 65–69, 73, 84, 114, 117, 120, 124–25, 133–34, 144, 146

Magnificat, 60n20, 81
Mennonite Biblical Seminary, 55n4
Mennonite Board of Missions, 55
Mennonite Confession of Faith, 137
Messiah, 10, 60, 70, 77, 87, 104, 114, 138
metanoia, 59–60
middle axioms, 9, 13, 74–80, 85–86, 89, 117, 136, 145
modernity, 2, 146–47

Nachfolge, 24
nonviolence, ix, x, 21n4, 30, 32, 47, 82, 104–5

obedience, 23–24, 28–34, 37, 41, 43, 47, 51, 70, 83n100, 91–92, 107, 119, 134
orthodoxy, 2–3, 5, 29–30, 41, 43, 110, 114, 143–44

pacifism, 5, 8, 12, 15, 17, 22, 33n43, 39, 53, 55, 63, 75n73, 91–95, 98, 105–6, 119
paradigm, 4, 9n26, 133–34, 136, 138, 142
parousia, 47, 67
Pentecost, 57n11, 91, 94, 137, 145
pietism, 42, 92
pneumatology, 40
polis, 70, 133n59, 138, 145
powers, 11n33, 63n36, 66–69, 80, 82–83
Protestant(ism), 12, 60n23, 83, 89, 91–92, 95, 99, 101, 104, 122, 130, 140
Puritan, 134

Realism, 57, 71
  Biblical, 36n54, 43n77, 80
  Christian, 22
Reformation, 12, 40, 80, 134, 141–42
  Radical, 44, 90–92, 94–96, 103, 106
Reformers, 21–22, 35, 43, 52n115, 126, 128, 141
Renaissance, 134
repentance, 30, 33n43, 38, 59–60, 70, 135
Resurrection, 33, 46–47, 50, 58n14, 67, 84, 104
revolution
  Kant's Copernican, 111
  moral, 61, 67
  original, 17, 55–64
  social, 69
Rockefeller Fellowship, 14n42, 105, 112n87

Roman
  authorities, 81
  Catholic, 40
  church, 22
  provincialism, 99
  Romanization, 94

sacrament(s), 17, 40, 46n89, 71, 107, 116–17, 120–22, 125–39, 142–44
sacramentalism, 103n62, 130–31
Schleitheim Confession, 44, 91–92, 127
sectarian(ism), 5, 11–14, 44, 51, 80, 85, 89, 95, 135, 139, 147
  anti-, 48
secular(ism), 4, 45n86, 71, 81–82, 112–13, 121, 124, 128, 137, 141–42, 146
sin, 23, 28, 30, 32–33, 38, 41n70, 46–48, 66, 71, 91
soteriology, 21, 25–26, 30–31
spiritualism, 40
suffering, 30, 47, 50–51, 62, 81, 98, 130, 135, 142
supersessionism, 56, 58, 142

Tantur Ecumenical Institute, 94–96, 101
theodicy, 31–33, 135
Toronto Mennonite Theological Centre, 7

universal charisma, 71n56, 132–33, 137
University of Basel, 16, 23
University of Notre Dame, 7n16, 55n4, 91n16, 94, 96, 108–9, 115n96

violence, ix, 24, 44, 46, 56–58, 62, 68–69, 76, 92, 98, 102n59

war, 55, 79, 100n51
   Cold, 54
   holy, 63, 82
   just, 55, 76
   of the Lamb, 47n95
   Thirty Years', 121
worship, 12n38, 14n40, 24, 51, 62, 64, 92, 103, 116–17, 122, 124–25, 129–31, 139

Yiddish(ism), 15, 89, 108, 142

Zealot, 57, 93
Zionism, 93, 105n69